The Forgiveness Handbook

Spiritual Wisdom and Practice for the Journey to Freedom, Healing and Peace

Created by the Editors at SkyLight Paths

Introduction by
The Rev. Canon Marianne Wells Borg

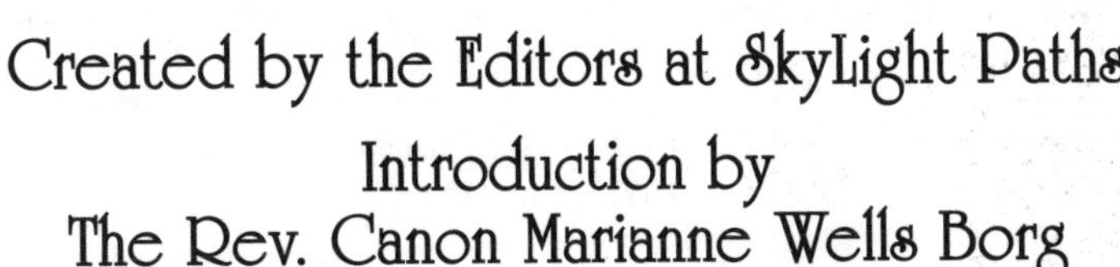

Walking Together, Finding the Way®

SKYLIGHT PATHS®
PUBLISHING
Woodstock, Vermont

The Forgiveness Handbook:
Spiritual Wisdom and Practice for the Journey to Freedom, Healing and Peace

2015 Quality Paperback Edition, First Printing

Page 236 is a continuation of this copyright page.

Library of Congress Cataloging-in-Publication Data
The forgiveness handbook : spiritual wisdom and practice for the journey to freedom, healing, and peace / [by SkyLight Paths Publishing].—2014 Quality Paperback Edition.
pages cm
Includes bibliographical references.
ISBN 978-1-59473-577-6 (pbk. : alk. paper)—ISBN 978-1-59473-581-3 (ebook) 1. Forgiveness—Religious aspects. I. SkyLight Paths Publishing.
BL65.F67F68 2014
205'.699—dc23
2014022301

10 9 8 7 6 5 4 3 2 1

Manufactured in the United States of America
Cover and interior design: Michael Myers
Cover background image: © Silvionka/ Shutterstock

SkyLight Paths Publishing is creating a place where people of different spiritual traditions come together for challenge and inspiration, a place where we can help each other understand the mystery that lies at the heart of our existence.
SkyLight Paths sees both believers and seekers as a community that increasingly transcends traditional boundaries of religion and denomination—people wanting to learn from each other, walking together, finding the way.

Walking Together, Finding the Way®
Published by SkyLight Paths Publishing
A Division of LongHill Partners, Inc.
Sunset Farm Offices, Route 4, P.O. Box 237
Woodstock, VT 05091
Tel: (802) 457-4000 Fax: (802) 457-4004
www.skylightpaths.com

Contents

Introduction ix
The Rev. Canon Marianne Wells Borg

Understanding Forgiveness 1

What's Stopping You? 3
Linda Douty

How to Let Go of Resentment 6
Rabbi Edwin Goldberg, DHL

Proverbs on Forgiveness 11
Translated by Rami Shapiro

Crossing the Bridge 12
Karyn D. Kedar

A Choice and a Gift 14
Rev. Timothy J. Mooney
Practice: What Am I Holding on To? 16
Practice: The Log in Our Own Eye 17

Letting Go 19

Leaving the Past Behind 21
Rev. Jane E. Vennard
Reflection: Looking Backward and Forward 23
Practice: The Courage to Forgive 23

Repainting Your Story 25
Linda Novick

The Qur'an on Forgiveness 28

Clearing the Wellspring 29
Nancy Barrett Chickerneo, PhD
Practice: A Clearing Experience 30

Four *R*s for Relinquishing 32
Kent Ira Groff
Practice: Emptiness as Space for God 33
Practice: A Focusing Exercise in Three Gestures 33
Practice: "Let It Be" 34

Naming Your Hurts and Fears 35
Nancy L. Bieber
Practice: The Naming Game 35
Practice: The Room 36
Practice: Accepting Love 36

Letting Go of Old Illusions 37
Jan Phillips

What Animals Can Teach Us about Letting Go 41
Diana L. Guerrero

Reconciliation and Forgiveness in Relationships 45

Reconciliation in Your Own Heart 47
Caren Goldman
Practice: Journaling with Others and Self 50

It Starts with You 51
Marcia Ford
Practice: Making the First Move 53

The Sacred Speech of Forgiveness 54
Rev. Donna Schaper

Listening for Reconciliation 59
Kay Lindahl

The Philokalia on Forgiveness 62

Prayer for Our Mothers 63
M. F.

Prayers for Marriage 64
Annotated by The Rev. Canon C. K. Robertson, PhD

Forgiveness in Caregiving 66
Marty Richards, MSW, LCSW

Setting Boundaries 77
Marcia Ford
Practice: Clarifying Your Boundaries 79

Finding Peace in Letting a Relationship Go 81
Susan Quinn

Forgiveness and Grace after Divorce 85
Rev. Carolyne Call

Forgiving Suicide 90
Rabbi Elie Kaplan Spitz
Practice: Journaling about Loss 93
Practice: Letter Exchange 94

A Prayer for Forgiveness 95
Rev. Steven Greenebaum

Forgiveness and the Divine 97

A God Who Desires to Forgive 99
Annotated by Rami Shapiro

Letting Go of a Vengeful God 100
Tom Stella
Reflection: The Moral of Your Story 104

You Accept Us—At Times of Self-Doubt 105
William Cleary

You Are Living a Good Story 106
Karyn D. Kedar

The Psalms on Forgiveness 108
Translated by M. Basil Pennington, OCSO

Offering All to God 110
Annotated by Paul Wesley Chilcote, PhD

Trusting God's Forgiveness 112
Rev. Larry J. Peacock
Practice: Forgiveness Dance 113

Accepting Forgiveness 115

The Privilege of Asking Forgiveness 117
Rabbi David Lyon

Humbly Embracing Imperfections 119
Tom Stella

Questions in Asking for Forgiveness 122
Rev. Carolyne Call

Ghazali on Forgiveness 123
Translated by Aaron Spevack, PhD

More Than Apologizing 124
Rami Shapiro

Developing Self-Compassion 128
Imam Jamal Rahman
Practice: Loving the Heart 129
Practice: Sacred Naming 130

Granting Yourself Absolution 132
Marcia Ford
Reflection: Being Drained of Self-Criticism 134
Practice: "I Can't Forgive Myself Because __________" 134

Laugh at Yourself 136
Rev. Susan Sparks
Reflection: Laughter and Forgiveness 137

Facing Brokenness 138
Terry Taylor
Practice: *Maitri*—Embracing Your Pain 141

Love Your Enemies 143

Hospitality to Enemies 145
Rev. Nanette Sawyer
Practice: Self-Examination 148
Practice: A Circle of Love (Draw It Large Enough to Include Your Adversary) 151

The Gospel of Matthew on Forgiveness 154
Translated by Ron Miller

Encountering the Heart of the Enemy 155
Rami Shapiro
Practice: Dining with the Devil 158
Practice: Dear Hated One 158

A Prayer of Forgiveness for Enemies 161
Nancy Corcoran, CSJ

A Moveable Feast 163
Katharine Jefferts Schori

Praying with the Angels 166
Imam Jamal Rahman

Forgiveness, Justice, and Peace 169

Seeking Justice on the Path to Forgiveness 171
Marie M. Fortune

Wise Justice, Merciful Hearts 175
Rev. Donna Schaper

The Book of Common Prayer on Forgiveness 178

Reconciliation, Retribution, and Justice in Islam 179
Annotated by Sohaib N. Sultan

Prodigals and the Path to Peace 181
Rev. Dr. Joan Brown Campbell

Reconnecting with the Earth 185
John Philip Newell

Interfaith Forgiveness 190
Pastor Don Mackenzie,
Imam Jamal Rahman, and Rabbi Ted Falcon

Peacemaking in Our Own Hearts 197
Molly and Bernie Srode
Practice: Affirmations for Personal Peacemaking 198

Dancing Peace and Forgiveness 199
Cynthia Winton-Henry
Practice: Inner Peace Dance—80 Percent Stillness 201

Intercession and Justice 203
Rev. Larry J. Peacock
Practice: Intercession Collage 204

Cultivating a Forgiving Heart 205

Lovingkindness Meditation to Open the Heart and Mind 207
Louise Silk
Practice: *Mettabhavana* Meditation 208

Escaping the Blame Cycle 210
Gordon Peerman
Practice: Working with RAIN 214

Meditations of Marcus Aurelius on Forgiveness 216

Bedtime Forgiveness Prayer 217
Tamar Frankiel, PhD, and Judy Greenfeld
Practice: Bedtime Forgiveness Meditation 218

The Fruit of Love 221
Nancy L. Bieber

Living in Love 223
The Rev. Peter Wallace
Reflection: Loving and Being Loved 226

Meeting Everyone as a Stranger 227
Diane M. Millis, PhD

Seeing a World Where There Is No "Other" 230
Yoland Trevino

Pursuing Kinship Rather than Estrangement 233
Rev. Nanette Sawyer

Credits 236

Notes 240

Introduction

by The Rev. Canon Marianne Wells Borg

> "Forgiveness can happen early or late—when we realize just how short life is, we usually want it to happen early. We want to [have] the goal of perpetual forgiveness already in our hearts."
>
> —Rev. Donna Schaper

Forgiveness was a difficult concept for me as I grew up. Raised in a non-Christian country until I was eight, I was not shaped by doctrines or belief systems of any sort. There was only "free spirit" as far as I was concerned. Although even as a child, when I thought like a child, "God" or what twentieth-century philosopher William James calls "The More" was something I knew about. I somehow sensed that, as the Scripture says, "God is the one in whom we live and move and have our being" (Acts 17:28).

After moving to the United States I slowly became enculturated by a ubiquitous "Christianity." But I resisted the notion of sin and forgiveness so interwoven in conventional Christian thinking. In my mind, sin and forgiveness were a package deal—you could not have one without the other. And they partnered with blame and apology, with judgment and the necessity for self-recrimination. I was burdened enough by a troubled self-esteem as I grew up in what is commonly called a dysfunctional family. My parents, fine as they were, mirrored my confused and troubled self: I was not enough. I was a disappointment. I should know better or certainly more than I did. My mother would so often say, "Love is understanding"—but, it seemed, I was lacking in both.

So, as the years went on, the freedom of living and moving and having my being in God became subject to a gravity that kept me emotionally captive. The very work that could have sprung me loose—forgiveness—was the very work I resisted. My soul longed for release. For a return to the Heart that recognizes that we are good, very good, and that this existence is precious, to be cherished for itself and for its very impermanence. As an adult, I sought emotional freedom anew. That freedom is not only a real possibility but a practice we can all engage in.

For you an opportunity for emotional freedom is here, to be discovered and explored in this book. Perhaps you think forgiveness is a trap of sorts, like I did, and doesn't really have liberating power, or perhaps you are now finding that your longing for integration trumps the claptrap you have been carrying for years. Perhaps the promise of emotional freedom has finally overcome the pull of the undertow. This book has come to you. Now is the time. Step through this door of wisdom. It will guide you to the freedom, healing, and peace that we all long for—and that the world sorely needs.

Let this book greet you, as it has me, with insight, tenderness, and practical assistance. Open its pages and open the way to a multitude of helps. There is a kindness and generosity in this collection. And a call for honesty. "The truth will set you free," it is written. The wisdom here will show you the way. You will find renewal in these pages, empowering you for love of self and love of others.

The authors include lights well known and lights lesser known but no less bright. They reflect wisdom from a spectrum of religious traditions. Together they provide an inclusive spirituality that will speak to everyone. Everyone. There is so much to be gained here, such valuable new perspectives on an old story.

You can delve into these pages wherever you would like. Each contribution is a self-contained gem. You will want to gather them all. Here is a treasure trove of spiritual wisdom and practices, a variety of lenses through which to see again. Sometimes these lenses overlap, calling attention to truths that bear repeating, truths we seem to forget so easily. Here is clarity and tenderness and just plain good teaching about human nature. This collection is a study in reorientation; to reorient, spiritual companion Kent Ira Groff reminds us, means "turning east again," to the place of sunrise, "where new insights dawn."

Augustine in reflecting on his relationship with God wrote, "How late I came to love you, O Beauty, O Wisdom, so ancient and so fresh." I can say the same about my relationship to forgiveness: How late I came to love you. Beauty. Wisdom. So ancient. And so fresh. This book has come to me late. But not too late.

Pulitzer prize–winning poet Mary Oliver writes of looking back on life and being able to say she was "married to amazement," taking the world into her arms. Let this handbook and its trustworthy guides be witnesses to such a marriage. Yours.

Understanding Forgiveness

> We move on because life is too rich and wonderful to waste on the negative feelings.... [We forgive] not because those who hurt us deserve this grace, but because we deserve it.
>
> —Rabbi Edwin Goldberg

Folk wisdom often pairs forgiving with forgetting—which, particularly to those who have sustained a great hurt, feels both impossible and flippant. The contributors in this section say, no, forgiveness is not forgetting—it is healing; it is freedom; it is being restored to wholeness; it is reopening our hearts to love.

This section equips you for the road ahead, offering encouragement, recalibrating your understanding of forgiveness, and preparing you for some of the obstacles you may confront. Linda Douty shares perspectives from later life, while Rev. Timothy J. Mooney examines examples of childlike forgiveness. Rabbi Edwin Goldberg challenges you not to spend another minute letting resentment take up room in your heart. Karyn D. Kedar offers a reminder that forgiveness is something you have to do over and over, layer by layer, but that it's a little easier each time. In each chapter, you'll find fruitful questions to ask as you contemplate the places in your life that need to be touched by forgiveness.

Take a deep breath. Don't despair at the depth of your wounds or the length of the process. The only thing necessary in this moment is to find within yourself the willingness to begin the journey.

What's Stopping You?

Linda Douty

I used to think that age sixty-five was the start of a slippery downward slope to the cemetery.... I've read a shelf-full of books telling me how to grow old gracefully—most of them with specific instructions on how to hold the appearance of Father Time at bay—eat like a bird, work out like an athlete, nip and tuck like a starlet, be incessantly positive, and stay busy. But those answers don't fit the deeper needs of later life.

Because I have a stubborn tendency to view everything through rose-colored glasses, I made a firm decision to approach this stage of life with a smile and a shrug. But my body and my contemporaries were saying, "Not so fast, Pollyanna—this ain't all a bed of roses!" So I decided to get real. After all, later life presents life's grandest opportunity for honesty.... I decided to get outside my own head to see what others were experiencing. Over a period of a few months, more than fifty articulate seniors agreed to respond to some pretty nosy questions (with a guarantee of confidentiality, of course)....

When I asked a question about any lingering forgiveness issues, one story made me catch my breath. "Years ago, when our nineteen-year-old daughter was murdered, my crash course in forgiveness began," remembered Walter. "It was quite an odyssey. I didn't think it was possible to do it, but it was. I had to see forgiveness as a process, not a onetime act. If I treated it as an event, it was too easy to fail, to admit defeat, to say, 'I tried, but I just couldn't do it.' It's closer to the truth to say, 'I'm willing to begin the *process* of forgiveness.'"

Linda Douty, a leading speaker on the topics of meaningful aging, personal growth, and spiritual formation, is the author of *How Did I Get to Be 70 When I'm 35 Inside? Spiritual Surprises of Later Life* (SkyLight Paths) and other books. Linda is also a spiritual director and a contributor to *Presence* (the journal of Spiritual Directors International).

First, he realized, he had to acknowledge what the anger was doing to him—to his body as well as his spirit. "I remember someone telling me that 'resentment hurts the vessel in which it is stored more than the object on which it is poured,'" he said. "Anger that is kept alive year after year does its toxic work on us. It's like scratching poison ivy—at first it feels good to scratch it, but all that does is spread the poison."

Walter admitted that the process took time. "I had to feel and own the anger and rage before I could begin to let it go," he recalled. "Even then, it was impossible to do it alone under my own steam. How could God forgive such a horrible thing—or expect me to forgive it? I had to wrestle with that for quite a while. My faith in God's forgiveness had to be strengthened and reaffirmed. I prayed the Lord's Prayer, especially the part about 'Forgive us our trespasses as we forgive those who trespass against us.' I read everything I could find that mentioned forgiveness—like the words of Jesus on the cross forgiving his own murderers."

Walter envisioned God's forgiveness as a rolling river, an ongoing reality of love. "We don't have to produce it ourselves," he added, "but we have to be willing to participate in it. It felt to me as if I were taking my boat and paddle and entering a river of forgiveness that was stronger than I was. What I needed to contribute was willingness, not power."

Another realization helped Walter's progress on the path to forgiveness. "At first, it seemed that if I forgave the murderer, I was somehow condoning what he did, saying that it was okay, that it didn't hurt that badly. And that was unimaginable, of course. I had to reframe it, to understand that we forgive people, not behaviors. And forgiveness is not forgetting, either. What I was really saying was that I didn't want to carry that burden of unforgiveness inside me any longer; it was destroying me."

In addition to this dramatic and difficult story of forgiveness, I encountered many whose forgiveness issues were directed toward themselves. "I made so many mistakes as a mother, and I can't do it over," recalled Sandra. "I loved my children, but honestly, it's hard to forgive myself for my own damaging words and deeds."

Remorse was reflected by Peter also. "It's hard to excuse some of the things I've done in my life. But we human beings are good at whitewashing our actions, justifying them with all sorts of rationalizations to get ourselves off the hook. Now that I'm older, it seems healthier to admit that most all of us have done some pretty rotten things, often from ignorance, sometimes out of anger and malice, and frequently with motives of self-interest—indulging our passions or trying to make ourselves look better at someone else's expense. But when we have the courage to stare our own demons in the face and admit them, the pathway of forgiveness seems to open up."

Marsha's comments on forgiveness had to do with the necessity of releasing the outcome. "It's unilateral," she insisted. "You can't control other people's responses, if you choose to forgive them. They may or may not want to move toward reconciliation with you. The point is, you can't let the littleness in others bring out the littleness in you."

One final word of wisdom came from Hannah, who mentioned the relationship between unforgiveness and martyrdom. "If you live long enough with an unforgiving attitude, it becomes part of your identity," she said emphatically. "You become a permanent victim, wearing it like a badge of honor. I had to quit chewing on the hurt and stop talking about it. Only then could I move toward forgiveness. Otherwise, I was sabotaging myself."

Writer and theologian Frederick Buechner's graphic description of the condition of unforgiveness provides powerful motivation to move beyond it:

> Of the Seven Deadly Sins, anger is possibly the most fun. To lick your wounds, to smack your lips over grievances long past, to roll over your tongue the prospect of bitter confrontations still to come, to savor to the last toothsome morsel both the pain you are given and the pain you are giving back—in many ways it is a feast fit for a king. The chief drawback is that what you are wolfing down is yourself. The skeleton at the feast is you.[1]

How to Let Go of Resentment

Rabbi Edwin Goldberg, DHL

All of us have names and faces of individuals we are not able to forgive. For instance:

- How can we forgive a relative who molested us?
- How can we forgive an ex-spouse who maligns us?
- How can we forgive a thief who has stolen precious memories from us?
- How can we forgive a murderer who has taken a loved one from us?
- How can we forgive a corporation that uses our talents and then discards us?
- How can we forgive a parent who abandons us?
- How can we forgive stupidity, hatred, bigotry, cruelty, and greed?

One of the tragic things about life is that, sooner or later, people will hurt us and we will find ourselves wondering whether or not we can forgive them. We will ponder how we can forgive those who have wronged us, insulted us, those whom we swore we would never speak to again.

On the one hand, we may feel we have no need to forgive. Indeed, those who have hurt us may not be asking for our forgiveness. They may not even know they have hurt us. They may not even still be alive. On the other hand, we also know that without forgiving those who have hurt us, we ourselves may carry a burden so heavy that every day is filled with needless pain and suffering. And we wonder: If

---

Rabbi Edwin Goldberg, DHL, noted lecturer, is author of *Saying No and Letting Go: Jewish Wisdom on Making Room for What Matters Most* (Jewish Lights), among other books. He is the senior rabbi at Temple Sholom in Chicago and the former spiritual leader at Temple Judea in Coral Gables, Florida.

we can forgive those who have hurt us, will this pain go away? Will we be relieved of the constant drain on our emotions?

One thing I do know: Nothing destroys a relationship or threatens our well-being faster than resentment. It is the cancer of our emotions. It is the poison of our spiritual life. The word *resentment* literally means "feeling again," and it therefore emphasizes a clinging to our past. Its meaning focuses on those who have hurt us and returning, over and over again, to this vision of our being victims. If we are honest, most of us will admit that we don't want such baggage with us throughout our lives. But how do we let go of our resentment? How do we forgive?

It may help to remember that forgiveness, although difficult, can work in relieving us of resentment. Donald McCullough, a pastor and author, once observed that forgiveness is like an antibiotic, "very rare and almost always effective, that saves relationships from death."[1] Of course, we won't want to use this medicine every day. It's not necessary to forgive most of the people who irritate us. Instead, we simply should learn not to let them bother us so much. We should learn to overlook the petty annoyances they cause and the frustrations they bring to our lives. For instance, the shopper in front of us in the express lane who has fifteen items instead of ten, or the channel-surfing spouse—their actions may be annoying, but they don't require forgiveness. Genuine forgiveness should be reserved for those who really hurt us. Forgiveness is for the deep and searing pain that involves betrayal, disloyalty, or even brutality. One sign of wisdom is learning to know the difference between meaningless irritations and devastating pain.

The Obstacles to Forgiveness

When it comes to forgiveness, even when true pain is involved, there is a fairly simple method to help you accomplish this most difficult task. The trick is to identify the obstacles in your way and then try to overcome them. Such work may not be easy, but it can be effective.

The first obstacle to forgiveness is the perverse pleasure we find in not forgiving someone. Being human, it's all too easy to cling to our resentment. A crucial component to forgiveness is deciding if the anger is a delicacy you would like to forgo.

Another obstacle to forgiveness is that often we don't understand what forgiveness really means. For instance, we tend to confuse forgiving with forgetting, but they are not the same thing. There are times when we will forgive those who hurt us, even though we cannot forget. Forgiveness is not saying, "I don't feel the pain anymore." Forgiveness is saying to the one who hurt us, "I do not feel the need to hold on to your involvement in my pain anymore." Forgiveness is not forgetting; forgiveness is choosing not to actively remember.

It's also important to note that forgiveness doesn't mean condoning an action. You don't have to tolerate what someone has done to you in order to forgive him. Forgiveness is not saying to the person who has hurt you, "You're okay." Forgiveness is saying, "I'm okay, and I am willing to let God deal with whether you're okay." If you're not okay, you actively look into how you can become okay. In other words, you can forgive someone and still not approve of his behavior. You can forgive him and still refuse to accept what he has done to you. At its core, forgiving is not about the people who have hurt us. Forgiveness is about healing ourselves after we have been hurt.

An additional obstacle to our forgiving—perhaps the biggest one of all—is that forgiveness offends the rational mind. If we think about it, this makes perfect sense. When someone wounds us, when someone has stolen something—or someone—from us, there is no reason why we should let that offense go. There is no reason why we should find compassion in our hearts for the perpetrator of these crimes. But the fact that we can find no rationale for forgiveness doesn't necessarily mean we should not forgive. It may mean we should simply stop being rational.

Or, perhaps, it is better to say that we should be rational and thereby "play out" what happens if we do not forgive. What kind of person or what kind of society do we become if we allow the search for vengeance to consume our lives? Consider the story of Bud Welch. His twenty-three-year-old daughter Julie died in the bombing of the Murrah Federal Building in Oklahoma City in 1995. Here's a statement he made prior to the 2001 execution of Timothy McVeigh, the man responsible for that bombing.

> The first month after the bombing, I didn't even want Tim McVeigh or Terry Nichols to even have trials. I simply wanted them fried. And then I finally came to realize that the reason that Julie and 167 others were dead is because of vengeance and rage. And when we take him out of his cage to kill him, it's going to be the same thing. We will keep the circle of violence going. Number 169 dead is not going to help the family members of the first 168.[2]

In essence, finding ways to forgive may seem like a terrible choice, but consider the upshot of not forgiving.

Stephanie Dowrick, author of *Forgiveness and Other Acts of Love*, suggests that to find our way to forgiveness, we may need to momentarily circumvent the rational mind, even though this is not easy. It means saying to the one who has offended us:

> I will attempt to go on loving the life in you, or the divine in you, or the soul in you, even when I totally abhor what you have done or what you stand for. What's more, I will attempt to see you as my equal, and your life as having equal value to my own, even when I despise what you do and everything you stand for.[3]

Obviously such an approach is difficult to maintain in the face of understandable resentment. "In emotional terms, it is Everest without oxygen, Wimbledon without a racket, La Scala without a score."[4] Such a challenge would frighten anyone. But it's necessary, for without giving up the resentment—even when such anger is reasonable—we can never free ourselves from the pain and suffering that we do not deserve.

Moving On with "Magic Eyes"

Let me share with you a story that reflects this irrational forgiveness. It's about a baker in a small village who lived a very righteous, upright life. His righteousness was so pure that it was hard to be around him. People respected him but found it difficult to love him. His wife was another matter. She loved people, and while she respected her husband's righteousness, there was an emptiness in her heart.

One morning, after working since dawn to bake his bread, the man came home and found his wife in bed with another man. Although the woman's adultery became the talk of the town, the baker didn't divorce her. He felt that the righteous thing to do was forgive her. Yet in his heart of hearts, he couldn't forgive his wife for the shame she had brought to his name. He let her live with him, but he hated her for what she had done to him. He only pretended to forgive her so he could punish her with his righteous mercy.

The baker's duplicity was recognized in heaven. Each time he would feel the secret hate for his wife, an angel came to him and dropped a small pebble into his heart. And each time a pebble was dropped there, the baker felt a stab of pain like the pain he felt on the day he discovered his wife and her sin. This made him hate her even more. His hate brought him pain, and his pain brought him hate. The pebbles multiplied and the baker's heart grew heavier and heavier with their weight. There were times when he wished he were dead.

Then one night the angel with the pebbles told the baker how he could eradicate the pain. The remedy was the "miracle of the magic eyes." He would need eyes that could look back to the beginning of his pain and see his wife not as a woman who betrayed him, but as a weak and lonely woman who needed his help. Only by looking at the world in this new way could he heal from the wounds of the past.

The baker complained, "Nothing can change the past. She is guilty, and not even an angel can change that." The angel replied to the baker, "You can't change the past. You can only heal the hurt that comes to you from the past. And you can only heal it with the vision of the magic eyes." The angel then told the baker how to have this vision: He simply had to try to see his wife in this new light. And every time he tried, a pebble would be lifted from his aching heart.

The baker tried to see the world with these new eyes. It took some time, but eventually the pebbles were removed. The baker's heart grew lighter, and he was able to invite his wife into his heart again.

There's nothing logical about the baker's choice, except for the fact that he was tired of the pain and his forgiveness ended the pain.

This is the true meaning of forgiveness. We do not pardon the one who has hurt us. We simply decide to move on. We move on because life is too rich and wonderful to waste on the negative feelings of anger and resentment that may be our right to own, but also will never let us be healed. So we bid them good-bye, not because those who hurt us deserve this grace, but because we deserve it. In short, as Rabbi Harold Kushner has observed, we get even by letting go. Ultimately, forgiveness is about refusing to let our resentment rent any more space in our minds.

Proverbs on Forgiveness

Translated by Rami Shapiro

Those who forgive insults keep their friends;
those who harp on faults are lonely. (Proverbs 17:9)

If you turn from evil and stand in awe of God,
then your kindness and honesty will bring
you forgiveness. (Proverbs 16:6)

Align yourself with godliness
and even your enemies will make peace
with you. (Proverbs 16:7)

Hide your wrongdoing and you will be exposed;
repent your mistakes and you will be forgiven. (Proverbs 28:13)

Rami Shapiro, a renowned teacher of spirituality across faith traditions and a noted theologian, is a popular speaker on the topics of religion, theology, and spirituality. He is author of the award-winning *The Sacred Art of Lovingkindness: Preparing to Practice* and *Proverbs: Annotated & Explained* (both SkyLight Paths), among other books.

Crossing the Bridge

Karyn D. Kedar

There is no comforting answer to the question *why?* Or *why not?* Because there is no God? Because life is cruel and random? Because evil-doers are punished and the good are rewarded in the world to come? Because God "needed" someone and cut his life short?

Every answer to *why* leads me to a deeper despondency. Those answers offer no solution, no resolution, no comfort. They make no sense to me. Life's tragedies do not demand an answer to *why*. Rather, they ask *how* and *what*:

> How can I make sense of my life?
>
> What have I learned about what is true and important?
>
> How do I turn my pain into compassion for others?
>
> Given what happened to me, how should I change my life?
>
> What am I supposed to do with the profound lesson I have learned?

"Why?" I have no idea. No one really does. This useless question distracts you from what you need to be thinking about. It keeps you in anger. Questions that begin with "how" and "what" lead us toward perseverance and resilience, toward a deeper understanding of life's meaning and purpose.

Tragedy elicits so much pain, and forgiveness can ease some of that pain. We can forgive what was unresolved before a sudden death. We can forgive what was not said or not done. We can forgive our own humanity and sense of helplessness....

Karyn D. Kedar teaches matters of the spirit to groups throughout the United States. She is senior rabbi at Congregation B'nai Jehoshua Beth Elohim in the Chicago area, and the inspiring author of *The Bridge to Forgiveness: Stories and Prayers for Finding God and Restoring Wholeness* and *God Whispers: Stories of the Soul, Lessons of the Heart* (both Jewish Lights).

Forgiveness is like a web. It is not a straight line of cause and effect. Remember—you tend not to forgive and forget. Sometimes you seem to be going in circles, as if you have made little progress. But you have. The progress in the world of the spirit is like a good refrain: it repeats over and over again. You heal, you feel anger, you accept, you learn, you forgive, you heal, and then life continues and you are soon called upon to repeat one or more of these steps. But each repetition is not in vain. It's not that you have not learned a lesson, rather, it's that the lessons of the spirit are learned throughout a lifetime, each time going deeper into the truth of it all.

Forgiveness is like a bridge you seem to cross over and over again. With every crossing, you discover that there is more. More darkness. More to forgive. More to learn. More light than we thought possible, just waiting to be released. More divine revelation to hear, to bear. More pain to feel, to bear. Another memory. Another layer to a memory you already had. All this is part of the journey. But here's the wonderful thing: having crossed the bridge once, it doesn't seem so narrow or dangerous the next time. There is great depth to healing and forgiveness, and, one by one, you will discover its various layers.

A Choice and a Gift

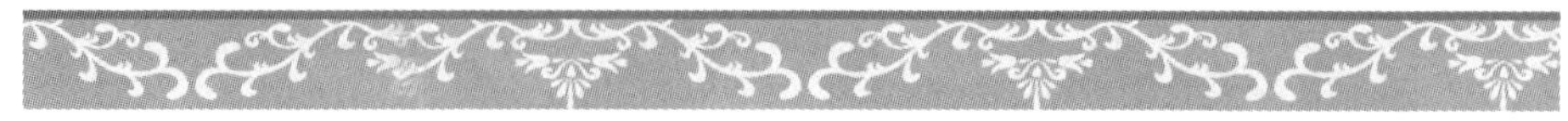

Rev. Timothy J. Mooney

> Then Peter came and said to him, "Lord, if another member of the church sins against me, how often should I forgive? As many as seven times?" Jesus said to him, "Not seven times, but, I tell you, seventy-seven times."
>
> —Matthew 18:21–22

> The root meaning of the verb "to forgive" is "to let go, to give back, to cease to harbor." Looked at this way, forgiveness is a restful activity. Far more work is required to cling to a judgment than to let go of it.
>
> —Hugh Prather

One day years ago, Matt, my five-year-old brother, came into the house crying. He ran into his room and as he slammed the door he shouted, "I *hate* Kenny!" The family made an unspoken, collective decision to let him cool down on his own. Thirty minutes later, at the dinner table, he was sullen and quiet. Dad asked what happened.

"Kenny called me a name and then he hit me, and so I hit him back!"

"Well, I'm sure you'll work it out," Dad responded.

"No! I hate Kenny."

Rev. Timothy J. Mooney, a Presbyterian minister, visual artist, and spiritual director, is author of *Like a Child: Restoring the Awe, Wonder, Joy and Resiliency of the Human Spirit* (SkyLight Paths). A pastor for over twenty-five years, he currently leads Community of ONE, a worshipping community in the heart of urban Denver, and offers retreats on spirituality and spiritual formation throughout the United States.

My brother stayed quiet throughout dinner and the conversation moved on to my sister's possible choices for a high school homecoming date, Mom's garden, and the difficulty I was having learning a new dive for the swim team.

Suddenly the doorbell rang. Dad pushed back from the table and saw Kenny's nose pressed up against the window on our front door. Dad looked at my brother and said, "It's Kenny." Matt jumped up and shouted, "Kenny!" He ran toward the door with a huge smile on his face. What happened between them was forgotten and forgiven. I can't tell you how many times that happened!

What is forgiveness, exactly? This illustration of my brother's easy forgiveness is not unusual among children. Unlike adults, children take life's bumps and bruises in stride. They seem to have a natural ability to move past grievances that only minutes before seemed grave and all-consuming. Whether a wrong has been done to them intentionally—someone threw a snowball at them—or unintentionally—a soccer ball spins off course and bonks them in the back—children are more likely to acknowledge the action, express their feelings (in anger, in tears), accept the apology, and move on. This doesn't mean children don't learn from their experiences. Rather, it means they are less likely than adults to let the facts of reality—that people make mistakes—negatively affect their mental and emotional well-being over the long term. Children choose to go forward, not backward.

We adults, on the other hand, often handle the wrongs that have been done to us—intentionally or unintentionally—differently than children. We're prone to harboring grudges and resentment, replaying offenses in our minds over and over again until what may have been an annoyance festers into rage and hate. We often long for vengeance—the offenders, perceived or real, getting payback for what they have done. As Christian theologian Lewis Smedes explains it, what makes forgiveness so difficult, so complex, is that it goes against our human nature of "ledger keeping." Forgiveness, Smedes says, "is outrageous. When we do it we commit an outrage against the strict morality that will not rest with anything short of an even score."[1]...

While forgiveness is an act performed by the person offended, it involves a gift rooted in grace for the offender. In the Gospel of Matthew Peter asks Jesus how many times he should forgive those who sin against him. Peter wonders if it could be as many as seven times. Jesus says to him, "Not seven times, but, I tell you, seventy-seven times" (18:21–22)....

When this grace finds you, touches you, convinces you—when it works its way underneath your carefully constructed defenses—it is liberating. The weight of guilt we carry for our wrongful actions is not fully understood until forgiveness lifts it and the freedom of grace *received* is experienced. How burdened we were! The same is true for the person who forgives. The burden of a grudge, resentment, or bitterness is not fully understood until the act of forgiving another lifts it and the freedom of grace *given* is experienced. How weighed down we are with being unforgiving! When you truly forgive from the heart, as Jesus describes forgiveness, you know it by the liberation of your own soul. The forgiveness is not simply spoken, not grudgingly offered; it is felt and real.

Peter's guess on the appropriate number of times he should forgive someone—seven—belies an underlying assumption about humanity that Jesus does not share. Peter assumes there is a limit, that others should, after a certain amount of time, get it right. Jesus assumes there is no limit, not only in our capacity for forgiveness, but also in our need for forgiveness....

We are called on to forgive, and that is extremely difficult. That does not mean we forget what wrongdoers have done to us. But it does mean we turn our rage into light, to build a better world.

And then, when we have forgiven, we often find an unexpected and grace-filled outcome. We find that we *have* forgotten in a sense—we've let it go. When we keep turning the offense over and over in our mind and heart—rehashing the bitterness, resentment, grudges, and desire for revenge—we keep the memory of the hurt alive. But when we offer forgiveness, we let it go in such a way that its emotional, energetic charge dissipates. We no longer obsess, dwell on, or return to it, and we discover that it vanishes from our mind. I want to be clear here. We are not the ones who do the forgetting; it's not an intentional act on our part. But the dynamics of genuine forgiveness, the letting go of the emotional charge, results in a kind of forgetfulness. It subsides because it is no longer being fed by our thoughts, emotions, and energy....

When we have offered genuine forgiveness, we find that we forget—we let go—but it is not of our own doing. It is a gift of grace.

Practice: What Am I Holding on To?

After a few minutes of centering and grounding, bring to your awareness the grudges you are holding on to, the people you have not forgiven. This may be difficult, but allow yourself to feel what you really feel, and bring to mind the wrongs you feel have been done to you.

Now consider what effects holding on to these grudges and the feelings associated with them are having on you.

What attitudes and behaviors result?

Are you happy with them?

Now ask yourself whether you are expecting something from these people first in order to forgive them or whether anything will enable you to forgive them.

Does the forgiveness depend on them or on you?

What are you willing to let go of?

What are you not willing to let go of?

Practice: The Log in Our Own Eye

In the Gospel of Luke, Jesus says to first take the log out of our own eye and then we will see clearly enough to help another take the splinter out of her eye. This parable helps us to recognize that often the very thing we do not forgive in another is a transgression we ourselves have committed. After getting into a contemplative place, ask yourself in what ways you have not forgiven yourself.

What are you still holding against yourself?

Where did those expectations and demands come from?

Are you willing to forgive yourself?

If not, what prevents you from doing so?

Just as forgiving others can often be a long process, so too is it with forgiving ourselves. This prayer practice can evoke difficult and tender emotions, so please be as patient and kind with yourself as possible, as you move toward forgiving yourself, rooted in God's forgiveness.

Letting Go

> To be on the path of the heart is to ... be light and unencumbered, emptied of debris and old illusions, knowing everything that ever happened to us got us to this moment, which is the only moment we have and the only place God dwells.
>
> —Jan Phillips

> By revisiting the events of our lives with fresh eyes, we can reframe our stories to see the course of our lives in a more empowering way. We have the ability to discern and choose those interpretations that are life enhancing rather than destructive, and each time we shed an unnecessary or limiting belief we can renew ourselves.
>
> —Linda Novick

The journey of forgiveness is essentially a search for freedom. Often this freedom comes through letting go—letting go of the past, of anger or bitterness, of defenses you may no longer need—so you can be free of resentment and open to love and healing.

As Kent Ira Groff writes, when someone advises you to "let it go," your heart may cry, "But *how?*" The contributors in this section offer practices to help you first of all determine what the "it" you'd like to let go of really is. And, if you find you're ready, they gently encourage you to release the emotion, hurt, or unhelpful story that you've identified.

If letting go doesn't seem to come easily once you've decided what you want to release, this section also contains a variety of practices to help loosen your grip—mantras, creative visualizations, breathwork—and tips on ways to take these letting-go practices into everyday life.

Through the practice of letting go, you'll find you can live each day just a little bit freer.

Leaving the Past Behind

Rev. Jane E. Vennard

How often we are pulled from experiencing the holiness of the present moment by thoughts of our past. You might remember a particularly wonderful time in your life, wish it were like that again, and despair at all the difficulties now surrounding you. Maybe you had a hurtful encounter with a friend last week and are rehashing what was said, what you wished you'd said, and wondering how it might have turned out differently. You could be carrying a deeply disturbing memory you can't seem to let go of, and when it comes to mind, you go back over the incident again and again, retelling the story and rekindling old hurt and anger.

Wishing things were as they used to be, reworking old conversations, and telling our painful stories of abuse and injustice is natural. But if we do so to place blame or dwell on another's guilt, our pain turns to resentment, and our lives fill with bitterness. Bitter people hold tightly to their past, remember every detail of the story, and sink into self-pity. Captured by past events, they are unable to move forward into new life. The possibility of forgiveness as a means of letting go of their hurt and bitterness may never have occurred to them.

Forgiveness keeps us from being stuck in the past and helps us find a way beyond the prison of bitterness. When we forgive, we let go of our emotional attachment to what has happened, but we do not forget or excuse the wrong that was done or the pain that was caused. Sometimes we are able to go to the person who has hurt us and offer them our forgiveness. Many more times forgiveness is something we do in our own hearts without engaging the other person face-to-face. Either way, forgiving

---

Rev. Jane E. Vennard, a popular teacher on prayer and spiritual practice, offers lectures and leads retreats in ecumenical settings. She is the author of *Fully Awake and Truly Alive: Spiritual Practices to Nurture Your Soul* (SkyLight Paths) and is ordained in the United Church of Christ to a ministry of teaching and spiritual direction.

another has no predictable outcome; it does not always lead to reconciliation, nor does it necessarily make a difference in the other person's life. What it can do is transform the person who has found the courage to forgive.

An emotionally abused woman went through the long, complex process of forgiving her ex-husband. "Holding the anger and resentment was hurting me and my children," she said. "Through forgiveness I have been released. Although I remember with sadness what we all experienced, I have moved on with my life. Through forgiveness I have let him into my heart. I will never again let him into my house."

Is there someone in your life you need to forgive? Are you willing to explore ways to do that? As you explore your ability to forgive others and seek the freedom that such willingness can bring, you will most likely become aware of some things you need to be forgiven for. When you recognize the hurt you have caused another, you may be able to write a letter or go to ask for forgiveness. But more often you will be faced with the hard task of forgiving yourself.

In my late thirties I let a dear friend down. She was counting on me, and I was not there for her. We did not speak of it, but we drifted apart. A few years later I learned she had died. I wept, wishing I had reached out to her, asking for forgiveness when she was alive. With her death, I felt there was no way to let go of the heaviness of heart that came from my betrayal. Over the ensuing years I have had to learn how to forgive myself. It has taken a long time. What I realized was that forgiving myself was not achieved through effort or willful action. Rather, forgiveness came through surrender—surrender to the reality of what I had done. I had to let go of my excuses, the rational reasons for my behavior, and my anger at her for her part in the friendship's end. When I was able to fully accept my guilt, I no longer needed to remain guilty. I was able to surrender into the arms of forgiveness.

The practice of letting go of past hurts, resentment, and bitterness may begin when we realize we have been holding on to something and turn to the process of forgiveness to set us free. As courageous as it is to forgive another or to forgive ourselves, the real challenge is to lead a forgiving and forgiven life. Rather than only attending to the large injustice or grievous hurt, are we willing to forgive the little mistakes and injuries that occur in everyday life? When another driver pulls into the parking space you were waiting for, can you nod pleasantly and move on? When the neighbor's child picks your spring tulips and comes to say she is sorry, can you forgive her? If you speak unkindly of someone and then recognize how unnecessary your words were, can you ask forgiveness for your thoughtlessness? There are an infinite number of opportunities every day to hold on to little annoyances, to let the words or actions of another lodge in our hearts to fester and to be brought out later for study, examination, and complaint. When we do this, we need the reminder from this vivid piece of Hasidic wisdom: "Rake the muck this way. Rake the muck that way. It will still be muck. In the time you are brooding, you could be stringing pearls for the delight of heaven."

Reflection: Looking Backward and Forward

Is it important for you to look to your past and begin or continue the practice of forgiveness? Where and how would it be wise to start? Only you can know. How attached are you to the life you have planned, making you unable to see the life that may be waiting for you? Spend some time looking back and then forward. Courage is necessary to look at these issues, to accept what you see, and then to transform old patterns of holding on to a new willingness to let go.

To remind yourself of the power of letting go, practice tightening your fists and gently opening your fingers wide, closing and opening, closing and opening. Do this anywhere and anytime. The wisdom of your body will guide you to the next step in the practice of letting go, freeing you for a life not yet imagined.

Practice: The Courage to Forgive

For this practice, I suggest you choose someone you wish to forgive for some small mistake or unintentional rudeness. In this way you can begin to become familiar with the process of forgiveness and start to develop a forgiving heart before you engage a person who has caused greater harm. You may wish to have writing materials with you.

Find a place where you can sit quietly alone and not be interrupted. If possible, you might place an empty chair in front of you.

Take a deep breath to settle yourself. Notice what you are feeling and thinking. Notice any bodily sensations.

When you are ready, imagine the person you wish to forgive sitting across from you. Pay attention to what he or she looks like—body posture, clothing, and facial expression.

Notice how you feel as you gaze at this person.

Now imagine the words you wish to say. You may do that silently, speak them aloud, or write them down. Don't try to "do this right." Speak from your heart.

Notice the effect your words have on the person opposite you. How does this make you feel? Might you wish to say more?

You may wish to end the practice here. However, you might want to hear what the other person has to say. If so, listen for his or her response.

This practice may turn into a dialogue, but only allow it to continue as long as it is helpful. Remember, you are in charge of this event.

When you feel complete with this session, let the image of the other fade from the chair, and turn your attention back to your own body—your feet on the floor and the chair supporting you. Pay attention to what you are feeling and thinking.

You may wish to end with writing what you have experienced and possibly a simple prayer of gratefulness for what you have learned about forgiveness.

Repainting Your Story

Linda Novick

What stories do you have in your soul that trouble you? This event or incident can be something that you have thought about a lot over the course of your life—a specific regret, disappointment, trauma, or harsh judgment.... I have found the this way of working with painful memories can bring healing and hope.

Step 1: Choose a Story You Want to Reinterpret

Begin by listing several possible stories that you would like to explore. Write them all down and then choose one. If you have trouble coming up with ideas, feel free to use the prompts below to generate some thoughts.

I can't forgive myself for ...

My parents were ... which caused me to ...

If I could live any day of my life over, it would be the day that ...

I still cringe when I think of ...

One of my favorite memories is the time that ...

When you have your list, narrow it down to a single story, so that your project will have a distinct focus. Which one do you want most to see transformed, or to at least view with a different interpretation? Which would make an interesting art project? Which can you envision being expressed with the materials you want to use for this project? If the story you choose is one that you have

---

Linda Novick frequently leads painting and yoga retreats in the United States and abroad. She is a professional artist who has been teaching painting to students of all levels for over forty years and is author of *The Painting Path: Embodying Spiritual Discovery through Yoga, Brush and Color* (SkyLight Paths).

already transformed in your mind, then creating an art project around it can be a wonderful way to deepen your new interpretation. If it is a story that you still struggle with, this art project can be the means by which you find new ways of seeing that old story.

Step 2: Plan the Form of Your Autobiography

Your next step is to write about how you see your autobiography taking shape. Take some time to really envision the project. Let it unfold in your mind, taking note of colors you want to use, objects you want to include, and anything else that comes to mind. Will you combine two or more media? If so, how? Use beginner's mind and approach both your story and the project with wonder and curiosity. Write down all your thoughts and ideas without editing them. Later, you can identify the ideas that will work best for this project and save the others for later.

Write down the theme for your autobiography: "I used to believe that ... but now I see that ..." If you aren't able to fill in the second part of that sentence yet, don't worry. This project itself can be a way of discovering how that sentence should end.

Step 3: Create an Action Plan and a List of Materials

Next, review your notes and write out a clear, step-by-step action plan in which you detail the specific steps you will need to take to put your project together.... It is important to plan carefully, because there's nothing more frustrating than being absorbed in a project, only to discover you are missing a vital color, brush, or other material because you forgot to note it! When your step-by-step list is complete, distill it down into a shopping list of the materials you will need, and then obtain any materials you don't already have.

Step 4: Create Your Autobiography

When you are ready, begin creating your autobiography, following the step-by-step action plan you created yourself. Let the project take as many hours, days, or

---

What would you like to declare about yourself?

If you do add words, consider the many ways you can incorporate them....

Will you handwrite your labels? Consider ways to use words that would add interest to your autobiography. You can use a computer to type explanations and narrative. You can use letters cut out from magazines. You can also use the resist process, by writing with oil pastels and painting over it with watercolor.

---

weeks as you need. If the story you are exploring is one that has not been transformed, allow this to be a time and space where you let your mind wander, looking for new ways of understanding that story.

Depending on the medium you are using for your autobiography, including actual words in your project may seem out of place. Yet the stories we rehearse and repeat to ourselves over and over are composed of words, even if only in our own minds. The actor James Earl Jones once said, "One of the hardest things in life is having words in your heart that you can't utter." "Uttering" those words by including them in this particular project can have an especially powerful effect on the psyche.

If you are tempted to explore the power of words, I encourage you to go for it and let your intuition guide you. For example, you could label the first part of your autobiography, "I used to believe that ..." and the second part, "But now I see that ..." Such words are a declaration in your project. A strong declarative statement can affect us deeply, as witnessed by the Declaration of Independence, or in Genesis 3: "And God said, 'Let there be light: and there was light.'" These examples powerfully demonstrate how declarations can transform countries, worlds, and universes.

One of the wonders of painting is that we can always make changes, wipe out portions we don't like, or even start all over again. Our lives are much the same way. By revisiting the events of our lives with fresh eyes, we can reframe our stories to see the course of our lives in a more empowering way. We have the ability to discern and choose those interpretations that are life enhancing rather than destructive, and each time we shed an unnecessary or limiting belief we can renew ourselves. The Chinese Zen poet Shih-wu reminds us, "Events and hopes seldom agree, but who can step back doesn't worry."

The Qur'an on Forgiveness

Righteous are] those who spend generously in times of ease and difficulty, those who control their anger, and those who are forgiving toward people. Surely God loves those who do good.

—Qur'an 3:134, from *The Qur'an and Sayings of Prophet Muhammad: Selections Annotated & Explained*

Clearing the Wellspring

Nancy Barrett Chickerneo, PhD

If you are thinking about clearing out the old to make way for the new, you need to know what your priorities are. What would you like to make space *for?* What would promote a clear, flowing wellspring for you? ... What things in your life are you trying to keep under control? In what ways does this limit you? What possibilities might open for you if you were to let go of this control? Does the idea excite you? Or scare you?

The reality is, sometimes open-ended possibilities can be a bit overwhelming, even a little threatening. So let's talk about fear for a minute.... Fear that there won't be enough, fear that we don't have what it takes, fear of what others will think, fear that we'll be alone. These fears seem to crop up most when we have lost our natural inner resilience, the innate confidence that we were born with, and don't realize we can get it back....

What does fear look like for you? What does it keep you from doing? How does it keep your wellspring from flowing clearly? Can you imagine what might open up for you if you could let go of fear?

Letting go is part of many religious traditions. For people of Jewish faith, the New Year festival of Rosh Hashanah is a practice of letting go, saying good-bye to the past year and hello to what life can become in the new year. For Muslims, the ritual of fasting during the month of Ramadan begins with the Night

---

Nancy Barrett Chickerneo, PhD, is director of SPA Sisters: Spirit, Place and Authentic Self, a nonprofit organization whose mission is to inspire, educate, and awaken women to their true selves through interaction with nature, creative expression, and connection with other women. A licensed clinical professional counselor and registered art therapist, she is also a professional watercolor artist and author of *Woman Spirit Awakening in Nature: Growing into the Fullness of Who You Are* (SkyLight Paths).

of Forgiveness, when arguments of the past are let go. Buddhists believe that the practice of nonattachment greatly reduces suffering because suffering is caused by craving and attachment. A classic Christian teaching of letting go is embodied in Jesus's invitation, "Come to me, all of you who are weary and carry heavy burdens, and I will give you rest. Take my yoke upon you. Let me teach you, because I am humble and gentle at heart, and you will find rest for your souls" (Matthew 11:28–29 NLT).

Yet, when it comes to lessons in letting go, I think my friend Gail might be right when she says that "God's world of nature is the most influential teacher of all." The natural world has a rhythm of letting go. The prairies burn so stronger grasses can grow. The leaves fall to make compost for new growth. Waves wash in and out, creating beautiful patterns in the sand on the beach. Nature is always living, dying, and resurrecting.

One day as I was sitting in my office, I looked out the window and caught a glimpse of this dynamic. Dead berries were still clinging to a tree's branches while new leaves were emerging. I was reminded, once again, that letting go of one part of life or way of being always opens us up to another. When we let go of what no longer serves us or no longer fits, we make room for something new and alive. Nature has not forgotten this grace-filled process.

Letting go can be difficult—even painful—but it can also be freeing. Letting go is a practice of faith, a beginning of hope....

Imagine that you are standing in an open prairie, your body firmly planted on the ground, your hands outstretched, open, not holding on to anything, reaching to the sky. This is the posture of letting go. The vulnerable front and center part of your body is "out there." This is the stance of freedom.

Practice: A Clearing Experience

Think of a place in nature that you can get to relatively easily. Dress for the outdoors and collect your journal and whatever pencils, pens, and art supplies you wish. Once you are outside in your chosen setting, find a place that attracts you and settle in. Look, hear, smell, breathe, and be aware. Then let yourself ease into this meditative exercise:

> I notice the air, the breeze, the wind, my breath. All speak to me of life, refreshment, renewal, rebirth, even birth. I find myself living in the moment as I concentrate on breathing in, breathing out, letting go of the old in order to create space for the new.

Give yourself some time to consider these questions:

> What do I need to let go of in order to clear my wellspring?
>
> What would I like to make space for in my life?

Now look carefully around you. Get up and walk about, if you like, and look for a symbol of letting go that you are drawn to in nature. When you have selected your symbol, find a place to sit quietly and consider:

> What can nature teach me about the natural path of letting go?

Begin to focus your thoughts on the specifics in your life:

> What is one thing I could let go of to begin to make room for something new?
>
> If I were able to let go of this, how might my life be different? How would letting go of this change the clarity of my wellspring?

Reflect on your thoughts through meditation (just being in the moment, aware of your senses), art, journal writing, poetry, movement, photography—whatever you feel inspired to do.

Four Rs for Relinquishing

Kent Ira Groff

How can you move through destructive experiences so they begin to metamorphose into life-giving gifts for yourself and your community? People often give advice: "You should just let go!" Sometimes you want to scream, "But how?" In *Praying Our Goodbyes*, Joyce Rupp outlines four continuing stages on the road to healthy relinquishment and new life.

Recognition of the loss or change and unresolved fear beneath it is the beginning step. Only by being aware and by naming the "demons" can they be offered to become what the Greeks called the *daemon*—a source of creative energy.

Reflection means meditating, praying—or playing with grief "like a child's toy," as the Russian writer Maxim Gorky put it. Playing with words in a journal, poem-making, walking with the loss or change, or talking it out opens the heart's eyes to see potential gain in the pain, which may also be aspects of spiritual direction.

Ritualizing means engaging in repetitive spiritual practices—physical, verbal and visual, musical—to notice gifts in the shifts of change and loss: a symbolic object of nature, a chant, a morning walk, centering prayer, tai chi or exercises where you breathe in and hold, then breathe out and release.

Reorienting literally means turning east again, to the Orient, the sunrise where new insights dawn. Any practices that help rejuvenate the resilient child in you will bear the fruit of compassion and courage to enter the dark tunnel of transition with hope.[1] ...

Kent Ira Groff, a spiritual companion for journeyers and leaders, retreat leader and writer-poet, is founding mentor of Oasis Ministries in Pennsylvania. He is author of *Honest to God Prayer: Spirituality as Awareness, Empowerment, Relinquishment and Paradox* (SkyLight Paths), among other books.

Practicing Relinquishment

In my experience, there are two main forms of relinquishment. You have experiences where at a point in time you're able to relinquish hurts or hopes. Other times, as with intense addictions and traumatic losses, you practice what I call a "twelve-step," day-by-day process of relinquishing. Either form can lead to reorientation.... The second form involves an experience of a continuous, day-at-a-time process of relinquishing. Life may deal you a wound that's so daily present that there won't be a once-and-forever relinquishment: traumatic injury, chronic disability, vocational crisis, suicide, tragic death or disappearance. You learn to practice repeated "twelve-step" relinquishing.

Sometimes there can be no closure. A person suddenly dies or disappears. That is when rituals can help. You may write an unsent letter, burn a letter, converse with a person not present using an empty chair, name the gifts from a negative relationship, or meditate on an object of nature that symbolizes your feelings. Write your way through the pain, using a dialogue in your journal. Act it out; dance with it; do physical exercise, tai chi, or yoga. Choreograph a gesture. Talk it out with a confidant. Release it with a repeated breath prayer. All of these activities aid in the work of day-to-day relinquishment....

The way toward genuine relinquishment is to recognize, reflect on, and ritualize weighty life issues so that your soul gets reoriented.

Practice: Emptiness as Space for God

I invite you to become aware of some emptiness in your life: an unfulfilled desire you may rarely express. Gently get in touch with it.

One somewhat private person said, "It's that my mother died and never got to see my husband and children. I think of it often." It may be a kind of a spiritual homing instinct, "a God-shaped vacuum." Once you name it, gently look at ways you may be using to fill it—some good, some not so good. Prayerfully begin to offer the emptiness by thinking of it as "space for God." Ask: What's the invitation in the emptiness?

Practice: A Focusing Exercise in Three Gestures

You may begin with a simple prayer or a chant. Now I invite you to close your eyes and get in touch with some area of stress or tension in your life: physical, relational, personal, or institutional (take a few minutes). Simply be with that tension or stress, not censoring it, just noticing it. Begin to focus on where in your body you sense the tension most (head, neck, shoulders, heart, stomach, groin, thighs, legs, feet, or elsewhere). Take a few moments of silence just to be with it gently in God's presence.[2]

1. Now see if you might place your hand or hands on that area of stress or angst; or you may place your two hands on slightly different areas. Again, the goal is just to be with that stress or tension, breathing slowly (a few minutes).
2. Find a second gesture … one of releasing the stress or tension … offering this area of angst to God, with several deep, slow, exhaled breaths (a few more minutes).
3. Allow a third gesture to emerge with your hands, this time one of healing … or one of integration … or of invitation … (a few minutes longer).

If you used a prayer or a chant at the beginning, softly begin to pray or sing again….

Practice: "Let It Be"

Listen to the Beatles' song "Let It Be" (on mp3 or the CD *Let It Be*). "Mother Mary" refers to Paul McCartney's dream of his mother, who died when he was fourteen. The title also might be heard as a subtle take on Mary's response when the angel Gabriel announced she would bear a child: "Let it be to me according to your word" (Luke 1:38). As you hear the words *let it be,* or repeat them in your mind, imagine letting go of an issue that you can't control, or accepting a challenge that may want to birth itself in you.

Naming Your Hurts and Fears

Nancy L. Bieber

Sometimes fear can keep you from progressing in the journey of forgiveness. These gentle practices can help you find, examine, and ultimately let go of the fears that might be holding you back. When you can look at your fears with respect, acknowledge them and learn from them, you diminish their power.

Practice: The Naming Game

We begin by facing and naming the resistances and fears that block our willingness to open to God and prevent us from receiving God's wisdom.

1. Create a name or an image for the fear you are focusing on. For example, you may be dealing with the "judge," or perhaps you decide to name your resistance something like Suspicious Sal. Perhaps you can create an image for your fear. (What does the judge look like, anyway?) Maybe you imagine it as a boulder blocking your path or a large, bristling cactus that you don't want to touch.
2. Take a good look at it. What does it look like and what do you know about where it came from? Has it been helpful to you in the past? Is there any part of it that is useful to you in your present life?
3. Consider what would be different about your life if you relinquished this fear or diminished its power. What might change about your life? Imagine your fear shrinking in size (the incredible shrinking boulder!) until it is the size you want it to be for now.

Nancy L. Bieber is a Quaker spiritual director, retreat leader, psychologist, teacher, and author of *Decision Making and Spiritual Discernment: The Sacred Art of Finding Your Way* (SkyLight Paths). She also teaches at Lancaster Theological Seminary and is a core leader with Oasis Ministries for Spiritual Development.

When you complete this exercise, take a couple of deep breaths, and then slowly release them. If you've been sitting, stand up and stretch; move around or go outdoors. This can help you bring the experience to a close.

Practice: The Room

This practice uses the imagination to move you beyond living in a room dominated by fear.

1. Imagine a house that has rooms for many experiences. There is a room for delight, a room for work, a room for playfulness. There are rooms for peacefulness and for anger, and one windowless room, down in the basement, for fear. Picture the house as completely as you wish, but without entering the rooms.
2. Without entering the fear room, state loudly and firmly, "I don't live there anymore." Repeat it several times. Perhaps you visit there occasionally, but let yourself feel what it is like to not live there anymore.
3. Picture yourself entering one of the other rooms of the house that you will find rewarding and satisfying. What do you find yourself doing there? How do you feel in that room?
4. After a little while, take a deep breath and release it slowly, bringing the practice to a close. You may want to stand and stretch, move around, or go outdoors.

Practice: Accepting Love

This meditative practice invites you to begin trusting a loving God. The only essential tool for the practice is your desire to relearn trust.

1. Sit quietly with the words below and let them sink into you. Stop reading and picture a loving God speaking with you gently and tenderly. Slowly reread these words several times.

> Do not fear, for I have redeemed you; I have called you by name, you are mine. When you pass through the waters, I will be with you; and through the rivers, they shall not overwhelm you.... You are precious in my sight, and honored, and I love you. (Isaiah 43:1–2, 4)

2. Allow one word or phrase to repeat itself in you. Recognize your yearning for it to be true and for you to trust it. Stay with this practice longer than you think you need to.

Letting Go of Old Illusions

Jan Phillips

The Persian poet Rumi writes:

> Keep walking, though there's no place to get to.
> Don't try to see through the distances.
> That's not for human beings. Move within,
> but don't move the way fear makes you move.[1]

To be on the path of the heart is to move the way courage makes us move. It is to be light and unencumbered, emptied of debris and old illusions, knowing everything that ever happened to us got us to this moment, which is the only moment we have and the only place God dwells. If we are still dragging pieces of the past into today, we may need to turn around, back up, and revisit people or places to free ourselves from entanglements that keep us from our path. And this may take some time.

In 1967, I entered the religious community of the Sisters of St. Joseph of Carondelet to become a nun, but I was a little too radical and was sent home after two years in the novitiate. For years after being dismissed, I was a furnace of raging anger.

The night my superior informed me that I was not to continue my novitiate, I was stunned into silence. When she said, "You know why, don't you?" I lied, trying to make this difficult job easier on her. "Yes," I said. "I guess so." When my parents were ushered into the room next door, I asked, "What am I supposed to tell them?" "Just tell them you don't have a religious disposition," she said, and

---

Jan Phillips is an award-winning photographer, writer, and national workshop leader. She is cofounder of *Syracuse Cultural Workers*, publisher of artwork that inspires justice, diversity, and global consciousness. She is author of *Divining the Body: Reclaim the Holiness of Your Physical Self* (SkyLight Paths), among other books.

that's exactly what I uttered as they walked toward me in that tiny parlor. But I was wondering why this had happened when I loved that life so deeply.

For months afterward, I'd go to the mailbox thinking maybe this was the day I'd get a letter from the convent saying it was all a mistake. But it never came. And I never forgave them.

And I never found my heart's path, because *that* was it, and they ripped me away from it. Or so I thought. I was so full of anger and resentment that it tainted everything. There was no space inside for joy. There was no way to carve out a new life because all my energy was going into the old one I wanted so desperately to have. I would not let go. Bad people had done bad things to me. I was a victim of a terrible wrongdoing. My whole life became this story. I joined the ranks of the walking wounded and stopped taking responsibility for the path I was on.

Eight years passed before I wrote to the community, asking for an explanation of why I was dismissed. I wrote about the hole in my heart and my inability to heal it without their help.

Would they please just give me the reason so I could begin my process of recovering? My novice director had died of stomach cancer, and I received a letter from the nun who had been director of the young professed sisters when I was there. She vaguely remembered me, and she was now the Mother Provincial, in charge of all the sisters in the Albany, New York, province. In her letter, she reminded me that according to canon law, the community did not owe an explanation to anyone who had been dismissed. But she'd gone to my file, and since it was so short, she sent along this passage: *Jan Phillips did not have a religious disposition and was dismissed because of her excessive and exclusive relationships.*

Finally. Something I could latch on to. It was a beginning, but only that. I had years to go to complete the process, to forgive them and move on. It helped me to have a reason, but the one they offered seemed ridiculous. They were just frightened by my passion, I told myself. No one was more inclusive than I when it came to relationships. And what did they mean by "religious disposition"? That you never questioned authority? That you memorized maxims and ate everything on your plate? That you recreated with someone different every day and finished the Stations of the Cross before 5 p.m.? Was it my attachment to the *resurrected* Christ, my lust for life in all its abundance that was really the issue? While my anger had dissipated over the years, I was still bound somehow, still resentful, still blaming them for banishing me from the one life that felt true to me.

I could not find the path of my heart because my heart was locked up, and I could not unlock it on my own.

It was in 1991, twenty-two years after my dismissal, that I called the sister who was the Mother Provincial when it happened. I asked if she would just sit with me while I told her the story of how it felt. That was all I wanted, a witness from the community. She agreed and we set a date. When I arrived at her convent, we went out to the screened-in porch and sat down, knee to knee.

"I'm going to start when I was twelve," I said, "when I first decided to be a nun. I'll probably cry through the whole story, but I just want you to listen from the beginning to the end, all right?" She nodded her head yes. For the next hour, we both wept as I drained out all my feelings and despair over the whole incident. I was honest about my broken heart, my shattered faith, my inability to find another path for myself while I was harboring all this sorrow and resentment. "I just want to let it go, Sister. I want to let it go, and I need your help," I sobbed. "Can you help me get free of this?" She took my hands in hers and said, "Jan, will you forgive me personally for the part I played in this deep and terrible pain of yours?" I nodded my head yes. "And will you forgive the community for the pain we caused you and for the mistakes we made in dealing with you while you were with us?" "Yes, Sister, I forgive the community," I blurted out, and with that forgiveness came the release, the freedom I needed to go on with my life and find the path that was calling me. With that forgiveness came a surge of energy, a rush of tenderness I hadn't felt in twenty years. It opened me up, unlocked my heart. It was a step into God I couldn't make while I was clinging to my pain and anger.

Only after I forgave could I understand there was nothing to forgive. They did not cause me pain. They just did what they did. Pain was my response to it. Pain was me holding on to it. Pain was me refusing to accept the life before me. Once I released it, I could bless that time I had. I could see that my two years in the novitiate was all I needed to get my footing in a faith I was meant to live out more publicly.

I was like a young eagle in a nest, peering over the edge, afraid to fly. And they nudged me out so I could soar. And I am.

Two years ago I returned to the motherhouse to give a workshop on creativity as sacrament. When I got to reconciliation, I used myself as an example. I told the story of my long journey to forgiveness and of how blocked I was for all the years I held on to my misery. In *A Course in Miracles*, the author Helen Schucman says that "forgiveness is the healing of the perception of separation." I only *thought* I couldn't have the life I wanted. Because my perception was of separation, I was living like something was being denied me, when I was free all along to construct a life that was like my life in the convent—a life that balanced silence and solitude with community and service.

I smile these days when I look at my life and see how much like a religious life it really is. I begin with morning prayers, work in solitude for the most part, give service by teaching and sharing what I know. And I've created a vital community of kindred spirits in my own town and across the country, so I have sisters around me everywhere I go.

There aren't that many steps to forgiveness, but sometimes it takes a long time to make them, or to figure out what we need to do to complete the process. The first step is to stop blaming others for our state of mind. If we feel someone is keeping us from being happy, then it's our responsibility to change the nature of the relationship. Clinging to a relationship out of habit or guilt or fear is a betrayal of our soul. Holding on to resentments weakens our immune system, steals our energy, and roots us in the past where there is nothing real, nothing to feed us, no sign of the Divine.

The step into God is a bold, clean step into now—this day with these people under these circumstances. If we sink our feet into the present moment and feel anything but joy, we're probably not on the path of the heart. It is time, then, to go inward, to ask our heart what it desires, and to move our feet in that direction.

What Animals Can Teach Us about Letting Go

Diana L. Guerrero

Chester was a naughty dog. He ran at, jumped on, and nipped anyone coming to visit. His owners were at a loss over what to do. When I arrived for the consultation, Chester didn't get any great attention for his poor behavior. Instead, he got a fancy dose of behavior modification and quickly learned that to get attention, he needed to sit.

Nancy, his owner, said, "Wow, I can't believe how fast he understood what you wanted." However, as with all new students, animals in school test the parameters. Sometimes they just forget and go back to the entrenched behavior. Chester was no exception and he soon got into trouble; he then made amends. I forgave him as quickly as he forgave me for correcting his poor choice. Nancy didn't understand and asked, "Why are you praising him so quickly?" Chester received a verbal correction and immediately adjusted his behavior, so he got praise. It is called "being in the moment," and what mattered most was his correct choice and behavior at that instant. He chose proper behavior instead of unacceptable behavior. When Chester tested the parameters, his behavior was more extreme, and so were the corrections. For such infractions, doggie etiquette dictates that canines make amends by licking. I accepted his apology by allowing it. We both forgave each other for any errors, reaching a place of harmony and understanding immediately. Animals teach us to be in the present moment, the only moment.

Diana L. Guerrero consults and lectures on animal behavior and related topics and publishes *Ark Animals*, an Internet magazine dedicated to wild and domestic animal behavior. She is author of *What Animals Can Teach Us about Spirituality: Inspiring Lessons from Wild and Tame Creatures* (SkyLight Paths).

A lioness guides, teaches, and protects her young. Although she might discipline one of her cubs for a transgression, she quickly forgives and does not hold a grudge. She watches as her offspring struggle with the lessons of life. Those educational experiences mold them and ensure their survival. She understands that schooling is necessary for their growth and success in life. She seldom intervenes, but she does respond to their cries. No matter what their actions, or expressions, she is always nearby in resilient support. Her relationship with her cubs is a reflection of how we should also behave in our relationships, and it parallels our relationship to the Divine.

Animals also are examples of how to move through life peacefully. They conserve their energy for matters of importance. The African lion spends a majority of his time sleeping. The rest of his efforts are focused on hunting or pride interactions. The African lion reminds us to focus our attention on our relationships, our friends and family. In addition, he is an example of what we need to strive for—being at ease instead of worrying about external circumstances and things beyond our control....

Although an African lion prefers to avoid a fight, he will bravely face an opponent and his fears. He is aware that it is sometimes necessary to take a stand to protect himself, his territory, or the pride of lions he claims as his family. Even so, he avoids a battle if given the chance, and he picks any skirmishes carefully.

We too must learn to pick and choose our battles. Some situations require that we take a stand and meet our challengers eye to eye, but our biggest demons are those we do not have the courage to face. Often, if we get closer and gaze at them from a new perspective, they end up less overwhelming than we thought. It doesn't matter whether our trials stem from another human being or an internal struggle: When our opponents are confronted, they withdraw under our concentrated focus. A colossal obstacle or problem often turns out to be a manageable situation.

An African lion injured in battle withdraws to lick his wounds, but once the dispute is over, no further energy is given to it. Members of the pride butt heads and rub each other in greeting, cooperative hunting efforts supply a feast, and life goes on. If only we recovered so quickly from our hurts and battles.

If we suffer from an encounter, we too need time to lick our wounds and sort out our priorities and feelings. If we feel wronged, or that we injured another, the best action we can take is to forgive. This forgiveness must be for our choices, our actions, and ourselves, as well as for the target of our hostility, decisions, or conduct. If we don't move on, then we suffer needlessly.

Emotions are powerful. When we harbor anger, resentment, or jealousy, we may feel the power of those emotions, but they are not usually constructive. These feelings need to be resolved before they fester and create larger problems. The inability to forgive or to release volatile feelings only prevents us from moving into a heart-centered equilibrium. Our decisions and actions are more reasonable and successful if we are compassionate and forgive.

Back in the early 1990s, a psychologist friend of mine proposed her theory: Dogs were angels put here on earth to teach us about unconditional love; after all, D-O-G is G-O-D spelled backward. I laughed, but I didn't dismiss the notion. Relationships between dogs and humans contain the amazing capacity to exchange love without restraint. Dogs greet everyone with gusto. They see the best and then translate it through their whole bodies. When greeting their companion, they often run in exuberance, spinning in circles and sometimes barking in excitement. No matter what the owner is like, a dog still loves him or her with all its being. Their actions show unconditional love and they do not harbor any resentment. Dogs forgive and forget quickly.

Humans are more protective of themselves emotionally. Some dogs and other animals find the need to do this, too. Animals with a history of repeated abandonment, or abuse, may start to protect themselves by withdrawing or by exhibiting defensive aggressive behaviors geared toward keeping strangers away. This goes against the true nature of the beast and only contributes to loneliness and isolation. Old emotional wounds must heal so the animal can truly function. This holds true for humans as well....

When we have our equilibrium on this rung of the ladder, we naturally become more inquisitive because we experience love, expect love, and feel safe. When we feel secure, we are more affectionate with one another, more compassionate, more passionate about life and others.

Reconciliation and Forgiveness in Relationships

Genuine forgiveness requires a profound reorientation of your heart. It is a deeply challenging act and also a deeply spiritual one.

—Rev. Carolyne Call

While much of the work of forgiveness is done in your own heart and soul, there is often a relational component as well. In all close relationships, sooner or later there will be a need to forgive, for offenses large and small. In this section you'll find encouragement and practical advice for specific relationships and situations: restoring a relationship by making amends and asking forgiveness for your own mistakes, or by having a heartfelt, healing conversation with someone whose mistakes have hurt you; choosing not to restore a relationship; dealing with both forgiveness and grief in the case of divorce or suicide; and the everyday work of forgiveness in situations like caregiving and marriage.

Sometimes on your journey to freedom through forgiveness you'll have to decide whether to restore a lost relationship. In that case, it is important to set boundaries for your own protection and for relational health, as Marcia Ford points out. Sometimes you may have to end a relationship before you can take a breath and begin the journey of forgiveness. Susan Quinn shares her story of deciding to let go of a relationship that was wounding rather than nourishing. In ongoing relationships, it's helpful to be reminded of concrete ways to make room for heartfelt communication. Rev. Donna Schaper and Kay Lindahl provide models for this in both speaking and listening. This section is packed with useful tools. Are you ready to dig in?

Reconciliation in Your Own Heart

Caren Goldman

During a long retreat I attended, participants from all over the country explored the gospels of Mark, Matthew, and Luke historically, literally, metaphorically, and experientially through the use of journaling, art, music, mime, and silence. Despite efforts to stay awake on this uncomfortably hot afternoon, my head bobbed and my eyes slowly closed as the leader read Jesus's teachings from Matthew's gospel: "So when you are offering your gift at the altar, if you remember that your brother or sister has something against you, leave your gift there before the altar and go; first be reconciled to your brother or sister, and then come and offer your gift" (Matthew 5:21–23).

Startled awake by what I thought I was hearing, I picked up my copy of the text and read it and reread it. Each time one word stunned me—the preposition *to*. By the time I put the passage down, I knew that word—*to*—was changing my life. I had always assumed the passage said, "be reconciled *with* your brother or sister." But it didn't. It said *to*. It said *to* over and over again as the Spirit of Reunion directed my mind to a slideshow of family members who had never again been seen after conflict. As each snapshot made room for the next, I kept curiously trying to figure out exactly what the word *to* was telling me about reconciliation.

Finally I got it. Long after everyone else had left the seminar room, I now knew that I could become reconciled *to* family members living and dead who had cut themselves off or been cut off by another. I could become reconciled *to* them even if I could never be reconciled *with* them. As I looked at what I could now see ahead of me, I prayed prayers of gratitude with all my heart, mind, strength, and soul.

Caren Goldman is an award-winning journalist, spiritual retreat leader, and conflict-resolution consultant to churches, synagogues, and not-for-profit organizations. She is the author of *Restoring Life's Missing Pieces: The Spiritual Power of Remembering and Reuniting with People, Places, Things and Self* (SkyLight Paths).

Gratitude for at last finding a way to narrow ancestral and domestic divides. Gratitude for a path to see hidden gaps forming traps in the family soul. Gratitude for a path where I could collect missing pieces that hopefully would bridge great gorges.

Being reconciled *with* another person implies mutuality and negotiation—that both parties have agreed to meet and enter a divisive space between them to attempt settling their issues. The process gets under way when they accompany each other into the divide and agree to negotiate difficult terrain to arrive at a new place. If emotionally mature, their desire to reach accord will be sincere and their common and personal agendas set in a spirit of reunion. But it will not be easy.

From start to finish, each person will try his or her best to manage anxiety so it doesn't escalate and cause a blowup. It will be a struggle. By their presence, the parties will be saying they agree to disagree. But can they do that? Each will be responsible for making "I" (not finger-pointing "you") statements about their feelings and experiences. Each will need to ask honest questions, avoid rhetorical ones, and resist lecturing.

The process entails asking each person to witness the other's truth, to listen carefully, and to take deep breaths to refresh their thoughts and inspire creative thinking. Moments of silence will call out for patience and the understanding that a pregnant pause may be preparation for birthing something new. Ultimately, to whatever degree they can, the transactors will offer transparency and vulnerability to one another to discover more than just the issue that separated them. They will dive into the river at the bottom of the divide and ride its unpredictable currents. They will pay attention to signs showing them that the issue on the surface may not have been the real issue or what *really* was the issue. It is there—in the discussions, gestures, and silence that follows—that reconciliation can happen. If it does and when it does, there will be only one other place to go. As the reunion draws to a close, forgiveness and expressions of gratitude will be offered, and with new hope each in his or her own way will go his or her own way.

Reconciliation *to* another is not the same, however. The road traveled to that place does not necessarily end in a physical reunion with the other—especially if he or she has passed away. Instead, being reconciled *to* means we journey psycho-spiritually to the person who comes "alive" within us. Through memories and memorabilia, we encounter the one who feels unapproachable, untouchable, and unreasonable. The one pushing buttons. The one who remains angry, sad, argumentative, or manipulative. The one with whom we still have unfinished business. The one who has no interest in finishing business with us. The one we hurt or who died before we could just talk, express remorse, ask for forgiveness, offer forgiveness, and mutually agree to move on.

Like all attempts at reconciliation, the choice to be reconciled *to* another begins with a yearning for the status quo to change. The process starts with willingness to be responsible and accountable. To look everywhere and at everything we can to see what precipitated the divide in a relationship. To accept and believe that whatever the Spirit of Re-union brings to mind can contain seeds of change—changes of attitudes, minds, hearts, beliefs, assumptions, and other things that previously grew out of control. And to trust that resurrecting events, words, images, and memories of feelings will help us find and fit together the missing pieces we need to reframe the past.

Next we begin retracing the steps we took and choices we made that may have led to the separation. We might ask: *How did I back away or move away emotionally from the relationship? Did I run from a truth? Did I move on because I felt the cost of the relationship wasn't worth the promise?* Along the way we also have to look at where the broken relationship took us afterward. *Did I leave feeling "right," relieved, happy, sad, confused, angry, revengeful, up, or down? Did I believe that "out of sight, out of mind" would serve me well? Did I ever take a moment to imaginatively put myself in the other's shoes to better see another's perspective?* If we explore those questions consciously, we can anticipate that our efforts to demystify the whole truth may result in *dis*-ease, pain, and suffering. If so, we must commit to staying the course—living questions and moving onward because we yearn to be in a new place within and see and experience this person differently. A place where, we can let go and take back our projections. A place where, in the end, we come to understand that by becoming reconciled *to* this other, our relationship with that person within us has changed forever. Someday, we may even choose to be reconciled *with* him or her. But we may also choose not to be—to just say no. No for the sake of a "yes" to new life in a new place that reconciliation *to* someone else can bring.

Whether we attempt to reconcile *with* or *to* family members or others, the Spirit of Re-union knows that hope in the heart must join with courage to mend a broken relationship. That without hope, attempts at reunion and re-union may falter and fail. In family relationships hope fueled by memories of those we've known even before birth helps us to keep living questions in blind alleys. Hope also pokes us with reminders that our efforts ripple across and affect something bigger than us. We take action to do our part to help restore balance, healing, and wholeness to a wobbly and tilted system.

Practice: Journaling with Others and Self

Some family disagreements last for a very long time or even a lifetime. Dialogic journaling offers a therapeutic way to imaginatively have a conversation with the other person. It can take the form of a scene from a play in which the characters are you and the "other." Plan to write your dialogue in a place where you feel comfortable, focused, and safe—at your desk, in a favorite chair, at the beach, in the woods, at a coffee shop or graveside. You do not need to write in an actual journal with a pencil or pen. You can write on loose sheets of paper or on your computer or some other electronic device. When you are ready to begin writing, recall or reread Matthew's passage about taking a gift to the altar (5:21–23). Then allow the Spirit of Re-union to bring to mind a thought, image, or sense of a family member who holds something against you.

Identify yourself as you open a conversation. For example:

> Me: It's been a long time since we had anything to say to each other.

After making your statement, patiently wait for a response. It may take a while before you hear the other person's comment. His or her words will come. When they do, write down exactly what is said. When ready, continue the conversation:

> Relative: I'm still angry about what happened and not sure I want to be talking to you now.
>
> Me: I can understand that. Part of me feels the same way. But I miss you and would like to try to figure out what we can do to talk about it and reconcile.

The conversation between you and the "other" continues. While writing, do not stop to edit or make judgments about the "quality" or veracity of the dialogue. Keep going until there is nothing more for either of you to say. Once you feel the conversation has ended, do what personally feels natural and helpful. There is no right or wrong way to revisit the dialogue. You may read and reflect on it immediately or put it aside and return to it later. If the conversation was left dangling, you may want to wait for the Spirit of Re-union to call you to pick up where you left off and begin conversing again.

It Starts with You

Marcia Ford

Barbara had been estranged from her brother for so long that she eventually lost track of him entirely. That would have been okay with her five years ago; back then, she didn't much care whether she ever saw him again or not. He had lived with Barbara and her husband for a few months after being released from rehab, but she had kicked him out after she smelled beer on his breath. Or what she thought was beer. She began to wonder if she had been wrong.

Some time later, Barbara and her husband began to realize that little things were missing—mostly small but valuable items like seldom-used jewelry and a few collectible coins. In anger, she called her brother and accused him of stealing from her; yes, he admitted, he had taken a few things and sold them so he could find a place to live. Furious, Barbara hung up and swore she would have nothing to do with him until he apologized and asked her forgiveness.

Within three years, both of Barbara's parents died, and she felt a compelling need to be reconciled with her brother, the only surviving member of her biological family. Today she lives with the regret that she never forgave him, sought his forgiveness, or attempted to reconcile with him when she had the chance. She prays regularly that he'll somehow reappear on someone's radar screen so she can contact him.

Barbara had learned a hard lesson about forgiveness and reconciliation: you can't wait for the other guy to make the first move. I suspect her brother was too ashamed of his actions to ever think she could forgive him, so he kept his distance

---

Marcia Ford is a former editor of *Christian Retailing* magazine, an Explorefaith.org columnist, and a frequent contributor to *Publishers Weekly*. The author of eighteen books, including *The Sacred Art of Forgiveness: Forgiving Ourselves and Others through God's Grace* (SkyLight Paths), she was the religion editor of the *Asbury Park Press* for ten years.

for a while and then dropped out of sight. By the time Barbara's heart had softened toward him, it was too late.

But even in situations where your offender—or a person you have offended—is still a part of your everyday life, you need to accept the fact that it's probably going to be up to you to begin the healing process. After all, you're the one reading a book on forgiveness, so the concept is apparently one you've been thinking about. That puts the ball in your court. Once you begin to get the first inkling that you need to forgive someone, or ask for forgiveness from someone, that's probably a fairly good indication that you need to take the initiative.

I cannot begin to relate the countless stories of regret that I've heard from people who wish they had done something that they knew they should do at the time, before it was too late.

Expecting someone else to get the message about forgiveness isn't exactly something you can count on. Look around you; television shows, commercials, movies, and music frequently sound out a message of revenge, not forgiveness. It's not impossible to find the inspiration to forgive, but there are an awful lot of messages out there trying to convince us that we need to get the upper hand on our offenders. The chance that someone will stumble on a message about forgiveness—a message powerful enough to penetrate their heart—is just that. A chance.

Don't take that chance. If you have offended someone and you want to ask their forgiveness, don't put it off. Barbara realized that too late; she never confronted her brother about the possibility that he'd been drinking again before she abruptly threw him out. She wanted—needed—his forgiveness for that. She may never get it now.

Likewise, she wanted to let him know that she had forgiven him for stealing from her. Most of all, though, she wanted to be reconciled with him. There's always the possibility, of course, that he would have rejected her, but at least she would have had peace in knowing she had tried. Living with that kind of regret is particularly painful; our sins of omission often cause more suffering than our sins of commission do.

"There are many persons ready to do what is right because in their hearts they know it is right. But they hesitate, waiting for the other fellow to make the make the first move—and he, in turn, waits for you," Marian Anderson points out.[1] If you are ready to do what in your heart you know is right, don't wait for the other guy. To him, *you* are the other guy—and he's waiting for you to make the first move.

Practice: Making the First Move

Think about what it is that holds you back from doing what is right. Consider all the possibilities: fear, pride, uncertainty, shame, embarrassment, and so forth. The fear of rejection is an especially powerful deterrent when it comes to forgiveness and reconciliation, for example. How can you get past those factors in order to take the initiative you know you should take?

Make a list of every situation in your life in which you are waiting for someone else to make the first move. It doesn't have to be related to forgiveness or reconciliation. Maybe it's another couple's turn to have you and your spouse over for dinner. Who cares whose turn it is? If you want to get together with them, invite them back to your house for dinner. We often don't realize the pleasure we deprive ourselves of—all because we're waiting for someone else to take the initiative.

The Sacred Speech of Forgiveness

Rev. Donna Schaper

If you have ever been forgiven, you know just how holy an experience it is. Doors that were closed, relationships that were ended, paths that were cut off suddenly face a clearing instead of darkness. We can go on. Very often, the words carry the clearing to us and us to the clearing.

Often it is not the "other" who is forgiving us so much as God who is forgiving us. God provides the energy. Sacred speech comes from our center in God and reaches for the center in others. It pays more attention to the vertical, the alpha, the omega, the source, and the important than it does to our horizontal relationships with each other. Sacred speech happens horizontally but is based vertically. It considers the urgent but stays centered in the important. Sacred speech makes choices about what matters and has as its chief antagonist the trivial. Sometimes even large things, such as an extramarital affair, for example, are small in the larger scheme of things.

We do not use speech to defend ourselves so much as we use it to open ourselves. "I" speech becomes safe. "I" can tell you I love you, treasure you, want to know you, and am disturbed by something you said. I have the permission and the commandment to enter difficulty with you in hope. I can open up things you might prefer to have closed. I know how to forgive—not by my power but by Spirit's power. Instead of "staying strong and firm," we become soft and vulnerable. That tenderness touches the tender part of others; we come out of the forest into a clearing. We can start again. No, we will never be the same. Some trust will

---

Rev. Donna Schaper is widely recognized as one of the most outstanding communicators in her generation of Protestant clergy. Senior minister at Judson Memorial Church in New York City, she is author of several books, including *Sacred Speech: A Practical Guide for Keeping Spirit in Your Speech*, and coauthor of *Labyrinths from the Outside In: Walking to Spiritual Insight—A Beginner's Guide* (both SkyLight Paths).

disappear. Some scars will take a long time to scab over. But scabs beat walking around with an open wound, a wound that only festers over time.

"The great irony of trust is that in order to rebuild it, one must take risks with the person who broke it," says Professor Robert Folger in an article on social psychology in the *Chronicle of Higher Education*. "You're trying to rebuild trust out of distrust ... part of the way you would do that would be to be vulnerable. It's tricky. You hate an enemy that you've feuded with for generations. Your first step has to be tiny. That's the fine line. You can't afford to get your throat cut." Folger argues that such tiny steps are particularly hard in places of great conflict, such as the Middle East, because people have been trying confidence-building measures there for a long time. "You try doing stitches," he says, "then over the past 18 months, 10 years of stitching together was ripped out. Once it's ripped out, it takes 10 years to make up."[1]...

Forgiveness can happen early or late—when we realize just how short life is, we usually want it to happen early. We want to know how to have the goal of perpetual forgiveness already in our hearts; then the right words come. Instead of saying, "I could never forgive you for that," we say, "I will be able to forgive you but not just yet." Some people can forgive their enemies and some cannot. Some people can forgive their parents for what they did or didn't do—and some cannot. Some cannot forgive the world's terrorists. Many live a foot away from forgiveness but can't quite break down into it.

Melting in forgiveness means going forward into a new world, in a new way. Most of us aren't very good at it. That's why Jesus's admonition that we forgive debt—even monetary debts—with grace and wit and gladness is more than a little difficult. We know he is right, but we don't know how to be like him.

Jesus argues that forgiving an unpaid debt is better than living without forgiveness.... What do we get from hanging on to our debts? Not much. The only result is separation from those whom we could love.

Speech That Carries Spirit

"I know I said I would never forgive you for having that affair. I know I said I never *could* forgive you. But the idea of going on in life without you is more than I can bear. We have children; they still love you. Thus I am forced, by the grace and power of God, to accept your apology and to trust that you won't go in that direction again. I speak not from my own power because alone I could never forgive you. Because God still loves you, I am going to try again."

It is possible that forgiveness is a form of the highest pragmatism. No, we don't always survive something as horrific as the death camps. Or the trouble of someone who has deeply hurt us. Or stolen from us. Or beat us. Or raped us. Or done something "unforgivable." But still, what do we get out of hanging on to the debt? When we let the debt go, we lean toward God. We do what we can't do. And God does the rest. God makes our speech sacred by doing what we think we can't do....

Sacred speech as forgiveness often means a good healthy connection to the word *I*. "I am sorry." "I forgive you." The whole person comes along in big sentences like that. In holy intimacy, I avoid "you" conversation.

I don't say, "You are really bugging me." Or, "You should never have had that affair in the first place." Instead I say, "I am really bothered or hurt by what you just said." Therapists speak about staying in the "I." When we know the grace of God that makes even the approval of our closest partner appropriately penultimate, we are able to stay in the "I." When we get scared, we start the "you" talk.

Religious professionals and spiritual people have an obligation to teach "I" talk at both the deepest and the most trivial levels. We incarnate sacred speech. We help people make it real in their ordinary lives.

Fear causes us to think that if we lose our lover's or best friend's approval we are finished, wiped out, destroyed. Sacred speech knows that no person can destroy us and that nothing can separate us from the love of God. Those who are capable of the most intimacy are those who are most centered—and therefore freer to take the most risks. Saying "I'm sorry" matters terribly to those who have little center. We slip into nothingness when we have done wrong.

Saying "I'm sorry" as a centered person is a loss of almost nothing. When confronted with difficult issues, the best thing intimates can learn to do is ask questions. A good one is, "Could you tell me more?" We urge the other to self-disclose; we don't expose or "uncloset" him or her. Especially if we are disturbed

Speech That Carries Spirit

"You are driving me crazy ... with that turning of the page while I am trying to sleep."
"I'm sorry, darling, I will go read on the couch—but I really want to stay close to you."
Notice the absence of defense: "I can read my paper if I want to ..." Notice the absence of advice: "No one can drive you crazy unless you let them." Notice the absence of excuses: "You say I am bugging you and I agree with you." Notice the moving closer while the other is distancing.
Notice that an apology always goes a long way to defuse a tense situation.

by something he or she is saying (or not saying), we need the simple tool of "tell me more." That phrase all by itself is godly. It means we are interested.

It means we are ready. It means we want to know. It imitates the relationship God has with humanity—where we are always urged to tell God more about who we are and where we are stuck. It is also the sentence that best walks the path to forgiveness.

Instead of trying to find out who is right and who is wrong—a dead end and an unspiritual act of the highest order—we agree to listen.

"Tell me more."

"Tell me more" is a way of granting the request for connection, which is what just about any complaint in any relationship really is.

Such a strategy also means that we have in our spiritual pocket an alternative to control. We learn these alternatives by living, by memorizing psalms, by studying Scripture, by being pragmatic about life at the highest level. "Don't tell me that" is the opposite of "Tell me more." Many of us shut down to our intimates without even knowing it because we don't want to hear what they are really saying. Many a partner stops being able to hear a loved one because he or she has begun to express unhappiness most of the time. We stop listening when we don't want to hear what the other has to say. When we don't hear what the other has to say, we also don't respond or speak well.

Sacred speech self-differentiates; it speaks plainly and personally and directly. It keeps good boundaries on behalf of good relationships.

Intimates use "I" language because it is fundamentally secure. No human can secure us. But Spirit and Source sufficiently secure us for relationships that are fair and just and caring. We develop into people who can use the "I" word well: "I, who am a real person with real capacity and realization of who I am, forgive you." "I, who am a real person with real capacity and realization

Speech That Carries Spirit

The barber said to his long-term client, "Those Palestinians are acting like animals. Do you see the way they terrorize and commit suicide just to keep Israel on high alert all the time?" The client excused himself from the barber's chair and said he would have to come back later. He returned the next day and said in a quiet voice, "I am very disturbed to hear anyone speak of anyone as an animal. It reminds me of what happened to the Jews under Hitler, when they were robbed of their humanity." And then he waited. His barber said, "I am sorry. I understand. I'm upset too. But let's not let it get in the way of our relationship. There is enough damage already done."

of who I am, am sorry." Sacred speech sets limits *and* tests boundaries: It is free to do both.

Out of our security, we are able to forgive. We are able to go on. We are able to do things that we, alone, "can't do." Spirit does them through us. Spirit keeps the air and water circulating in a relationship by a nearly constant process of forgiveness.

Speech That Carries Spirit

"I wish our relationship had more excitement ..."
"Tell me more... about what you want ..."
"I want to see more plays, make love more, go for long walks, have a sense that you really know me, through and through ..."
"Tell me more ..."
"I want to linger over dinner and laugh. I want you to think I'm the best-looking person you ever met ..."
"Tell me more ..."
Notice the refusal to defend. Most people hear the need for more excitement as a straight-out accusation. "What, didn't we have lots of excitement just last week ... and what about that trip last summer?"
Notice the absence of self-justification.
Notice the genuine interest in hearing.

Listening for Reconciliation

Kay Lindahl

Creating Safe Spaces: Listening with Love

What defines a safe space? Why do we need one? And how do we create one? Safe spaces are especially important to facilitate listening when sensitive or controversial issues are being discussed. People need to feel that it's safe to express their opinions, that they can trust each other. It's harder to listen in tough situations if we don't first know the parameters of the conversation.

When I think I might be confronted about something or if I have to make a controversial decision, I will usually be busy planning my response instead of listening to the issue as it is presented. This changes if I know that there are guidelines for the conversation—that it's not going to be a free-for-all.

One of the first steps in creating safe space is finding a common commitment. A commitment can take many forms, but I find that a verbal understanding at the beginning of the conversation is the minimum for people to feel at ease. For instance, if I am meeting with a friend to dialogue about a recent incident that has troubled our relationship, our first task is to discover what we hope to accomplish. In this instance, it could be to heal our relationship, not necessarily to rehash the incident.

Another quality of safe space is respect for each other and for differing ways of expression. Even when we don't agree, we can honor the dignity of the human soul. It's not always easy to hear that which is counter to our opinions. And yet, it is important for all to feel safe enough to share their ideas.

Kay Lindahl teaches the sacred art of listening to a variety of groups all over the world. She is the author of *Practicing the Sacred Art of Listening: A Guide to Enrich Your Relationships and Kindle Your Spiritual Life* and coeditor of *Women, Spirituality and Transformative Leadership: Where Grace Meets Power* (both SkyLight Paths), among other books. She is a cofounder of Women of Spirit and Faith and the founder of The Listening Center in Long Beach, California.

Perhaps the key quality of a safe space is love. One way to be sure that love is nurtured is to check in before you begin. Offer the opportunity for each person to say whatever he or she needs to in order to be present.

Risk being vulnerable to deepen the possibility for connection. The trust that is generated from this process becomes a foundation for the rest of the conversation.

Presence: Listening from Your Heart

One of the foundations of spiritual community is relationship. How do we relate to each other, especially to those who are not like us? By sacred listening, we can learn to be more present with each other.

Two aspects of being present in a conversation are listening and speaking. Many people are familiar with guidelines to conscious listening such as suspending assumptions and judgments and listening to understand rather than to agree or believe.

Another guideline for being truly present in our relationships is to speak from personal experience and to use "I" language. In our culture this is an amazing challenge. Too often the subject of our conversations are "you," "we," "everyone," or "they." This amounts to speaking from the head or the intellect, and sounds a lot like a lecture.

Speaking from the "I," the true self, the soul, is speaking from the heart. "I" language implies being accountable for what is said. It requires reflection to get to that place. It is the kind of speaking that connects us. Practice this and notice how it connects you to others.

Listen to the difference between these two ways of speaking. "You know how it is when you're feeling down and you want some support and inspiration and you just can't seem to get yourself motivated." Now listen to the true self in the present: "I know when I'm feeling down and I want some support and inspiration and I just can't seem to get myself motivated, I feel really lonely." Notice the use of pronouns in conversations. In your own speaking, be a listening presence.

Conversations of the Heart: Listening for Soul

"Heart listening" is the spiritual practice of listening from the heart and listening to the heart. Being truly listened to is one of the greatest gifts we can give each other. Heart listening is more than simply not interrupting others when they are speaking or not finishing their sentences for them. It calls upon many of the skills that we have already discerned: patience, silence, presence, and appreciation.

Heart listening may sound a lot like a meditation practice—it incorporates many of the same principles. Listening from the heart is being open and waiting for the other to speak what is really in their heart. As you practice, you will learn to be a heart listener and to know when you are hearing words from the heart.

Listening from the heart allows for silence and reflection. Conversation slows down and there is time to relax and feel a sense of peace. An actual sacred space is created between two people when we heart listen.

Listening to the heart also is part of this holy work. We become present to the other in such a way that they feel safe to speak what's in their heart. We practice having a sense of wonder and curiosity about another. The experience is almost as though I, as the listener, can call forth the full expression of the "listenee" simply by the way I listen to them. Sometimes I don't have to speak or ask questions but simply listen to their heart with my heart.

Listening to my own heart before speaking is another aspect of heart listening. It does not happen very often in ordinary conversation because it opens us up in ways that may be uncomfortable. Risking vulnerability with another takes courage. What if they take what I say and use it against me? What if they laugh at me? What if they ignore me? The rewards of taking that risk are extraordinary. First, I experience the wonderful feeling of fully expressing my true self. Then I feel the intimacy and sense of relatedness with another. Connecting with someone on a heart level is a holy experience. Heart listening opens up what is sacred inside us, releasing love. Speaking and listening from the heart is the art of dialogue. The more I experience this kind of speaking and listening the more natural it becomes.

When I practice this sacred art I discover that the skills I learn can translate into my personal and professional lives. I find myself appreciating other points of view rather than being suspicious of them. I find others opening up to me in different ways. I feel more connected.

The Philokalia on Forgiveness

Has a brother been the occasion of some trial for you and has your resentment led you to hatred? Do not let yourself be overcome by this hatred, but conquer it with love. You will succeed in this by praying to God sincerely for your brother and by accepting his apology; or else by conciliating him with an apology yourself, by regarding yourself as responsible for the trial, and by patiently waiting until the cloud has passed.

—St. Maximos the Confessor II, *Fourth Century on Love,* Sec. 22, from *Philokalia—The Eastern Christian Spiritual Texts: Selections Annotated & Explained*

Prayer for Our Mothers

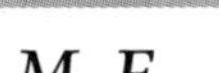

M. F.

Mother God, Creator, Wisdom,
Thank you for the mother who gave me life.
Thank you for her imperfect love.
Where she faltered, give me direction.
Where she neglected, help me grow.
Where she wounded, heal me.
Lead me into the womb.
I choose the pain of rebirth.
Bitter grief dissolves.
Waters flowing freedom and forgiveness.
Wail bringing release.
Breast offering life.
Joy and pain.
Milk for mother and child.
Thank you, Mother
For pouring your life.
Blessing me.

—from *Honoring Motherhood: Prayers, Ceremonies & Blessings*

Prayers for Marriage

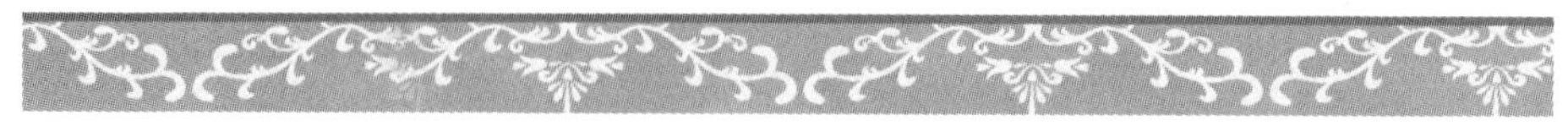

Annotated by The Rev. Canon C. K. Robertson, PhD

> Eternal love never fails; our love needs to forgive and be forgiven. As we pray and forgive we minister reconciliation.
>
> Those who marry are God's ministers to each other of reconciliation and change. As they grow together, wife and husband foster one another's strengths, they provide each other with the reassurance and love needed to overcome their weaknesses.
>
> —from the 1989 New Zealand Prayer Book

What a beautiful image! Spouses as "ministers ... of reconciliation and change." Love is manifested in forgiveness and reassurance, and so each spouse can dare to dig deeper and be challenged.

> Give them wisdom and devotion in the ordering of their common life, that each may be to the other a strength in need, a counselor in perplexity, a comfort in sorrow, and a companion in joy. Amen.
>
> Grant that their wills may be so knit together in your will, and their spirits in your Spirit, that they may grow in love and peace with you and one another all the days of their life. Amen.
>
> Give them grace, when they hurt each other, to recognize and acknowledge their fault, and to seek each other's forgiveness and yours. Amen.

The Rev. Canon C. K. Robertson, PhD, is canon to the presiding bishop of The Episcopal Church, a noted scholar, and a distinguished visiting professor at the General Theological Seminary in New York City. He has published many books, including *A Dangerous Dozen: 12 Christians Who Threatened the Status Quo but Taught Us to Live Like Jesus* and *The Book of Common Prayer: A Spiritual Treasure Chest—Selections Annotated & Explained* (both SkyLight Paths).

Make their life together a sign of Christ's love to this sinful and broken world, that unity may overcome estrangement, forgiveness heal guilt, and joy conquer despair. Amen.

Give them such fulfillment of their mutual affection that they may reach out in love and concern for others. Amen.

—from "The Celebration and Blessing of a Marriage,"
The Book of Common Prayer

Before their family and friends send the newly married couple off amidst a hail of thrown rice and congratulatory cries, they first pause, take a quiet moment, and together pray for them. Here we find a series of prayers that are appropriately used not simply at the start of a couple's life together, but throughout their shared journey. For we always need wisdom and devotion in the ordering of our common life, to grow in love and peace, the grace to forgive and be forgiven.

Each of these prayers can be used on a different night of the week so that, interestingly, the prayer about mutual forgiveness comes midweek—by that point, the two persons probably need to be forgiven for something! In any case, these prayers can be an ongoing gift for the couple, better than anything bought through the bridal registry. For here we have tiny nuggets of grace to get us through each day ... together.

Forgiveness in Caregiving

Marty Richards, MSW, LCSW

Forgiveness is a basic need for all of us. Because we are human, we can make hurtful mistakes. We may say or do things that bring pain and suffering to others emotionally, spiritually, mentally, or physically. And others may injure us. By the time we are older or struggling with chronic illness, or caring for someone who is, we may have a huge room in our hearts filled with accumulated hurts and frustrations.

The issue of forgiveness is not often spoken of in terms of a major health issue in caregiving—or "caresharing," which I prefer. Although it has been long discussed in religious and counseling circles as crucial to spiritual well-being, forgiveness is now recognized as pivotal to physical health as well....

The Past Gets "Stirred Up"

In a caresharing situation, the hurts of the past may resurface or take on a new significance. Past wrongs may be stirred up in the intimate contact that comes with personal physical care. For example, if your care partner was abused by someone in the past, the intimacies of receiving care may bring those old wounds to mind.

Alternatively, if you are caring for a parent who has abused you in the past, a renewed awareness of that old hurt and anger can bubble up, and you may feel bent over by the heavy load of collected injustices. Or, if you and your care partner have an unresolved marital issue from early in your marriage, this may haunt you in the caregiving situation.

Marty Richards, MSW, LCSW, is a clinical social worker, an affiliate assistant professor at the University of Washington School of Social Work, and a popular speaker on the topics of chronic illness, Alzheimer's disease, elder care, and spirituality and aging. She is the author of *Caresharing: A Reciprocal Approach to Caregiving and Care Receiving in the Complexities of Aging, Illness or Disability* (SkyLight Paths).

End-of-Life Issues Become Clearer

If you are caring for someone who is facing a terminal diagnosis or imminent death, they may have a pressing sense of making amends before it is too late. This is a critical time of heightened awareness of hurts and wrongs. Many seriously examine whom they need to ask forgiveness from, and whom they want to offer forgiveness to. They may realize how much they need to do, or should have done in the past, on forgiveness work. Because they are aware of how little time is left to sort things out and become reconciled, their need to work on unfinished business may be increasingly urgent. At the end of life, things that once seemed important in a personal argument or a business dispute or a family feud may not matter in the way that they did when people were younger....

The Barriers to Forgiveness

Forgiveness is a complex process that calls for coping skills, problem solving, and learning from past experiences, both positive and negative. So it is not surprising that many barriers may stand in the way of asking for forgiveness or giving forgiveness. Over the years of working with caresharing partners, I've encountered many who want to forgive (or be forgiven) but just don't think it's possible anymore. Alternately, I've seen others who feel that they were "right," so why should *they* ask for forgiveness! Either way, the resentments still linger, the pain still hurts, and the need for forgiveness still exists.

"It's Too Late"

Perhaps the one you are caring for has told you about an experience in the past that still hurts. They may have expressed a wish that things could be different now, yet they fear that too much time has passed to approach the other and ask for forgiveness. Or perhaps you have a forgiveness issue with your care partner, but, given their failing health or cognitive abilities, you are thinking it's too late—they're too frail or confused or in too much pain to deal with this.

If there is one thing I emphasize in the caresharing setting, it is that *it is never too late*! I have learned this important lesson from families I have worked with over the years, and from my personal experience. The healing that needs to occur is indeed possible.

"It's Just Not Worth the Effort"

Perhaps you've heard your care partner say something like this: "They're not going to change anyway, so I'm not even going to try to say, 'I'm sorry.' It's just not worth the effort." This stance assumes that relationship healing is not possible before even attempting to look at who and what needs forgiving. For some, this belief comes out of years of failed attempts and a certain life weariness at this point.

But I also think it is important to recognize that this protest (and the next one as well, "It's no big deal") might also be a cover for a variety of underlying feelings. Some may be afraid of punishment if they ask for forgiveness. Some may feel too ashamed to approach someone they have wronged. Others may fear rejection and would rather not take the risk. It is true that we always take a risk in asking for or offering forgiveness, and we may not achieve our desired outcome. But it is also true that we are changed by the process of seeking and granting forgiveness, even if we don't always gain our hoped-for end result. There is value in the process of forgiveness in and of itself.

"It's No Big Deal"

Perhaps your care partner has mentioned an issue with someone that's bothering them but has shrugged it off, saying, "It's no big deal." Denying the seriousness of a festering issue, or being unwilling to admit that an unresolved issue creates other concerns, is a little like leaving a wound untreated and expecting it to heal. Maybe someone in your care partner's family keeps promising to visit but never seems to show up. Or perhaps someone whom your care partner used to consider a "close friend" now manages to find any number of excuses not to call or come by. Or the issue might be between you and your care receiver. I've seen instances where a carer unwittingly acts or speaks negatively toward their care partner, but the partner never mentions it. Instead, the unspoken tension is suspended uneasily between them.

It has been my experience that, if there are needs for forgiveness—even things that are "no big deal"—that are not dealt with, they pop up somewhere else. Taking one step forward in the forgiving process, by acknowledging directly what has transpired, can move the relationship down the path of forgiveness.

"But I Was *Right!*"

Sometimes people feel justified in what they did and do not see the need to ask for forgiveness, even if another person took offense or was hurt by it. Or some may fiercely cling to the notion that they were the "innocent" victim in a situation, rather than a perpetrator, and fiercely hold on to their hurt. But in caresharing, these self-protesting and self-protecting stances are counterproductive. If, for example, you feel that your care partner has done something against you in a situation where you had the right perspective, this kind of self-righteousness may keep you from fully interacting with your care partner. Hanging on to being "correct" will fester in your heart and keep you from connecting with your care partner. You will be limiting the depth of your relationship because the unspoken protest will be hanging between you.

"I Don't Deserve to Be Forgiven"...

Perhaps your care partner has a family situation where they feel so bad about something they've done that they don't believe they deserve to ask for pardon. I see this with people who have thrown a family member out of the house, or have abused drugs or alcohol, or have been in trouble with the law. At this point in their lives, they may have done considerable inner work, become sober, or made restitution, but they may still want to work out issues with partners, parents, or siblings. Yet, at the same time, they may feel that what they have done is unforgivable. This can be very difficult to work through, but I hold to the same premise that I emphasized above: *It's never too late!* This may be a time when a counselor or spiritual adviser can be especially helpful in clearing the way for forgiveness to happen.

"He Can't Understand What I'm Saying Anyway, So Why Should I Bother?"

The whole issue of forgiveness can get even more complicated if one of the parties does not have the mental capacity to understand. What do you do, for example, if you are caring for a parent with dementia whom you would like to offer forgiveness for past abuses? Or from whom you would like to receive forgiveness? Yet you know that their limited cognitive abilities would prevent them from any meaningful comprehension and exchange.

It does not take full cognitive ability to say "I'm sorry" to another, or to understand it at some level. Although we can never be sure what gets through in dementia, my stance is this: If there is a need to say "I'm sorry," say it! And know that there may come a time when your loved one with dementia will say it to you. Listen and accept their statement, however they phrase it. At some level, however basic, there can be a sense of healing....

These barriers to forgiveness, and others you might identify, may be tough to consider. They require you and your care partner to be honest with yourselves and about your situation. But there are steps you can take to help you and your care partner, and the potential for physical, emotional, and spiritual healing is well worth the effort....

Family Forgiveness

Because our family relationships are the most long-standing and the most intense, often the greatest needs to forgive and be forgiven occur in families. Family struggles and a lifetime sense of injustices can build up and be passed on from generation to generation.

In the emotional overload of the caresharing setting, long-suppressed issues, family secrets, and "unfinished business" are more likely to surface and are often at the heart of the need to work on forgiveness.

As you work with your care partner, pay attention to the family issues and names that seem to be arising. They might identify someone within the family from whom they want to ask forgiveness, such as an estranged brother who hasn't been in touch for years because of an old feud or a misunderstanding. Or there may be someone in the family, such as a child who "abandoned" them at an early age, to whom they want to offer forgiveness.

If your care partner is a family member, it is also important for you to pay attention to your own family forgiveness needs. For example, if you are doing hands-on caring for an aunt who has always favored other nieces and nephews in the past but who are not part of the caring now, you may feel mad about the unfairness of the situation you're in. If you can forgive them, you can give yourself the gift of letting go of the anger, resentment, and frustration so you are better able to be present to the one who needs your care.

Care Partner Forgiveness

Caregiving situations can catch us off guard. You might have been living your life, and all of a sudden, there was a crisis, and you were expected and needed to step in as a caregiver. Or the need for care may have evolved slowly, and your role as a caregiver somehow seemed to evolve right along with it. Either way, you might find yourself in a position of caring for someone with whom you have had a past conflict, or for someone who has hurt you deeply in the past. In order to move ahead, you need to find a way to forgive them or your deep resentment could compromise the actual giving of care.

This need for forgiveness may be especially critical if the one you are caring for is a spouse or life partner. Over long-term relationships, issues arise. This is to be expected, and it is normal. You and your long-term partner have experienced a good deal together over the years, but maybe you have been carrying a silent hurt or anger....

Unresolved hurts and wrongs can have very negative effects on how care partners treat each other, but forgiveness can remove some of the barriers that get in the way of healthy caresharing. I've seen forgiveness connect people in surprising ways. The deepening and promoting of personal relationships may, in fact, be the prime reason why the work of forgiveness is so important to the health and well-being of you and your care partner.

If you are identifying with any of these situations as you read, I want to insert this word of encouragement: Just as there are many possibilities in relationships for hurting, so too are there many opportunities for forgiving and, ultimately, reconciling with each other. There is *always* the possibility of making peace with the past; there is *always* the potential for growth and change emotionally and spiritually.

Daily Matters

Because we are human, we are in need of forgiveness—sometimes on a daily basis. Forgiveness for issues from the past happens over an extended period, and may include a variety of people, but the issues of today are right in front of us. When there is something that needs forgiveness in the day-to-day process of caresharing, we have an immediate opportunity to say "I'm sorry," and do what we can to right the situation.

Forgiving Your Care Partner for the Difficulties of Caregiving

Caresharing creates hardships. That is a reality, and you may be having a wide range of feelings in response to this. You may be angry at the changes that the illness has brought, especially if the one you are caring for is a soul mate and confidant who used to support you through bad times and is now causing you the most difficult time you have had to face. And you have to face it alone.

If you keep these feelings locked up, they can come back to haunt you. You need to find a way to honestly acknowledge how you are feeling and find a place in your heart to forgive the person you are caring for so you can go on. Even if their illness is a direct result of not taking care of their own health over the years, it does no good to hang on to your anger about the past. What *is* is now, in the moment, and needs to be dealt with on that basis.

Forgiving Your Care Partner for Hurtful Behavior Caused by the Illness

If your care partner is dealing with dementia, or is in great pain, or is simply worn down by the relentlessness of treatment and isolation, they may say or do things that are very unkind to you as their carer. Recognize that it is often the *illness* that is causing this behavior. It is often the illness "talking." Your care partner's abusive words are not something they would normally say if their social graces were still intact, and their behavior may stem from a loss of the control they once had.

It is easier to forgive them if you remember that it is the *illness* that has changed the behavior and, indeed, changed the very person they used to be. However, that is not to say that you won't be hurt or angered by their behavior or remarks. The gift of forgiveness is that it can help you get beyond the hurtful actions or words. You will be freeing yourself from the potential to hurt back or withhold care and forgiveness opens ways for compassion to keep flowing.

Forgiving Yourself for Not Doing "Enough"

In the intensity of caresharing, it is easy to feel pulled apart inside by all that is happening. I've seen many carers set expectations for themselves that are not realistic and, in the process, set themselves up to fail and end up feeling terrible about not meeting their own expectations. They may even end up feeling as if they have failed the person they care about.

It is okay not to be perfect in your caregiving role! The first person you may need to forgive is yourself. Maybe you've been frustrated and said some angry things in the heat of the moment—and then felt bad about being angry. You may blame yourself for not being a better care partner, or feel a great sense of guilt about not doing a good job in this role that was thrust upon you. You feel even worse if others, especially other family members or friends, have little understanding of how hard it is to be a carer and seem to be critical of the job you're doing. You need to realistically consider what is "good enough" for your caregiving situation. That does not mean you care any less, only that you are more realistic in your expectations.

There may also come a time, in working through the problems confronting you in the caresharing situation, when you need to make a decision that you cannot be a primary caregiver for someone. Others may be pressuring you, saying that they think you "should." However, I've seen many times where someone's decision not to take on full-time caring is the best for all concerned. Only you can know the path you have walked with your care partner. Only you can make the decisions that you need to make.

Asking Your Care Partner for Forgiveness

There may be times in the caresharing process when "forgiving yourself" for your actions (or lack of action) is not enough. Situations may arise in the day-to-day give-and-take of caregiving when you need to ask your care partner for their forgiveness.

In any caresharing setting, there is a lot of room for mistakes. Some are "legitimate"; that is, they come out of not knowing what to do or how to handle a situation. Some are understandable, when everyone is stretched to the limit of trying to handle pain or loss or restrictions or frustrations. Some days, you may need to recognize that your heart is not in the caring, or even the relationship.

And there may be times when you need to look at the situation and acknowledge that you did not do the right thing. None of us is perfect; however, there is work to be done. When you can identify the problem and ask for, or offer, forgiveness, you will be able to keep your focus on the issues that matter most.

Where to Start

In the dance of caresharing, there are many tricky steps in the forgiveness process, and how forgiveness is helped or hindered can affect the delicate balance in caring. In the forgiveness process, taking that first step is crucial.

Do Not Wait

If you need to say "I'm sorry" to your care partner, do it now! If you have not seriously considered what might be done to ameliorate the situation, think about it carefully, now. Do not put it off. If your care receiver has expressed a need to forgive or be forgiven, do what you can to facilitate the process.

Make the First Move

If there is an issue between you and your care partner, you may need to make the first move. Waiting for them to initiate the process is a prescription for failure. If it is in your heart to forgive them for hurting you, you need to make the approach. And if you are the one who has hurt them, all the more reason for you to take the first step. Keep in mind, however, that you cannot force someone to forgive you. But the process can begin only when someone makes the first move. By taking the initiative, you can gently help begin the journey.

Look for Catalysts

Because the issue of hurts and forgiveness can be so delicate, it can be difficult to suddenly open a conversation on this topic. Oftentimes, it is helpful to pick up on "catalysts" from other conversations or events to help introduce the process.

One catalyst for a forgiveness discussion can emerge out of the stories that your care partner tells about their life. They might reminisce about significant events and, as part of the process, do some reflecting and reexamining of their life. They may express some regret about something they did, or a wish that they had done something differently. If they say—even in a passing comment—that they wish they could change the way things were left in a situation, or talk to someone they felt they have wronged, this is the time to respond and explore with them the possibility of pursuing this.

As stories are told, issues between you and your care partner may also arise. These narratives can take on a new significance and urgency in light of their declining health or impending death, and I have often seen these life reflections become catalysts for family members to work on forgiveness.

Sometimes situations happening in the "outside world" become catalysts for discussions of forgiveness. Any major catastrophe, for example, may lead you and your care partner to a broader examination of what really matters in life. As you and your care partner discuss any world events or disasters, either of you may realize anew the need to say "I'm sorry" to those you have wronged.

Other catalysts for forgiveness discussions can arise out of family and networks of friends. The unexpected death of a well-loved friend, for example, might make your care partner more aware of their own vulnerabilities and intensify their wish to seek out the people with whom they need to make amends.

Ask Reflective Questions

Sometimes the best path to a forgiveness discussion is the most direct. If your care partner has told you they are concerned about past hurts or wrongs, you might want to use some gentle reflective questions to help them consider whom they need to forgive, or request forgiveness from. As a carer, you might also find that taking some time with these questions can clarify your own thinking about the issues.

> Is there someone who has hurt or angered you whom you would like to forgive?
>
> Think of times when have you forgiven someone else. What happened as a result?
>
> Is there someone you have hurt or angered from whom you need to seek forgiveness?
>
> Remember the times in the past when people have forgiven you. What did that feel like?
>
> Are there lessons from these experiences that you could use now?
>
> What are some of the steps you could take to initiate this forgiveness?

Remember, even small steps in moving through the process of forgiveness are important. The sense of healing can be a powerful goal and gift.

Keep a Journal

Putting thoughts and feelings into written form is a good way to sort out what the real issues are so that they can be explored frankly. If, for example, your care partner is having trouble talking to you directly about a painful issue from their past, you might suggest that they write down a description of their experience and make note of their thoughts and feelings about it. They can always destroy the papers, if they choose. You can affirm to them that, by putting their issue into writing, they will at least have acknowledged their concerns to themselves, which is an excellent first step toward dealing with a difficult issue and exploring what and who needs forgiveness.

Seek Out Support

Sometimes it can be very helpful to talk through forgiveness issues with a trusted adviser, counselor, clergyperson, or spiritual director before approaching the person whom you are seeking forgiveness from or offering forgiveness to. A neutral "third party" can gently reflect back to you what they understand the main issues to be and help you sort out the options in your situation. If your care partner has limitations, a support person can also help you consider what is appropriate to say directly to your partner and what things you might want to channel in other ways. Being extra sensitive to your care partner's limitations is especially critical when there are forgiveness issues between the two of you....

Rituals of Forgiveness

Many of us benefit from structured observances to forgive and be forgiven, and our various religious traditions have rich rituals to help us do that....

You might also consider developing your own personal rituals and rites of forgiveness. At times, I have encouraged people to write a letter to the person they want to forgive, or to the person from whom they need to ask forgiveness. The goal is to record all the issues *for themselves* as specifically as possible, expressing their real feelings about the incident or event that led to the hurt. They can then choose to send the letter, burn it and scatter the ashes, bury it, or tear it up. It is a way of letting go, which is a key part of the healing process of forgiveness. You or your care partner might find this personal ceremony very meaningful. If your care partner is not able to write, you might offer to be a scribe for them, to put their words in writing (assuring them of complete confidentiality, of course). This kind of letter-writing ritual might also be healing for other family members or people involved in the caresharing situation.

Prayers for Forgiveness

Prayer can be a very meaningful part of the work of forgiving and being forgiven. Prayer is important on many levels, and for many people it offers strength and support throughout life.

When it comes to forgiveness issues, many people pray by name for those who have wronged them, or for those whom they have wronged. Others make their personal petitions first, asking God to forgive them, before they ask forgiveness of another. Many find that dealing with the difficult issues of forgiveness in prayer first helps them do the difficult work of forgiving and being forgiven. The formalized prayers of various religions can provide helpful templates for your forgiveness prayers. Prayer can be very effective for those who believe in its power. The specific wording or style of prayer is less important than the practice and intention of prayer. Prayer not only offers a connection with a Source of Love and Power beyond human limits, but the familiar words and routines also provide a comforting place to start the process of forgiveness, especially when you are under stress.

No matter how it is configured, forgiveness is an ongoing process. No person has only *one* event in a lifetime where forgiveness or forgiving is required. Making mistakes and hurting another is part of the human condition. And forgiving those mistakes and hurts does not happen overnight, nor does it happen easily. Forgiveness involves many steps and requires a true willingness to face the concerns and to move forward.

Setting Boundaries

Marcia Ford

Mark and Cathy—not their real names—were long-ago acquaintances of mine from a church in New Jersey. At the time that I knew them, I was between marriages and prone to find a happy couple at every turn. Some of you know what I mean. When you're alone and miserable, all the world's a couple—a deliriously, blissfully ecstatic couple. You, on the other hand, seem to be the only unattached person left on the planet.

Cathy and I probably could have been good friends, except for the fact that there she was happily married and all. It was hard seeing her husband lavish so much affection on her, so I kept my distance. He wasn't sappy or anything; he just appeared to be genuinely in love with her, even after nine years and three children. After we all went out for pizza one night, I rode home with Lynn, Cathy's closest friend. "Mark is one of the good guys," I said. "I can tell." Right.

A year or so later, after I learned that Mark had been unfaithful to Cathy pretty much since their honeymoon, I remembered Lynn's silence in response to my astute observation. When Mark and Cathy separated and later divorced, I immediately joined the chorus of critics who denounced Mark's despicable behavior every time we talked to Cathy. We were in her corner, cheering her on to a better, Mark-free life.

Problem was, inexplicably and unknown to us, Cathy still loved Mark. And in spite of himself, Mark still loved Cathy. Since they weren't exactly on good terms or even speaking terms—she had moved out of state and taken the kids with her—neither one knew how the other felt.

Marcia Ford is a former editor of *Christian Retailing* magazine, an Explorefaith.org columnist, and a frequent contributor to *Publishers Weekly*. The author of eighteen books, including *The Sacred Art of Forgiveness: Forgiving Ourselves and Others through God's Grace* (SkyLight Paths), she was the religion editor of the *Asbury Park Press* for ten years.

Mark's guilt nearly crushed him, but before the damage was complete, he broke down and got into some committed therapy for a serious amount of time. Meanwhile, Cathy began to see a counselor in her new church, which proved to be a much safer place to confess her love for Mark than among her Mark-hating friends. With his therapist's blessing, Mark drove a thousand miles to tell Cathy how sorry he was and to ask her if she thought she might someday be willing to consider the possibility of forgiving him. He decided that the best he could hope for was that she would not shoot him, which he felt she had every right to do.

Cathy didn't shoot him. To Mark's surprise, she forgave him.

He had no way of knowing that for nearly a year she had been working toward forgiving him. He was so shocked, in fact, that he blurted out a question he'd never had any hope of asking: "Does that mean you think we can get back together?"

Now, Cathy still loved the man, but she wasn't what you'd call stupid. Her incredulous look was all the answer Mark needed. After spending some much-needed time with the children, Mark returned to New Jersey, figuring it was all over once again.

Back in her counselor's office, Cathy identified the behaviors—aside from the obvious one—that had troubled her about Mark all along, actions that she now realized should have tipped her off to her husband's affairs. With her counselor's help, she created a list of nonnegotiable conditions that Mark would have to fulfill before she would consider reconciliation.

Her list started out like this:

1. Continue seeing his therapist. Cathy credited him with challenging Mark to take a hard look at himself and make difficult but necessary changes.
2. Exhibit faithfulness and responsibility in other areas of his life—toward God, toward his employer, toward his biological family, toward his children.
3. Find an accountability partner, a man who would make a commitment to meet with Mark weekly to help him maintain his integrity through open and honest dialogue.

In all, the list included seven conditions. By defining what she expected of Mark, Cathy established the boundaries that would protect her as they took their first small steps toward rebuilding a relationship. Mark's willingness to abide by her wishes helped restore her trust in him. Only after Mark had proven himself over an extended period of time did Cathy even consider a full reconciliation. Four years after their divorce, Mark and Cathy remarried.

Mark agreed to a new set of requirements that applied to their married life ... and Cathy did the same. Over the years, she had examined the behaviors of her own that had contributed to the failure of their first marriage. Mark and her counselor collaborated on a list of conditions Cathy would have to meet. Both Mark's list and Cathy's included this item: participate in regular marriage counseling sessions. The last I heard, Mark and Cathy had celebrated twenty-three years of marriage, give or take that four-year break.

Establishing clear, measurable, and realistic boundaries is a sound practice for all of us to follow. It's especially important for anyone seeking the restoration of a relationship that was broken by infidelity or abuse or a similar serious offense. Just as important is maintaining the boundaries you have set. If you agree to reconcile with your abusive father on the condition that your only contact is by phone, for example, then you need to be prepared to stand your ground if he shows up at your door, playing on your sympathy in the hope that your good nature will win out over your resolve.

This is one of the greatest obstacles to releasing women from the control of the abusive men in their lives. Some women either fail to draw clear boundaries that define what they absolutely will not tolerate in a relationship, or they manage to forget those boundaries when their abusers show up with empty promises and an uncanny ability to convince them that things will be different this time. It's all well and good to forgive your abuser, but make it clear that you have regained control of the situation by drawing a huge and unmistakable line that he is never to cross.

It's a mistake to think of boundaries in a negative way, as if they were the walls of a prison. They're not. They're more like the walls of a fortress. They are not meant to restrict you but to protect you. When it comes to you and your emotional—and perhaps physical—well-being, living within boundaries gives you control over not only who may enter your life but also the conditions under which they may do so. You may permit entrance to someone who once hurt you, but he must leave his weapons behind.

Practice: Clarifying Your Boundaries

Visualize your life as a fortress designed to protect you and not to isolate you. There will be times in your life when the drawbridge is down, when your welcoming and generous spirit allows others to enter freely. At other times—especially after you've been hurt—the drawbridge will be up, the gates closed, the doors padlocked. What will it take for you to allow someone—anyone—into your fortress under those circumstances?

No matter what your present situation is, it's a good idea to get clear about what your boundaries are in all relationship categories—friendship, romance, work-related, family, and so on.

You won't be able to cover every possibility, because you often don't know what your limitations are until someone comes right up against them—or violates them. But you can have a pretty good idea what you will and will not tolerate, based on your previous experiences. Say you work in an environment where your coworkers routinely trade favors—you flip the burgers for me when I'm overloaded, and I'll cut the tomatoes for you when you're overloaded. But then there's Sam, who never, ever gets those sesame seed buns toasted without imposing on you and me, which puts us on overload when we return to our own work. The line you draw will be right at the point where Sam's inability to do his own work begins to affect yours.

Write down everything that comes to mind as you're doing this exercise. Later on you can delete those things that either don't really bother you all that much or that seem excessive compared to everything else on your list. The main point is to clarify what your boundaries are—for yourself right now, and for others later on.

Finding Peace in Letting a Relationship Go

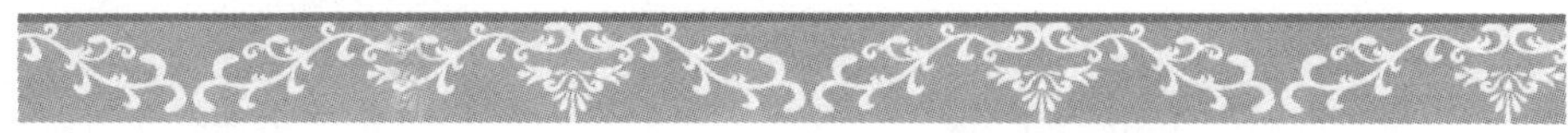

Susan Quinn

Faith in the Transitions of Not Knowing

A short while ago—it seems so much longer—I made one of the most difficult decisions of my life: I ended my relationship with my Zen teacher.

She and I had worked together for fifteen years, and I was in the final stages of becoming a *sensei* (teacher) when I realized that it was necessary for me to move on. Although I was certain that I had made the right decision, it was nevertheless a painful one, and I am still going through the grieving process. Even so, my spiritual practice has served me well through this time of transition; it has helped me understand how I arrived at this decision, how to work with the raw emotions that have arisen and otherwise heal in so many ways.

My spiritual practice has empowered me to reflect deeply on where I am, who I am, and where I am going. Zen practice has been my most profound teacher and my healing balm during this period. It has provided me with many tools—experiential as well as philosophical—to both learn from and heal from my experience. Although my relationship with my teacher has ended, I am more committed than ever to my personal practice. I'd like to share how it is guiding me through this time.

Sitting through My Sorrow

In Zen Buddhism we call meditation *zazen,* or "sitting practice." Zazen is central to Zen, and it has grounded my life in peace and, often, clarity.

Susan Quinn, a contributor to *Women, Spirituality and Transformative Leadership: Where Grace Meets Power* (SkyLight Paths), leads a meditation group in Poinciana, Florida, and teaches several types of meditation.

Medical research validates my belief that when I meditate, I change my brain! Early on I experienced calmness and less stress, as I incorporated meditation into my daily life; over time I have continued to experience more openness and joy in my life. In the past when times were tough, I had convinced myself that meditating was the last thing I wanted to do.

After all, with my mind going crazy, why bother! Over time and with a deeper understanding, however, I realized that *not* meditating was simply not an option. Choosing not to meditate would be like not getting out of bed in the morning. So after leaving my teacher, I continued to meditate.

Sometimes my mind flew everywhere, remembering the past, worrying about the future, with sadness welling up along with disappointment about all that had occurred. But in between those thoughts were moments of peace, solace, even joy; although my practice reminds me that the "good emotions" can't be held onto either, I recognized that as the days and weeks went by, I was comforted by more periods of spaciousness and lightness.

Recognizing and Embracing Loss

I knew that by ending the relationship with my teacher, I would be filled with anxiety, sadness, anger, confusion, disillusionment, and a myriad of other emotions. But knowing the results of my decision was completely different from allowing myself to experience them. At one level I knew that I had to allow myself to experience whatever arose in order to move through my grief, but who really wants to embrace misery? Instead, one of the first things I recalled was the basic premise of Zen, the Four Noble Truths. These truths reminded me that life is filled with suffering, disappointment, and loss; that we suffer, not because of these experiences, whether they are annoying or excruciatingly painful, but because we hold on to our desire to keep things safe, predictable, and consistent; that we don't have to live in these constant cycles of loss and clinging; and that there is a path to moving through them to freedom. I gently and regularly reminded myself that everything is impermanent, and how I responded to the outcomes of change was up to me. With all that said, though, I was still suffering! By continually reminding myself that my grief was also impermanent, however, I could breathe into my fragile and vulnerable condition and discover that even moment to moment there was also peace and well-being.

Nevertheless, I'm human, and the paradox of life is that even when we have tools to deal with difficult times, we still feel our deepest emotions.

As grief, tears, sadness, anger, and confusion arose in me, I allowed myself to fully experience these emotions. As the days went by, I noticed the ever-changing quality of these emotions, how they came and went, intensified and dissolved.

Zen has taught me that all the thoughts and feelings I was experiencing were ungraspable, empty of any fixedness, and would pass. I was especially surprised to notice my feelings shift regarding my teacher. Although I felt we both had contributed to the tensions in our relationship, and my desire was to credit her with "most of the blame," when I let go of blame and simply owned my contribution to the breakdown in our relationship, compassion for both of us suddenly had the space to emerge. I knew that she too was experiencing grief and loss, and I recognized that the sadness I was going through was the loss that everyone in the world experiences not only from time to time, but actually in every moment.

Practice Is Not Enough

Although my Zen practice was a key to my transition, I knew that it was not the only step I could take in this healing process. I'm one of those people who tends toward introversion; although I love being with others, I replenish my energy by taking time to myself. In the past, during stressful times I would tend to withdraw; no one wants to be around an unhappy, hurting person! I've realized that much of my spiritual growth has been a result of being in relationship with others. My husband, bless his patient heart, is my teacher and dear friend, and over time I have come to treasure my friendships with others as well. Rather than pulling into my cocoon, I chose to reach out to my closest friends and ask them to help me through my grief. They were extraordinary. They bore witness to my decision and my experience, offering comfort, a ready ear, even laughter. Along with my practice, they have been a balm to my aching loss and have reminded me often that I am loved and treasured. My practice serves me well in teaching me that we are not separate, but in relationship with everyone and everything.

And in the midst of suffering is also growth and well-being.

And Then There Is the Future

During this time of transition, I also experienced the unavoidable question: What next? I asked myself every imaginable question, so that I could bear witness to all my choices and opportunities; I put all possibilities on the table. Did I want to continue my Zen practice? Did I want to continue leading my meditation group? Did I want to find a new teacher? Was I motivated to complete my teacher training? A part of me wanted to know the answers to all these questions immediately. Being in the place of not knowing is such an uncomfortable place to be! I knew, though, that this not-knowing place was the perfect place to be. I have trained all these years to learn how to rest in uncertainty, to open to possibilities, to be curious.

This time of my life offered me the perfect opportunity to just not know. I also realized, however, that some of those questions might already be answered, because of who I am and how I live.

In the everydayness of life, I am a wife, consultant and trainer, meditation teacher, friend, daughter, sister, writer, and speaker. Intermingled with every single role that I play, I am a Zen practitioner. There is no way for me to separate that from who I am, so I still practice. I love providing a space for meditating and leading my meditation group, so I still welcome them into my home. To be in that leadership role responsibly, I feel that participants and I would benefit from me having a teacher in my life, a person to consult with, with whom to explore ideas. At this writing, I am investigating finding a new teacher. Finally, because there are a number of hurdles to overcome and steps to take if I decide to pursue and complete my training, I am letting go of my need to make that decision right now. Instead, I am free to move through whatever life presents in the days and weeks ahead.

Where I Am Right Now

So here I am: writing this piece for you; feeling a gentle breeze drifting from the fan overhead; sensing the heat of the Florida afternoon; wondering what is next. I am healing: my breathing is easier, my heart is lighter; my fingers tap on the keyboard. I notice my thoughts shifting: lighting on the past, touching to the future. My Zen practice reminds me that with all of that, there is just this unique and precious moment, here with you.

Forgiveness and Grace after Divorce

Rev. Carolyne Call

> To forgive is to set a prisoner free and discover that the prisoner was you.
>
> —Lewis Smedes

At a public lecture on the topic of healing, author and pastor Sara Miles was asked a question by a young audience member: "Do you believe in miracles?" After a reflective pause, Sara shared the story of a woman in her parish who had been coming to the food bank for groceries. This woman was homeless and had lost her hearing due to sustained physical abuse from her former husband. After visiting and coming to know some of the people there, she started to get involved at the food bank and began attending church. Sara went on to say that her own hopes for the woman were that she would be healed—get an education, start a new life, go on to do amazing things. This, to Sara, would have been miraculous and wonderful. However, none of these things happened. The woman continued to struggle and her life was far from Sara's vision of a renewed existence. "However," Sara remarked, "she forgave the man who abused her." She paused and then added, "Isn't that the real miracle? Forgiveness is the real miracle."

Of all the steps we can take in the aftermath of divorce, forgiveness is the one people find the most challenging. Some would hear Sara's story above and argue that the woman's husband should never be forgiven for what he had done. And yet for the nameless woman in the story, her ability to forgive demonstrates just how far she has progressed in her own spiritual journey.

Rev. Carolyne Call, a minister and spiritual adviser for those in the process of divorce, also conducts workshops and retreats on spiritual, psychological, and moral development and is author of *Spiritually Healthy Divorce: Navigating Disruption with Insight & Hope* (SkyLight Paths).

Are you willing to consider forgiveness as a goal on your own horizon, too? Before we begin, I want to acknowledge the difficulty of this subject and the defensiveness it can create within us. Of all the discussions I have had with individuals involved in divorce over the years, forgiveness is the one topic that prompts the strongest emotional reactions. Regardless of your initial reaction to the idea of forgiving your spouse, you must take a long look at this facet of the spiritual life. As you will discover, it is a central component of spiritual health and one of the best ways to manifest a life committed to loving God and others....

How Divorce Undermines Forgiveness

Divorce disrupts your ability to forgive in several ways and for several reasons. First and most important, it ruptures your primary social unit. This is the pair-bond formed by you and your spouse that is at the very center of your daily life. This bond is the source of companionship, affection, and physical and emotional intimacy. Many of us perceive marriage to be a sacred bond, established on faith-based vows that imply permanency.

Divorce is the breaking of that bond, whether it occurs through a sudden shattering or a slow disentanglement. Various betrayals and hurts may surround the end of a marriage, creating multiple fissures within the breakup.

At the heart of divorce is, ultimately, the experience and reality of rejection or exclusion. Whether you initiate the rejection, you are on the receiving end of it, or you arrive at a mutual decoupling, this is always a damaging aspect of the divorce process. You have been excluded from a private, special emotional reality, and the negative feelings tied to rejection occur whether you sparked the divorce action or not. This puts you in a defensive position with tremendous vulnerability. When you are in the throes of this situation, forgiveness rarely figures in your reflections. When you are emotionally raw and experiencing hurt, you are unable to consider forgiveness.

For some of you, divorce is the primary rupture in your life and one of the most significant emotional events. It can cut suddenly, with force and depth, or it can rub you raw over time. Either way, the wounds are usually profound. Survival is generally the first thing on your mind, not forgiveness.

Second, during the divorce process you may be on the receiving end of hurtful behavior toward you or your children. As a result, your own protection (or the protection of your children) is seen as paramount. Forgiveness is difficult to contemplate when you hold another person fully responsible for the difficult situation you are in. Related to this, you may also focus on the unfairness of the whole thing, ruminating on what you have sacrificed already for this marriage and believing the other is largely to blame for the divorce. This is a natural place in which to find yourself, as you seek to protect yourself and shield your own vulnerabilities. However, with help you can move forward out of this emotional bunker. Your perspective can become more balanced and you can consider the goal of forgiveness....

Revisiting Forgiveness in Spiritually Healthy Ways

Genuine forgiveness requires a profound reorientation of your heart. It is a deeply challenging act and also a deeply spiritual one. The spiritual nature of the act is attested to by the world's major religions and is considered fundamental to your spiritual journey.

When someone very close to you hurts you, that hurt can become the primary object of your attention. You become invested in the pain and the status of yourself as a wounded person. This is not to say that the pain is not real—it certainly is. But healthy spiritual life is gained by maintaining a balance between the three aspects of the dynamic triad. While you should be concerned with the nature of your relationships with others (including hurt to a relationship), that cannot be the only object of your concern or focus. Without the third side of the triad—the Divine—you face the possibility of remaining stuck in a wobbling dyad that cannot grant you the perspective you need to move forward in healthy ways. In each of the world's major religions, forgiveness is connected to the Divine, to the ground of our being. The relationship between yourself and God can allow you to shift your orientation away from a limited concern with your own pain and toward healthy spiritual life....

Moving Forward

Almost all the divorced or divorcing people with whom I have worked acknowledged that forgiving their spouse was something they felt was necessary in order to move forward, but they found the actual process very difficult. Those who were Christian felt the added weight of Jesus's command to forgive others and to love your enemy. Forgiveness is not to be taken lightly. It requires commitment and a reorientation of your thoughts, feelings, and behaviors. Like grief, it can be a cyclical process, one you move through again and again. This cyclical nature can be hard to face. You tend to believe that once you have been able to forgive, the situation is over and done with. This may be true for some transgressions in your relationship. But divorce is a deep and complex emotional experience. Because of the multiple levels and experiences, you may need to revisit forgiveness from time to time.

Over time, with strength drawn from your network of support and spiritual habits, you may find that this cycle ends and you have truly arrived at the end of the forgiveness journey. This may take years. Your willingness to take even one step on this journey is an indication that you can regain spiritual balance in your life.

What can you expect from forgiveness? You can expect it to be difficult, but you can also expect it to be healing. Forgiveness usually brings about a change in attitude toward your spouse and toward the divorce. Kate remembers that "learning to forgive, whether it was for me or others, played a huge part in coming to terms with the divorce. It wasn't until I was able to forgive [him] and myself for our roles in the divorce that my attitude and behavior changed." There can be a resulting change in feelings, from negative to neutral or more positive, but it will be different than the feelings you knew before.

Jon picks up on this subtlety when he notes, "I had to get to a place of forgiving my ex-wife. When we got to a point of forgiving each other for our failures, it was powerful and healing. But it didn't mean that we could just go ahead with our marriage. Forgiveness felt different than bondedness." Jon acknowledges that even though they were able to forgive each other, they could not go back to the relationship they had known previously. This may seem like an obvious statement, but it is an important point to remember. One of the false expectations of forgiveness will be that it will take away all the bad feelings and everything will go back to the way it was before.

This will not happen. A fundamental breach in a relationship means things are changed permanently. However, forgiveness can bring you to a new and better understanding of what actually happened in the course of your marriage and divorce.

How Forgiveness Works

How does the process of forgiveness actually work? In many ways it is mysterious. A combination of factors moves you to a change in perspective over time. This change in perspective is seen as "reframing" the situation—you come to view the person, the action, or the situation in a new light and with a more open heart. Empathy and compassion come to the fore while anger and judgment retreat. Jared's description of his own shift is quite dramatic. Sometimes the shift can come in one moment; for others, the change comes over time with an accumulation of factors, such as a change in lifestyle or circumstance, time in therapy, religious reflection, and so on.

Joining a support group, talking with a compassionate mirror, and reading spiritually oriented books were all named as effective starting places by people I have counseled. These resources can help you change your thinking and they can also facilitate a shift in feelings.

One of the most effective means, however, for moving yourself forward is prayer or meditation. In my own practice, I draw on images from a powerful story about the Buddha's life. In combating anger and hatred toward his enemies, the Buddha would meditate at length. In his meditative imagery he would see lines of soldiers facing him with arrows drawn. When the arrows were released, they flew toward him in the air, but before reaching him they morphed into flower petals and fell harmlessly to the earth. This image helped me to stay true to the direction I had set in my own spiritual map. The Buddha's actions highlight an important dynamic of forgiveness. The soldiers (or your spouse) may still have arrows. The arrows may still be aimed at you and they may still be released in your direction. The change is in how you perceive the arrows and the soldiers.

The Buddha strove to love the soldiers by recognizing their common humanity and by turning their hatred away with compassion. He demonstrates that the key to transformation lies within your own heart and mind. It is here that you must focus your efforts, not toward changing the other person. And while I cannot boast of having his skill at meditation, I do know that directed meditation can transform the heart if done regularly and with a skilled teacher. Prayer can also bring the same kind of healing over time, especially if you commit to the practice of praying for your spouse.

Both prayer and meditation can become cornerstones of the final test of forgiveness—your behavior. When you have fully forgiven your spouse, you no longer seek to hurt him, you refuse to rise to provocation, and you have a sense of disconnection that is healthy and empowering. The flame of vengeance dies and turns to ash. Your focus becomes something completely new—an open vista whose view is no longer blocked by your own anger, fear, or despair. You may well feel some residual sadness.

Grief for the "death of a hundred dreams" may always stay with you. But your life has new direction and new hope.

In time, you may finally be able to say with Frances, "I have discovered that forgiveness is everything. Forgive … again and again and again. It is the only way to freedom."

Forgiving Suicide

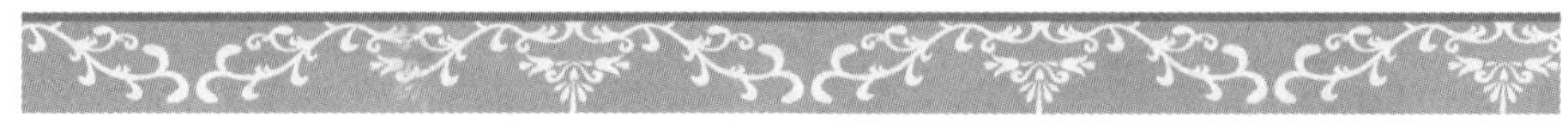

Rabbi Elie Kaplan Spitz

In my counseling, I have seen how an act of suicide leaves mourners with soul-searching, unanswered questions that often begin with the word *why*—Why did she kill herself? Why didn't I see it coming? Why didn't I make a difference? These questions make the mourning period brutal, and they make the process of healing long and difficult.

The profound emotional impact presents obstacles to gaining perspective: guilt at not having prevented the death, and anger at the lost one for having inflicted such enormous pain. I have been asked: Isn't taking your own life the most selfish possible act? While I am aware that it is perhaps the most painful deed, I know that it arises in a soul that is detached from the rational. We strive to forgive, to understand the suffering soul who was overwhelmed by the compulsion to end the pain, who lived with a sickness of the soul that rendered rational thinking impossible, and who could not comprehend the harm his or her deed would cause.

I remember the first person I knew who took his life. Sam was just twenty-three, enormously talented as a student and athlete, popular, handsome, the boy who had literally told me at the Jewish Community Center pool, "Anything you can do, I can do better." From hindsight, I wondered whether unreasonably high expectations and striving for perfection had led him to feel a sense of failure When I learned of his death, my first thought in the midst of my profound sadness was, "If I had been his friend, I could have made a difference."

When my rabbinical colleague took his life a few years ago, I thought of the last time we had been together, after eighteen years of friendship, and wondered: "Why didn't I recognize his pain? Why didn't I see the clues?"

Rabbi Elie Kaplan Spitz is a spiritual leader, scholar, author, and speaker to a wide range of audiences. He is the author of *Healing from Despair: Choosing Wholeness in a Broken World* (Jewish Lights) and currently serves as rabbi of Congregation B'nai Israel in Tustin, California.

Two sons recently came to see me with unanswered questions upon the loss of their mother, a woman who had suffered from chronic depression for many years. As they sat before me, the older son asked, "Is it true that Judaism teaches that to take your own life is a major sin? Does God reject my mother for having committed this act?" I responded that a soul who takes her own life does so as a compulsive, irrational act. If their mother could have understood the pain that she would inflict on her loved ones, she would not have taken her life. I answered that the God that I honor embraces their mother and her pain, knowing that it was the need to escape unbearable suffering that drove her to take her life. The mourning rituals performed in her honor would be the same as those for any loved one.

The shock of losing a loved one to suicide is made even more difficult if we believe that even God detests this act. However, a review of the Jewish tradition reveals a God of compassion and understanding. Suicide is tragic, but the person who takes his or her life is not rejected.

To Destroy a Gift from God: Portraits from Scripture

In the Hebrew Bible, there are five figures who committed suicide. Strikingly, there is no specific word in Hebrew scripture for suicide, nor is there an explicit condemnation of the act. The most famous of these personalities is Samson. Betrayed by Delilah, deprived of his strength, and blinded by the Philistines, Samson chose to die rather than entertain the Philistines at a celebration of their god Dagon. In Judges 16:28 Samson called out to God asking for strength to wreak vengeance on the Philistines. With one hand on each of the central pillars of the Philistine temple filled with three thousand people, Samson cried out, "Let my soul die with the Philistines," and pulled down the pillars, killing himself and all the guests present. The Rabbis identified Samson's deed as a heroic death intended to thwart Israel's enemies, an act of *kedushat ha'shem*, sanctification of God's name....

This and other cases of suicide in the Bible do not portray the irrational, compulsive need to turn off emotional pain that usually prompts people to kill themselves. What is fascinating is that while we often look to the Bible for guidance on the crises we face, in the case of suicide there is no direct precedent or clear example that reveals to us the Bible's perspective on suicide....

Today rabbis emphasize the lack of conscious intention in the act of self-destruction. This approach is reflected in an influential code of Jewish law from 1835, the *Arukh Ha Shulkhan*, in which the author, Rabbi Yehiel Epstein, stated:

> Generally, when someone takes his own life, we blame it on any reason at all, for instance, fear or troubles, or insanity, or the belief that suicide is a better alternative than getting involved in other transgressions. Suicide is truly a remote prospect for a person in his right mind.[1]

In Judaism's approach to suicide, viewed as a whole over more than three thousand years, we find several lessons. First, our bodies are a gift from God and our responsibility is to preserve life. Second, we are vulnerable, subject to despair and unbearable pain that may lead to compulsive, irrational acts. Third, the Rabbis recognized this lack of intent when they referred to suicide as "destroying oneself with knowledge." This awareness led the Rabbis to presume a lack of rational intent and to avoid condemning suicides as intentional, with a wisdom that foreshadowed a much later recognition in Western society that spiritual suffering rendered lost souls incapable of choosing freely.

The Aftermath: Understanding the Unnatural Death

From this brief examination of the biblical and rabbinic traditions, let me return to the sons whose mother had committed suicide. After speaking to them of the evolving Jewish view of suicide, I asked about their mother, seeking to touch on the four different planes of loss. I wanted to learn from them the physical facts, a description of the unfolding of the events. Mourners may find that retelling a story of trauma brings them a sense of closure. I offered comfort as a caring listener, acknowledging the intensity of their anger, guilt, pain, shame, and horror. I wondered about the questions running through their minds: Why didn't I see it coming? Why didn't I do more?

Rabbi Harold Kushner, who has brought comfort to the many readers of *When Bad Things Happen to Good People*,[2] once shared with me that he has in his library an entire shelf of books on the topic of suicide. He said, "You know, all the books seem to say the same thing. The first half of each book provides all the signs to look for to help prevent a suicide from occurring. And the second half of each book says that if a loved one has taken his or her own life, know that you shouldn't blame yourself. And both are true." The way I understand this paradox, from my own experience on the brink of the abyss, is that for a person who is in deep pain and grappling with suicidal thoughts, there is a conflict between the desire to end the pain and the will to live. The soul in pain may effectively mask the internal anguish with everyday conversation or withdrawal. For the observer, the internal struggle is impossible to recognize....

I spoke to the sons from my own knowledge of despair and from the stories told to me. I acknowledged that it is only human to grapple with guilt and anger on losing a loved one to suicide. I described how it is only with the perspective of hindsight that we may recognize signs that danger was imminent. I explained that once a family member decides to take his or her life, there is often very little anyone can do to change that decision, especially when the compulsion to end the pain is kept a secret. I observed that with suicide—as with an accident—the family suffers the overwhelming sense that the death could have been prevented, that the tragedy is unnatural. Guilt, shame, and secrecy make healing a complex and difficult process....

From Loss to Forgiveness: Remembering the Holy Sparks

The loss of a loved one to suicide leaves a tangle of emotions. We address betrayal by understanding that the soul we loved was overwhelmed, possessed by compulsion. We come to peace by accepting that our loved one was at once two people: one familiar to us and the other a stranger who was unable to reason due to illness. We forgive by remembering that our loved one contained holy sparks and by gathering up those sparks so as to identify a legacy of goodness.

Healing takes time, demanding patience and humility to process loss. By drawing on our collective Jewish memory, we remember that, as a people, we come out of the darkness of slavery into the light of freedom. Our individual lives are part of an ancient tradition of emerging from despair with the motivation and capacity to repair the world.

Practice: Journaling about Loss

Consider responses to the following questions about your loved one, whether mourning a death by suicide or either a protracted or sudden illness. Set aside a time each day, such as early in the morning or before bed, or each week, such as just before Shabbat or on Sunday night. Putting your thoughts on paper aids forgiveness, healing the broken parts of your relationship, honoring goodness, and integrating another's life into your own as a source of blessing.

How would you like this person to be remembered?

What do you miss about her the most?

What do you imagine he would say if he could speak to you now?

What action would she want you to take?

How would he want you to live in recalling his memory?

What was your loved one's legacy to you?

Practice: Letter Exchange

When loved ones die we cannot converse with them, but we can still express ourselves to them. Write a letter to your departed loved one to gain greater perspective and assist healing.

Describe the mix of emotions—loneliness, anger, grief, guilt, love—that you are experiencing. As an act of empathy, write back to yourself "as if" you were your loved one responding. Write a final letter back to your loved one. This exercise may be repeated periodically in the course of the mourning process, bringing a profound sense of your loved one's legacy and of your own progression toward healing.

A Prayer for Forgiveness

Rev. Steven Greenebaum

Allow me to forgive,
For I am imprisoned by my bitterness.
Allow me to be forgiven,
For I am shamed that I have done another harm.

I earnestly pray that we may all forgive and be forgiven.
May we love and be loving.
May we strive to see the right, to do the right;
And to be generous with others as we would be with ourselves,
This day, this week, this life.

Amen.

Rev. Steven Greenebaum, an Interfaith minister and founder of Living Interfaith Church in Lynnwood, Washington, is the author of *Practical Interfaith: How to Find Our Common Humanity as We Celebrate Diversity* (SkyLight Paths). Featured in the *New York Times*, he speaks and leads workshops on Interfaith and compassion as the core of our diverse spiritual traditions throughout the United States and Canada.

Forgiveness and the Divine

> When a discomforting intuition alerts us to the fact that we are not being true to ourselves, guilt is good. But most religious guilt is the product of neurotic fears that emphasize our imperfection and God's presumed wrath.... When we realize the full, sacred extent of our personhood, and when we live not from our ego but from our true, God-infused self (let go and let God), we will be in sync with the Tao, at one with God, in right relationship with the world, virtuous people, truly moral human beings.
>
> —Tom Stella

When you think of God's forgiveness, what comes to mind? When you think of seeking forgiveness from God, how do you feel?

If you think about needing forgiveness from God at all, you may have a tendency to find fear or condemnation in that thought. And pain can make you feel distant from God—whether it's the pain of betrayal or the pain of guilt or feeling unworthy. The contributors in this section gently show the way to a new perspective on the Divine, seeing God not as a condemning judge of our moral failings, but as a loving presence giving you a clearer understanding of the world and helping you grow into a better human being.

Not surprisingly, many of the chapters in this section contain prayers: prayers to open your heart in gratitude to the forgiveness God freely offers; prayers asking for help in accepting your own mistakes; prayers of penitence. These can help you find words to express whatever it is you need to declare to or ask of the Mystery of the Universe. But first, Rami Shapiro offers us a beautiful passage from the Qur'an—God's declaration of compassion and forgiveness for *you*.

A God Who Desires to Forgive

Annotated by Rami Shapiro

So much theology is wrapped up in a judging God saving some and condemning others. We frighten ourselves into conforming to one religion or another, each religion promising salvation from the wrathful God of its own imagining. The Prophet Muhammad reveals a different vision, a vision of God who desires only to forgive:

O humans, so long as you call upon Me and ask of Me,
I shall forgive you for what you have done,
and I shall not mind.
O humans, were your sins to reach the clouds of the sky
and were you then to ask forgiveness of Me,
I would forgive you.
O humans, were you to come to Me
with sins nearly as great as the earth,
and were you then to face Me, I would bring you forgiveness
nearly as great.

—A Divine Saying of Prophet Muhammad

Rami Shapiro, a renowned teacher of spirituality across faith traditions and a noted theologian, is a popular speaker on the topics of religion, theology, and spirituality. He is author of the award-winning *The Sacred Art of Lovingkindness: Preparing to Practice* and *Recovery—The Sacred Art: The Twelve Steps as Spiritual Practice* (both SkyLight Paths), among other books.

Letting Go of a Vengeful God

Tom Stella

> Morality is a redemptive process. In the light of God's revelation in Jesus Christ, human life is not a purely natural reality. Human life is always supernatural. God is redemptively present in the process by which man becomes more truly human.... God is present to man in the faith, hope, and love which are the basis of all moral life.
>
> —Gregory Baum, *Man Becoming*

What a novel thought it is that "human life is always supernatural" and that morality has to do with becoming "more truly human." If, like me, you think this is odd, perhaps it is because you were taught what I was taught: that being human is merely natural, not supernatural, and that morality is the process not of becoming more truly human, but of keeping our human nature in check....

The moral air I breathed as a child created in me a sense of anxiety, the ingredients of which were fear and guilt. When a discomforting intuition alerts us to the fact that we are not being true to ourselves, guilt is good. But most religious guilt is the product of neurotic fears that emphasize our imperfection and God's presumed wrath. Like the bumper sticker that reads "I saw that. God," I was given the impression that when it comes to seeing our misdeeds, God has 20/20 vision. This way of thinking has kept some of us from attaining spiritual maturity but has, for countless others, been emotionally crippling....

Tom Stella is a hospice chaplain, retreat facilitator, former Catholic priest, and a cofounder and director of Soul Link, a nonprofit organization whose mission is to bring spiritual seekers together. He is also author of *Finding God Beyond Religion: A Guide for Skeptics, Agnostics & Unorthodox Believers Inside & Outside the Church* (SkyLight Paths), among other books.

Some people were fortunate not to have lived under that oppressive cloud at home but, like Sam, experienced the same thing in parochial schools or within a church community. This was the case in my own life. My family was more functional than most; never once do I recall the fear of God being used to keep me in line. But the formal religious education I received in a Catholic school and the air I breathed at the church where my family worshipped had a decidedly negative bent. The emphasis of moral teachings was on avoiding sin and its "near occasion" and on the punishment that awaited me if I failed to do so.

When the tyrannical voice of moral righteousness rules a family or a classroom, or when the word of God is preached with unbending harshness from the pulpit, what is communicated is that our worth as people and our acceptability in the eyes of God depend on our compliance with particular norms of behavior. Whether intended or not, the message is that we are not loved or lovable until we get it right.

Abiding by Rules or Abiding in God

In grappling with the negative notion of morality, I have tried to recognize and rescue the baby in the bathwater—that is, to embrace the importance of moral parameters without ceding power to the guilt and fear associated with them. This endeavor has made me realize that morality is essentially about right relationship rather than appropriate behavior. It is more about abiding in God than abiding by rules. Living a moral life is not merely a matter of obeying religious laws, but of recognizing in them the articulation of a higher directive (love) that is written on our hearts. Jesuit priest William Johnston echoes this notion when he writes, "And this, I maintain, is the very apex of Christian morality. No longer fidelity to law but submission to the guidance of love."[1]

My reading of the gospels leads me to believe that Jesus knew that abiding in God was more important than abiding by rules.

Many Christians tend to see Jesus as having been a good Jew, which he was. He was familiar with the Torah, he attended synagogue services, he gave alms, and he tended to the less fortunate. But what often fails to register with us is that he broke as many religious rules as he kept. He healed on the Sabbath, befriended sinners, welcomed women as close disciples, and challenged the righteousness of religious authority figures. In this he did not thumb his nose at the rules and rituals of Judaism, but he demonstrated what it meant to be a truly good Jew—namely, to be faithful to the inner promptings of the Spirit even when doing so put him at odds with conventional religious morality.

There are times and circumstances in which breaking the letter of the law is the right thing to do. I believe that naturalist John James Audubon may have had this idea in mind when he said, "When the bird and the book disagree, always believe the bird." When the voice of conscience is at odds with the law of the land, the church, or any other authority, we must believe and act in accordance with the voice. In one example of conscience trumping law, friends of mine were arrested for trespassing at an air force base while protesting the U.S. participation in space weaponry development. They were obviously in violation of civil law (the book), but their actions were in keeping with the Spirit (the bird) that called them to stand up against anything that could cause harm to any human being.

In Harmony with the Tao

My belief that morality has to do with right relationship has been influenced by Taoism, an ancient philosophical and religious tradition of Chinese origin. It developed in part in response to Confucianism, which, like most religions of the West, stressed the primacy of virtue: it is by right actions that we become good. The Taoist philosopher Chuang Tzu (369–286 BCE) taught that being attuned to the Tao (Way), not virtuousness, was the essence of goodness. Being at one with the guiding principle of life, the simple good underlying all things, the order beneath chaos, is the way to a fulfilling life individually and an ordered life collectively. In the introduction to his work on Taoism, Thomas Merton states the following:

> For Chuang Tzu, the truly great man is therefore not the man who has, by a lifetime of study and practice, accumulated a great fund of virtue and merit, but the man in whom "Tao acts without impediment."[2]

Being a person in whom Tao or God acts without impediment does not minimize the importance of traditional morality, for without an objective reference point, our moral compass can easily take us off course. The term *following our conscience* can be a euphemism for doing whatever we want. A relational understanding of morality changes the emphasis from compliance to congruence, from striving to be good to resting in God, from keeping rules to growing toward a harmonious union with the Sacred both within and beyond our selves.

This same emphasis can also be found in Western religions. Terms like *union of wills*, *purity of heart*, and *dying to self* so common in the lexicon of Christianity refer to a relationship with God in which no trace of the ego or false self is to be found.

Through meditation and other spiritual practices, we are invited to undergo a transformation that closes the gap between God and our soul. In fact, there is no gap, only a lack of awareness of our oneness with God. But the failure to realize the truth of this union has resulted in a kind of busy morality characterized by the pursuit of virtue rather than a more contemplative, mystical communing with God.

Because I was taught that being virtuous was synonymous with being moral, I find it nothing less than revolutionary to think that morality has less to do with the attainment of virtue than with being in union with God. But as I reflect on the unfolding of my life, I can see the wisdom of this teaching. My experience is that morality, understood as striving for virtue, has served only to focus attention on myself. When my attempts to be virtuous succeed, I am uplifted. When they fail, I am deflated. It's all about me. But when my focus is on being in sync with Tao, God, or Spirit—the essence of which is love—I tend to forget myself and live, instead, with a higher consciousness and a freer spirit. I have also found that the virtue I once strove to attain has now begun to manifest itself independent of my efforts—true morality is more about grace than willpower, more about God than it is about us.

Free from Self, Free for Others

When we abide in God and live attuned to the Spirit, we become liberated from self-preoccupation with its focus on sin, repentance, sacrifice, and the like. Our attention shifts from concern only about the state of our souls before God to one that includes the "state of the union," the condition of the world and the quality of our relationships with others—especially those in greatest need....

Although I believe with St. Paul that "nothing will be able to separate us from the love of God" (Romans 8:39), the need for repentance, for a change of heart, can be appropriate, for despite our best efforts, we all stand in need of forgiveness for offenses of omission and commission. It is also true that in a broader understanding of sin, we are responsible for the general brokenness, the less-than-healthy condition of humanity in which we participate and to which we contribute by our selfishness, greed, judgmental attitudes, and the like. But moral people, while being appropriately concerned with their own faults, do not overlook their responsibility to and for the world.

The Moral of Our Story

Another way to think about the important notion of morality has to do with learning the deepest truths about ourselves: who we are and how we are to live. When a story conveys a truth about life, we say it has a moral. This is the case with Greek myths, Aesop's fables, and Jesus's parables, to name just a few examples.

Perhaps morality can be looked at in this way, rather than being thought of only as religious prescriptions having to do with right and wrong behavior. Life's unfolding is a story full of lessons to be learned, truths to internalize and apply to our endeavors and relationships. As we integrate and live what we learn, we grow in moral maturity.

The moral of our lives is revealed when we open ourselves to the shadow and light within as well as to all that we encounter in life. Our strengths and weaknesses, altruism and selfishness, faith and fears, successes and failures, loves and losses, and joys and sorrows can bring us to the humbling awareness that despite our folly, we are the locus of the Divine. Thomas Merton, speaking with full awareness of the poverty of his attempts to achieve holiness, once expressed this truth in a journal entry:

> I am noisy, full of the racket of my imperfections and passions, and the wide open wounds left by my sins. Full of my own emptiness. Yet, ruined as my house is, You live there![3]

That God lives in us even when we are at our worst can be a transforming realization. To embrace this truth, instead of dwelling on the "wide open wounds left by [our] sins," can enable us to pick up the broken pieces of our lives and move forward in faith. This movement, this sometimes awkward staggering toward and with God, is the spiritual journey wherein we discover the moral and meaning of our lives....

When we realize the full, sacred extent of our personhood, and when we live not from our ego but from our true, God-infused self (let go and let God), we will be in sync with the Tao, at one with God, in right relationship with the world, virtuous people, truly moral human beings.

Reflection: The Moral of Your Story

Describe the feelings that accompanied your first exposure to moral teachings.

What positive purpose do moral teachings like the Ten Commandments and the Golden Rule have in your life?

Describe a time in your life when being true to the Spirit may have required you to go beyond the law.

How would you put into words the "moral" of your life? What life lessons have you learned? What meaning have you discovered by experiencing life's ups and downs?

You Accept Us—At Times of Self-Doubt

William Cleary

Thank you, God of All,
cocreator of our world,
for allowing us to be imperfectly made—
because it makes us, if we are wise, forgiving.
Do you accept us as we are?
We condemn people too quickly:
we judge them for flawed thinking, disguised egotism,
unworthy acquisitiveness, or skewed opinions.
But we can forgive them once we accept our own shadow,
and realize how well we ourselves fit
into the ranks of a less-than-perfect human race.
You, Holy God, accept each of us,
prophets tell us, just as we are—
provided our moral judgments of others
are reciprocally generous and compassionate.
Imperfection fits this evolving reality,
for the universe thrives on diversity,
including random failure,
one of the very preconditions for the unfolding advances.
May it be so.

William Cleary is a former Jesuit priest, filmmaker, and composer. He is the author of many books on spirituality, including *Prayers to an Evolutionary God* (SkyLight Paths). His musical *Chun Hyang Song* was performed at the Seoul Olympics.

You Are Living a Good Story

Karyn D. Kedar

We have so many regrets. There were so many times that we could have—or should have—chosen a different path or gone in a different direction. Every time we use the word *should,* we accuse ourselves of not doing our best. Every time we say "I could have," we second-guess ourselves, blaming ourselves for not choosing a different path. Guilt and regret are heavy on our souls. Imagine how much energy we would have if we did not let them weigh us down: energy to create, energy to love, energy to move on.

I was recently having coffee with someone who had been a friend for many years. Every time we get together, we begin by recounting the story of our lives, as if we were telling some sacred narrative. At one point, we began to wonder how life would have been different *if we only....*

We looked at each other and instantly recognized that we had it all wrong. We were wrong to regret any part of the story. The "good" decisions and the "bad" decisions were all the "right" decisions because they led us down a path that was filled with meaning. There were so many lessons learned from the mistakes, so much growth from the bad experiences, that we honestly wouldn't change a moment. *Should have* and *could have* were futile phrases that did not recognize that *all* is for a reason and that we did the best we could at the time.

"It's not enough to forgive others," I said. "We must forgive ourselves."

For the next several hours, we retold the "sacred narrative," this time recounting the lessons in the turns in the road.

Karyn D. Kedar teaches matters of the spirit to groups throughout the United States. She is senior rabbi at Congregation B'nai Jehoshua Beth Elohim in the Chicago area and the author of *The Bridge to Forgiveness: Stories and Prayers for Finding God and Restoring Wholeness* and *God Whispers: Stories of the Soul, Lessons of the Heart* (both Jewish Lights).

"That's what 'repentance' means in Hebrew," I said. "The word for repentance is *teshuvah* and it means to turn toward the right path, the path that leads to an understanding of God."

She smiled. "Then let's *turn* from accusation toward understanding. In the turning, we can head for the goodness of God. Let's take 'should' and 'could' out of our vocabulary."

As we chatted, we became more inspired to understand the choices we had made and began the process toward self-forgiveness.

Together, we wrote this prayer:

> God, thank You for helping me see
> That each phase of my life is perfect.
> That I have arrived,
> That I've always been where I need to be
> Living perfect moments ...
> With Your help, I relinquish my need to judge.
> Embrace my heart as it beats, even as it bleeds.
> Help me grow with love, acceptance, and curiosity.
> Thank You for lighting my way
> For gently illuminating a path in the darkness ...
> Let it now be and always be
> Yet another exquisite phase.
> For the crimes against myself, I am sorry.
> For all my slips and slides, I forgive myself.

At every stage in my life, I did what I knew how to do. If I would have known better, I would have done better. But every day I must remember to be kinder to myself and more forgiving of my imperfections, because, at every point along the way, I am blessed. Everything I have done and seen has made me who I am in this moment. It's okay to have been me. I forgive.

The Psalms on Forgiveness

Translated by M. Basil Pennington, OCSO

It was not an enemy who reproached me,
  otherwise I could have borne it.

Nor was it he who hated me that rose up against me,
  or I would have hid myself from him.

But it was you, a man of my rank, my companion and confidant.

We took sweet counsel together
  and walked together in the house of God.

Let the death come upon them;
  let them go down alive to Sheol;
  for evil is in their homes and in their hearts.

As for me, I will call upon God and the Lord shall save me.

Evening and morning and at noon I will pray and cry aloud
  and God shall hear my voice.

God will give my soul peace, delivered from the battle,
  for there are many against me.

God shall hear and will humble them, the God who abides from of old,
  because they have not changed, they fear not God.

My companion has turned against one who was at peace with him;
  he has broken his covenant.

The words of his mouth were smoother than butter,
  but war was in his heart;

M. Basil Pennington, OCSO, was a monk for more than fifty years. He lived at St. Joseph's Abbey in Spencer, Massachusetts, and was the author of many modern spiritual classics, including *Finding Grace at the Center: The Beginning of Centering Prayer* and *Psalms: A Spiritual Commentary* (both SkyLight Paths).

his words were softer than oil,
yet they were drawn swords.
Cast your burden upon the Lord and he shall sustain you.
God shall never allow a good person to be overcome.
You, O God, shall bring them down into the pit of destruction;
bloody and deceitful men shall not live out half their days.
But I will trust in you.

—Psalm 55:12–23

Offering All to God

Annotated by Paul Wesley Chilcote, PhD

Wholehearted surrender to God involves the confession of all one's sins. We offer our brokenness to God. But such a surrender includes the acknowledgment of our goodness as well. We offer our good works to God. The good in life offered freely to God entails every aspect of the disciple's life of prayer—adoration, repentance, thanksgiving, and intercession—the deepest moaning of the heart. We offer our very souls to God. Below is a prayer of surrender from *The Imitation of Christ*:

> "The earth is the Lord's and all that is in it, the world, and those who live in it" (Psalm 24:1) I desire to give myself to you as a free offering and to remain yours forever. O Lord, in the simplicity of my heart, I offer myself to you today—a sacrifice of perpetual praise, to be your servant forever.
>
> I offer you all my sins and offences, O Lord, on the altar of your mercy.... Consume them all with the fire of your love and wash out all the stains of my sins. Cleanse my conscience from all offences and restore your grace to me, which I lost by sin. Forgive all my offences and receive me mercifully with the kiss of peace!
>
> I also offer you all that is good in me, although there is very little and it is far from perfect. Amend and sanctify it. Accept all my good works and perfect them more and more. I offer you all my prayers, especially for those who have wronged, grieved, or slandered me in any way and made my

---

Paul Wesley Chilcote, PhD, is an academic dean, professor, and a Benedictine oblate at Mt. Angel Abbey in Oregon. He is the author of many books, including *The Imitation of Christ: Selections Annotated & Explained* and *John & Charles Wesley: Selections from Their Writings and Hymns—Annotated & Explained* (both SkyLight Paths).

life uncomfortable or unbearable. I pray also for all those whom I have at any time troubled, grieved, or scandalized by words or deeds, wittingly or unawares. Please forgive all our sins and offences against one another. Take from our hearts, O Lord, all jealousy, indignation, wrath, and contention, and whatever may preclude or diminish love. Have mercy, O Lord, have mercy on those who crave your mercy. Give grace to them who stand in need and grant that we may be counted worthy to enjoy your grace and attain life everlasting. Amen.

— Thomas á Kempis, *The Imitation of Christ*

Trusting God's Forgiveness

Rev. Larry J. Peacock

Be mindful of your mercy, O Lord, and of your steadfast love,
  for they have been from of old.
Do not remember the sins of my youth or my transgressions;
  according to your steadfast love remember me,
  for your goodness's sake, O Lord!
Good and upright is the Lord;
  who therefore instructs sinners in the way,
And leads the humble in what is right,
  and teaches the humble the way.
All the paths of the Lord are steadfast love and faithfulness,
  for those who keep God's covenant and decrees.

—Psalm 25:6–10 (author's paraphrase)

Learning to follow the paths of the Lord requires an awareness of the times we have strayed from doing what is right and good. "Forgive the many times I have walked away from You, choosing to walk alone" (v. 7, *Psalms for Praying*).

Not only do we need forgiveness for the sins of our youth, but we also need forgiveness for all those times we have turned our back on God. The psalmist asks God to "remember me" (v. 7), not all our wrongs, sins, and faults. The psalmist counts on God's steadfast love, which abounds in forgiveness. To move from sin to right living, the psalmist counts on God's instruction and guidance. "You are honest and merciful, and you teach sinners how to follow your path" (v. 8, CEV).

Rev. Larry J. Peacock is a retreat leader, writer, and advisory board member at the Academy for Spiritual Formation. He is the author of several books, including *Openings: A Daybook of Saints, Sages, Psalms and Prayer Practices* (SkyLight Paths), and is executive director of Rolling Ridge Retreat and Conference Center in North Andover, Massachusetts.

Create in me a clean heart, O God,
  and put a new and right spirit within me.
Do not cast me away from your presence,
  and do not take your holy spirit from me.
Restore to me the joy of your salvation,
  and sustain in me a willing spirit.
Then I will teach transgressors your ways,
  and sinners will return to you.
Deliver me from bloodshed, O God,
  O God of my salvation,
  and my tongue will sing aloud of your deliverance.

—Psalm 51:10–14

This beautiful psalm, often used on Ash Wednesday, ushers the faith community into a time of repentance. It deserves a place in our daily life of prayer. The psalm moves from heartfelt confession to honest petition and asks for enough wisdom to teach God's way of forgiveness. We ask God to create in us "a clean heart ... a new and right spirit" (v. 10). We ask God to restore our joy and strengthen our will. We pray that our sin will not keep us away from God's Spirit. We trust in God's forgiveness, and we promise to live and teach God's way and to sing God's praises.

Practice: Forgiveness Dance

I invite you to try a forgiveness dance. Dancing offers another way to pray without words, to let our bodies express what we feel. People who feel self-conscious about dancing in public often find that creating their own dance in a private space becomes a wonderful way to pray. Others, like King David, dance their joy and praise comfortably in the presence of the community of faith (2 Sam. 6:5). Today many sacred dance troupes create dances for worship celebrations.

I invite you, in whatever way you choose, wherever you choose, to dance your sense of God's forgiveness. You might read portions from Psalm 51 and then close your eyes and let your body dance what it feels like to have a clean heart and a new spirit, and to have joy restored. Closing your eyes may help you be less critical of your dance. Dance your prayer.

Accepting Forgiveness

> When you ask someone for forgiveness, you place yourself in a position of radical vulnerability.... It is an invitation for healing for both you and the person you have harmed.
>
> —Rami Shapiro

Asking for forgiveness—and then accepting it—may be even more difficult than forgiving others. And sometimes the hardest person to accept forgiveness from is yourself. But, as Rabbi David Lyon encourages, it is not your job to go through life making no mistakes. It is your job to grant others the privilege of forgiving you when you do make mistakes. And it is your job to accept that forgiveness.

Accepting forgiveness means letting go of regrets, should haves, if onlys; it means facing your pain, your shame, your shadow side, and being brave enough not to hide any longer. It also means thinking of yourself with compassion. When you can see yourself both clearly and with compassion, that is the basis for true transformation, for true formation in love.

The Privilege of Asking Forgiveness

Rabbi David Lyon

"To err is human." Indeed, making mistakes is normal and natural. Usually we learn from our mistakes and move on. Sometimes we need some help. We find help from sources like therapists and close friends. But healing also comes from sources inside us, like renewed self-esteem and budding self-respect.

Remember, we were created in God's image, and the soul that God implants within us is a pure soul. When we don't help ourselves up and over stumbling blocks, we diminish the creativity God instilled within us. We have to make the effort.

"To forgive divine," concludes the familiar quotation. We have come to believe that forgiveness is something only God can provide. God does provide forgiveness when we seek it, just as God responds courteously when we bring courtesy to God. But it is not the case that God alone has the privilege to grant pardon.

When we make apologies for our actions or explain our transgressions to those we have offended, we begin the process of helping others to forgive us. Next, we come to God seeking the same forgiveness. And yet, despite it all, we are still the ones who can't forgive ourselves completely. We linger in a self-made world cut off from all the blessings God wants us to enjoy when God lives with us along the way.

The Jewish poet Abraham ben Samuel Abulafia (thirteenth century) wrote:

> I have tested the hearts of those who hate me, but no one hates me as my own heart does. Many are the blows and wounds inflicted by my enemies, but no one batters me and wounds me as my soul does.... To whom can I cry out, whom can I condemn, when those who are destroying me come

---

Rabbi David Lyon is an innovative spiritual leader and educator and an active participant in interfaith activities. He is author of *God of Me: Imagining God throughout Your Lifetime* (Jewish Lights) and senior rabbi at Congregation Beth Israel in Houston, Texas.

> from within myself? I have found nothing better than to seek refuge in Your mercy ... God who sits upon the Throne of mercy![1]

When we truly despair and see nothing of value within us, the poet writes, we have to look to God.

We cannot despair. Who taught us that we had to be perfect, anyway? Our parents? Our teachers? Were they perfect? Our task is not to err so that we may be forgiven. Our task is to do the best we can and to know that when we miss the mark, and we will, we have the privilege to speak up and to be heard.

Humbly Embracing Imperfections

Tom Stella

I am a mystic, and so are you. We may not have attained the spiritual heights we strive for or that others have reached, but we are mystics nonetheless. This is so because mysticism is not about dwelling on the mountaintop or having peak experiences. It has to do with the astounding yet simple truth that God is the spiritual Ground of our being. No matter where we are on the climb, we are one with the One we seek. Philosophy professor and author Kerry Walters claims that historian and theologian Rufus Jones, one of the founders of the American Friends Service Committee, believed this to be true:

> For Jones ... the soul is inherently "conjunct" with God, inseparably linked with Spirit and thus by its very nature open to the Divine. There's no need for the distracting razzmatazz of esoteric techniques and visions and ecstasies, because God is already here, encountered in the everyday course of life or not at all.[1]

Being only halfway up the mountain, it is easy to forget that "God is already here." But when we lose sight of this truth, we may fall prey to the illusion that we must strive to be "there"—at the summit, where we can experience the Divine in a flash rather than stumbling upon the sacred in the flesh.

And it can be hard to imagine that we are mystics when our introspection reveals darkness rather than light, confusion rather than clarity, a mess rather than a sacred mystery. If we are an incarnation of God, should not the opposite be evident? The spiritual path that leads to the discovery of our interior union with

---

Tom Stella is a hospice chaplain, retreat facilitator, former Catholic priest, and a cofounder and director of Soul Link, a nonprofit organization whose mission is to bring spiritual seekers together. He is also author of *Finding God Beyond Religion: A Guide for Skeptics, Agnostics & Unorthodox Believers Inside & Outside the Church* (SkyLight Paths), among other books.

God meanders through a murky mess. Those aspects of ourselves of which we are not proud and that we try to keep hidden from sight lurk just beneath the surface of our personas.

When we stop, when we allow ourselves to be alone, when we muster the courage to take an honest look at who we are, we come face-to-face with the shadowy self described by C. S. Lewis as a "zoo of lusts, a bedlam of ambitions, a nursery of fears, a harem of fondled hatreds."[2] How can anyone filled with the likes of these monsters be even a mediocre mystic?

Annie Dillard writes about the journey through darkness to light:

> In the deeps are the violence and terror of which psychology has warned us. But if you ride these monsters down, if you drop with them farther over the world's rim, you find what our sciences cannot locate or name, the substrate, the ocean, or matrix or ether which buoys the rest ... our complex and inexplicable caring for each other, and for our life together here.[3]

A few weeks before the release of the film based on her book *Dead Man Walking*, I saw Sister Helen Prejean interviewed on a television talk show. When asked why she worked with death-row prisoners, she replied, "Because everyone is always more than the worst thing they've ever done." We are more than the worst aspects of ourselves. Beneath the darkness there is light.

Before we are the complex, self-defeating, anything-but-holy people we may have become in our actions and relationships, we are one with God: spiritual beings, mediocre mystics who need to wake up to the wonder of ourselves as the locus of the Divine.

It is the embrace of the inner darkness, not its exclusion, that gives birth to the peace of mind and heart that characterizes mystics. It is brokenness humbly accepted, not perfection, that makes room for God. I have discovered that it is better to embrace myself as one who is imperfect than it is to demand perfection as a criterion for self-acceptance. It is second nature for everyone I know to strive for perfection. When we identify a fault, a shortcoming, or an aspect of our character that is problematic, many of us instinctively attempt to root it out so that we can be the person we want to be, one who resembles the ideal presented to us by family, church, and society in general. But this striving doesn't usually result in achieving our goal. Rather, it ends in frustration as we remain the flawed person we have always been.

Life will be a battleground until we become wise enough to make peace with ourselves—flaws and all. This does not preclude attentiveness to our faults.

Self-compassion is a radical acceptance of our goodness despite our imperfections. In religious language, this is a willingness to surrender to God, whose love for us is unconditional. All our attempts to change for the better will be short-lived unless they begin with this truth, for we soon tire of the task when our goal is to be rid of our imperfections. The humble embrace of the crack, the flaw, and the imperfection allows Divinity's light to both get in and shine forth from us as compassion.

Questions in Asking for Forgiveness

Rev. Carolyne Call

All theistic religious traditions teach followers to repent after committing a violation against God or one of God's creatures. Your decision to ask another person for forgiveness is laudable if it is done solely for the purpose of seeking peace for yourself or reconciliation and/or closure. Here are some questions to use in the process of discerning whether asking for forgiveness is appropriate at this point in your journey.

1. Clearly articulate the reasons why you wish to ask someone for forgiveness. Why forgiveness for this? Why now?
2. Are you seeking closure for yourself or have you been focusing on the desired reaction of the other person?
3. In asking for forgiveness, can you be content with making your request, even if the reaction of the other person is negative or hostile?
4. Can you disengage yourself emotionally and spiritually, if the reaction to your request for forgiveness is one of hostility?

Rev. Carolyne Call, a minister and spiritual adviser for those in the process of divorce, also conducts workshops and retreats on spiritual, psychological, and moral development and is author of *Spiritually Healthy Divorce: Navigating Disruption with Insight & Hope* (SkyLight Paths).

Ghazali on Forgiveness

Translated by Aaron Spevack, PhD

If you backbite, you must seek forgiveness from Allah Most High, and then go to the one whom you have slandered and say, "I have oppressed you, so forgive me."

—Ghazali, *The Forty Foundations of Religion*, Book III

Aaron Spevack, PhD, assistant religion professor at Colgate University, specializes in Islamic intellectual history, including law, theology, and Sufism. He is the translator and annotator of *Ghazali on the Principles of Islamic Spirituality: Selections from* The Forty Foundations of Religion—*Annotated & Explained* (SkyLight Paths).

More Than Apologizing

Rami Shapiro

As much as you try, you cannot go through life without causing pain. Rather than being depressed by that reality, you can seek to repair brokenness and restore relationships, paving the way to receive forgiveness for yourself. Whether you are recovering from addiction or not, the twelve steps of AA contain rich wisdom for cultivating the humility and courage needed to ask for forgiveness and make amends.

> Step Nine: We made direct amends to such people wherever possible, except when to do so would injure them or others.

Some people," said Dr. Valerie Goode—a Miami-based psychologist and friend with decades-long experience working with addicts of all types—"hope to use Step Nine as an escape hatch to avoid feeling the depth of another's suffering, and their own guilt for causing it. They think that by saying they are sorry they can manipulate people into forgiving them. Or they think that by saying they are sorry they deserve to be forgiven and if the other cannot forgive it is no longer their responsibility to make amends. This is cheap grace and counterfeit healing." Cheap because it costs us very little: All we have to do is say we're sorry. Counterfeit because simply saying we're sorry doesn't change us or offer the people we have harmed any hope of healing....

Rami Shapiro, a renowned teacher of spirituality across faith traditions and a noted theologian, is a popular speaker on the topics of religion, theology, and spirituality. He is author of the award-winning *The Sacred Art of Lovingkindness: Preparing to Practice* and *Recovery—The Sacred Art: The Twelve Steps as Spiritual Practice* (both SkyLight Paths), among other books.

It is only after listening, only after making ourselves absolutely vulnerable to another's pain, that we have any idea as to the suffering we caused. And only when we do know that suffering do we have a genuine opportunity to ask for forgiveness.

"You have to be very mindful when engaging in asking for forgiveness," [a friend] told me. After listening to the pain and suffering you caused another human being, your natural tendency is to say "I'm sorry," but this, he said, is often a dodge. After apologizing, you expect the other to say, "It's okay." In fact, the reason you apologize in the first place may well be to elicit this response, and in this way to skim over the deeper work of Step Nine. But unless and until we are willing to do the deeper work, real amends making cannot happen. And to do that deeper work, you have to be clear about the difference between asking for forgiveness and apologizing.

The difference was made clear to me by a middle-aged meth addict named Phil, who spoke about making amends to his wife.

> The details don't matter as far as what I'd done, but what I learned working Step Nine was a real eye-opener for me. I kept telling her I was sorry for this and sorry for that, but she kept on being pissed at me. And that was making me angry as well. Here I am apologizing and she just doesn't seem to care. In fact, the more I said I was sorry the more pissed she got. So I kept asking her what she wanted and she kept saying she wanted me to apologize and I kept apologizing—you know saying I'm sorry—and we got nowhere. And then it just happened: Instead of saying I'm sorry during one of these attempts at amends, I asked her to forgive me. It wasn't that I planned to say something different, it just came out different. She was suddenly like a new woman. She started crying and saying how much she wanted to forgive me and how much she still loved me and that it would take time but she thought that my behavior was better and that she could and would forgive me.

Saying "I'm sorry" gives you power over the other person. You are affirming that you have made your peace with the past, and the other should do so as well. There is nothing more you can add to "I'm sorry," so there is nothing for the other person to do but acquiesce or push for something more. But what more can you offer, other than "I'm sorry"? When we ask for forgiveness we admit that we are powerless.

We cannot forgive ourselves; we need the other to offer forgiveness to us. Asking for anything is a humbling act. We ask for what we do not have and cannot get for ourselves. We ask because we are powerless to achieve our goal without another's help. After we have truly listened to another's story of suffering; after we have grasped beyond a shadow of a doubt our role in producing that suffering; after we have seen the damage we have caused and how we caused it, we are humbled. But not humbled enough. We must dare to lower ourselves even closer to the earth, to metaphorically prostrate ourselves before another and ask for forgiveness.

What if, however, in the process of telling her story, the other has forgiven you? You heard her say so. She is being magnanimous, so shouldn't you be grateful, accept her gift, and move on without actually asking for forgiveness yourself? No.

Some people cannot bear to tell their story if that story causes another pain, even if the person being hurt is the person who caused the original hurt in the first place. Despite the fact that we are the cause of the pain, the other person cannot bear to hurt us, and so forgives us prematurely. This is an act of self-protection on the other's part that will short-circuit the Step Nine process.

If premature forgiveness is offered, do not reject the gift, but do not be satisfied with it, either. Say something like "Thank you for that, but I'm trying to understand what meaning my actions have for you that I might better understand how my behavior causes suffering and change my behavior more thoroughly. If you would, please tell me more." You need not force the issue, but encourage the person to tell you enough of the damage you caused to make it clear to you that saying "I'm sorry" is insufficient, and asking for forgiveness will, in fact, be a humbling and potentially healing act for both of you.

Receiving another's forgiveness isn't the goal of Step Nine; asking for that forgiveness is what matters. When we ask, we help restore the other's self-worth. By requesting something that only he can give, we help him discover that he is valuable, that he has a role to play in our healing, and that playing it will promote his own healing as well.... When you ask someone for forgiveness, you place yourself in a position of radical vulnerability. You not only admit to having caused the other person harm, but you admit that you cannot move on with your life without the other person's forgiveness. It is another example of admitted powerlessness. But this does not mean that you turn your life over to the other. Asking forgiveness isn't an invitation for retribution and abuse. It is an invitation for healing for both you and the person you have harmed. If the other doesn't want to heal, or cannot heal, you cannot allow yourself to be held hostage to her illness. If you sincerely ask for forgiveness and it is not given, wait and ask again, and then again. But if after three times the other is still unwilling or unable to forgive, move on.

While there may come a time when you once again have an opportunity to make amends with this person, you need not, indeed must not, allow the other's state of mind to dictate your recovery.

If some of the people we have harmed choose to hold on to their pain, if they choose to bear a grudge even in the face of our sincere request for forgiveness, then we are free from the burden of the wrong, and the other is left carrying it alone. But when forgiveness is genuinely beseeched and genuinely bestowed, the burden is lifted from everyone. This is why forgiveness is as good for the giver as for the receiver. Both are freed from the crippling weight of the past. Both are free to move on.

Developing Self-Compassion

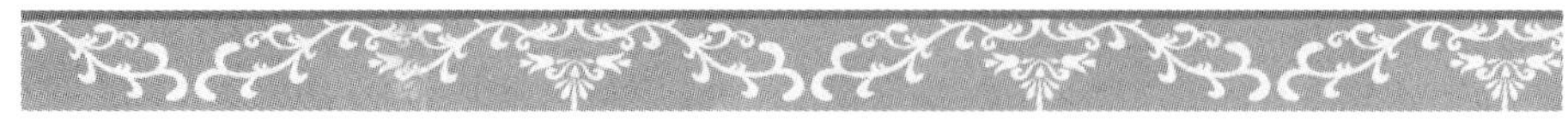

Imam Jamal Rahman

> In the Name of God, Boundlessly Compassionate and Infinitely Merciful
>
> —Qur'anic invocation known as the Basmala

Islamic spirituality focuses on the abiding need to understand the majesty and beauty of compassion, and to practice it in our inner and outer lives. Bereft of mercy and gentleness with self, it is difficult to transform the ego and open the heart; without compassion for others, life becomes dreary and burdensome. A Bedouin once pleaded with the Prophet to reveal to him how the Basmala might be bestowed on him, and the Prophet replied that when we are compassionate with ourselves and others, the grace of Infinite Compassion will be bestowed upon us.

The transformative powers of compassion are easily illustrated by the element of water in nature. The Qur'an calls it the best metaphor or "sign" of divine compassion. "O my people! Ask forgiveness of your Lord and turn to Him [in repentance]: He will send you the skies pouring abundant rain, and add strength to your strength" (11:52).

The special power of that phrase, *add strength to your strength,* can best be appreciated in the context of another Qur'anic verse revealing that water is the very essence of life: "We made from water every living thing" (21:30). In other words, the water of divine compassion adds strength to our sacred essence; it makes us even more of what we already are.

Imam Jamal Rahman, beloved teacher and retreat leader, is author of *Spiritual Gems of Islam Insights & Practices from the Qur'an, Hadith, Rumi & Muslim Teaching Stories to Enlighten the Heart & Mind* and *Sacred Laughter of the Sufis: Awakening the Soul with the Mulla's Comic Teaching Stories & Other Islamic Wisdom* (both SkyLight Paths), among other books.

We merely have to observe the effects of water in nature to realize that it is indeed a perfect metaphor for compassion. In a gentle rain, water is soft and yielding, even life giving: it mists the flowers and cools the skin on a sultry day. "Thou canst see the Earth dry and lifeless—and [suddenly] when we send down waters upon it, it stirs and swells and puts forth every kind of lovely plant!" (22:5).

But just as it is easy to underestimate the power of water, so too is it easy to undervalue the power of compassion. In torrents, water has the power to wash away continents; and in "torrents," compassion has the power to wash away the detritus of the false, self-protective ego. In fact, Sufi teachers say that those who are gentle and merciful are the ones who have authentic power. They are the ones who most emulate the life-affirming power of our Creator: "He is the One that sends down rain [even] after [men] have given up all hope, and scatters His Mercy" (42:28).

Clearly, then, compassion for self and others is the foundation for all other spiritual practices. But it is axiomatic that we can only truly be compassionate with others when we have learned how to be compassionate with ourselves. The following reflections and practices are useful in developing this life-giving attribute for our own precious souls.

If we seek to tame the ego and align it with our higher self by sheer willpower, the ego will resist our efforts with creative excuses for maintaining the status quo. But if we focus the light of awareness on the ego with mercy and gentleness, the ego slowly begins to relent and allows itself to be transformed, just as the hardest stone eventually yields to a steady trickle of water. The practices described here are the ones that my friends and congregants have found most effective in their work to cultivate the gentle but essential art of compassion for self.

Practice: Loving the Heart

In an exquisite revelation that came to the Prophet Muhammad in a dream, God said to him, "Neither my Heaven nor my Earth can contain me, but the soft, humble heart of my believing slave can contain me." Think of it: The Divine Heart of the All-Compassionate God dwells in the chambers of the human heart! Sages and poets tell us that the human heart yearns to open the window of the heart and gaze incessantly upon the Beloved. It begs to become illumined with love, compassion, light, and delight.

Loving the Heart is a meditative practice that will help build awareness of this heart-to-Heart connection. In silence, focus your attention on your physical heart. With your consciousness, embrace your heart. Remind yourself that the Beloved resides in that space. Then, when you are ready, tell your heart, "I love you." Say the words with feeling—with humility and sincerity. You might also want to say, "Thank you. I am so grateful." Choose words that resonate with you.

If it feels narcissistic to say "I love you" to your own heart, remind yourself that the words are directed to Divinity. It may feel awkward at first, but persist with it. Very often, the discomfort dissolves. Spiritual teachers say that as you continue with this practice, a mysterious, divine vibration goes from the tongue into the mouth, into the throat, into the chest, deep into the heart, deeper still into the hidden, and then into the "hidden of the hidden," healing and empowering your sacred essence. Faithful practitioners have reported that in times of difficulty or affliction, they have been astonished to hear a reassuring voice rising from within and telling them the same words that they have repeated so often: "I love you."

Practice: Sacred Naming

Of all the relationships we experience in our lives, the most fundamental one and yet the most neglected is the relationship with our own dear selves. Without our even realizing it, we talk to ourselves often and, sadly, much of this self-talk is quite negative. We castigate ourselves for not being smart enough, quick enough, beautiful enough—the list is long and hurtful. If we are serious about pursuing a relationship with our sacred essence, it is helpful to become more aware of our internal dialogue and practice "spiritual intervention" to transform our negative self-talk by addressing ourselves with affection and compassion.

One of the most effective ways of doing this is a simple practice called Sacred Naming, in which we soften our self-criticisms by directing them not to our "stupid" selves but to our "child of grace" selves. Choose your own term of endearment, something like "Sweetheart," "Dear One," "Brother + your name" (for example, I say, "Brother Jamal"), or whatever feels genuine and evokes compassion for yourself. It may be a loving nickname used by a treasured grandparent or a favorite aunt. The key is to find a sacred name that brings up feelings of mercy and gentleness. Know that there is sacred beauty and power in being named with affection. If the naming is said in a tone of voice that emanates from the heart, it creates a sacred vibration that leaves an indelible imprint on your soul. Recall the sweet vibration of, say, your grandmother's voice when she called you by a pet name with the energy of love and kindness. That is the sweetness we need to use when addressing ourselves.

Having chosen your sacred name, be on the lookout for any opportunity to use it. The moment you become aware that your internal dialogue is beating up on you, immediately intervene by addressing yourself with your sacred name and continue the conversation with the gentler energy that it evokes. Whenever I interject the heartfelt name Brother Jamal, I feel a wave of mercy come over me, and I reinforce that feeling by saying, "Brother Jamal, I'm so sorry you're experiencing difficult feelings right now. Please know that I am here to support you," or words to that effect. Invariably, the direction and content of the negative inner conversation change for the good.

Friends and congregants who perform this practice report several major shifts. The sharpness of the ego palpably begins to soften and the ego actually enjoys the moments of collaboration with the soul. Also, there is the added benefit that with continuous practice, you will find yourself naturally naming others with kindness, and this often results in outer harmony and cooperation.

Granting Yourself Absolution

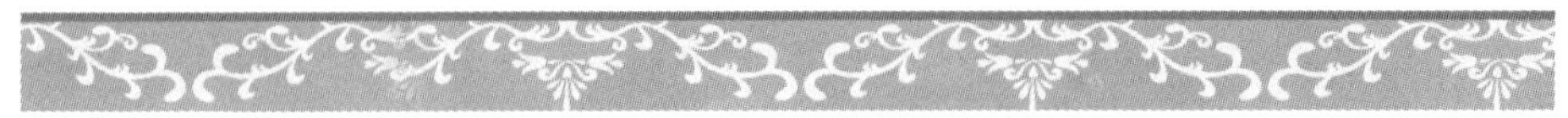

Marcia Ford

Union organizer Dolores Huerta was once quoted as asking this succinct question: "If you haven't forgiven yourself something, how can you forgive others?" Had I been anywhere in the vicinity when she said that, I would have been the one jumping up and down, both arms flailing about in the air, begging her to call on me to respond. I have the answer, and it's equally succinct: "Easily. Very, very easily." My unscientific, statistically unreliable observation of many of my fellow Americans has convinced me that we are a peculiarly masochistic lot. Our penchant for introspection and self-criticism makes us especially unforgiving of ourselves. Given the choice, a lot of us would sooner forgive a serial killer for his heinous crimes than forgive ourselves for making an insensitive remark to a friend sometime in the last century. The reason is fairly obvious: we don't have to live with the serial killer.

There's another reason why we're unable, or at least reluctant, to indulge in a bit of self-forgiveness. That's because the need to forgive ourselves is so doggoned daily and so annoyingly long term. I speak here with authority and from a great deal of personal experience. For people like me, learning to forgive ourselves is a lifelong lesson, one that I seriously doubt I'll master during my own lifetime. Forgive you? No problem! Forgive myself? Big problem! The obstacles to self-forgiveness go by many names. Perfectionism. Shame. Guilt. Failure. Blame. Weakness. Regret. Add your own words to the list. What they all add up to is the word *human*. We have a hard time accepting our own humanness.

Marcia Ford is a former editor of *Christian Retailing* magazine, an Explorefaith.org columnist, and a frequent contributor to *Publishers Weekly*. The author of eighteen books, including *The Sacred Art of Forgiveness: Forgiving Ourselves and Others through God's Grace* (SkyLight Paths), she was the religion editor of the *Asbury Park Press* for ten years.

We think we should be above making the mistakes we've made throughout our lives, but we have this head full of negative memories that keep surfacing to make sure we never forget that we're not above it after all. The same brain that cannot recall what I had for dinner last night is the very brain that cannot let me forget the offensive comment I made at the Millville High School Holly Ball in December 1965, a not-so-funny remark that still makes me cringe and brings tears to my eyes when I let it.

So what are we to do about this lifelong dilemma? No one has helped me learn to forgive myself more than author and psychology professor Lewis Smedes. Since I'm still a learner in the self-forgiveness classroom, join me in gaining some insights gleaned from the wisdom of Professor Smedes.

Thankfully for us, Smedes believes the difficulty we have in forgiving ourselves is not such a bad thing. Were it any easier, we'd be inclined to dismiss our serious offenses all too readily.

But as difficult as self-forgiveness is, it's also essential to our sense of wholeness and well-being. Here, the good professor brings logic into play: since it take two to play the blame game, we end up with a divided self—the one doing the blaming, and the one deserving the blame.

"We feel the need to forgive ourselves because the part of us that gets blamed feels split off from the part that does the blaming.... We are exiled from our own selves, which is no way to live," Smedes writes in *The Art of Forgiving*. "This is why we need to forgive ourselves and why it makes sense to do it: We are ripped apart inside, and forgiving ourselves is the only way we heal the split."[1] Ripped apart inside—that's exactly how we feel when the memories of our bad behavior and the consequences of our bad decisions join forces to condemn us. The image of being the peacemaker who is able to mend the rift between the blaming self and the blamed self is one we would do well to carry with us throughout our lives. Forgiving ourselves becomes an act of self-restoration; we're putting ourselves back together again, making ourselves the whole person we are meant to be.

After imparting this wisdom to us, Professor Smedes doesn't abandon us in the lecture hall; he leads us out into the world where we can apply self-forgiveness principles to our everyday lives. Among his suggestions: Clarify specifically what you need to forgive yourself for. You have the power to grant yourself absolution, so look in a mirror and tell yourself, "God forgives you and so do I"—the sentiment Catholic priests express when granting absolution during confession. Act like a forgiven person acts. Do something impulsive, extravagant, for another person. "Do anything nice that the practical part of you will tell you is nutty," he writes. "Celebrate the miracle you are performing on yourself by creating a little miracle for somebody else."[2] Perhaps the most important suggestion of all is to keep granting yourself absolution day after day after day, any time and every time those negative memories crop up. As with forgiving others, it becomes easier to forgive ourselves the more we do it—so those recurring memories may in fact serve a positive purpose in our lives.

Finally, it helps to remember this: If God has forgiven us, who are we to veto his ruling? To do so is tantamount to usurping God's authority and power in our lives—which gives us yet another misdeed to forgive ourselves for. Better to agree with God that we're forgiven and be done with it.

Reflection: Being Drained of Self-Criticism

Self-forgiveness can be an empowering experience, while self-criticism is a particularly draining experience. But maybe you need to be drained of all that self-criticism in order to be filled with power. Close your eyes and criticize all those things you find it so hard to forgive about yourself ... but only under this condition: imagine God watching you in amusement the entire time. The things we find so hideous about ourselves are usually trifles to God. And all those memories that are so shameful and so embarrassing? You can be fairly certain no one else remembers them. They're too busy mentally replaying their own shameful and embarrassing moments.

Practice: "I Can't Forgive Myself Because ___________"

One of the obstacles to forgiving ourselves is our inability to understand why we have such a hard time with the concept, as well as our unwillingness to take the time to discover precisely what it is that prevents us from forgiving ourselves. You can start to tear down that obstacle right now by completing the following sentence: I have a difficult time forgiving myself because ______.

Make a list if you have to. You may realize that there are many reasons why you have trouble with self-forgiveness.

Some of the most common are the negative messages you may have received as a child, even if you had the best of parents.

Nearly all are related in some way to a combination of low self-esteem, a misunderstanding of what forgiveness is, and a misreading of what the Scriptures have to say about forgiveness.

When you're finished with your sentence—or your list—talk it over with God. Imagine a loving God pointing out all the misconceptions you have that are preventing you from forgiving yourself. Then imagine the Spirit leading you into the truth about how and why you should forgive yourself.

Laugh at Yourself

Rev. Susan Sparks

Humor offers a revolutionary, yet simple, spiritual paradigm: If you can laugh at yourself, you can forgive yourself. And if you can forgive yourself, you can forgive others. Laughter heals. It grounds us in a place of hope.

Perhaps most important, laughter fosters intimacy and honesty in our relationships with each other and with God. In fact, laughter and faith are mutually dependent. Theologian Conrad Hyers explained, "Faith without laughter leads to dogma, and laughter without faith to despair." It is in these words that we begin to see a tiny glimmer of the power that can come from the merger of humor and the sacred.

As a trained theologian, my favorite movie is, of course, *Kung Fu Panda*. The best part is when tortoise Zen master Oogway tries to convince Po that even though he's an overweight panda, his true destiny is to be a great dragon warrior. "Our destiny," he tells Po, "is usually found on the road we take to avoid it." And there, in one sentence, is my life as an ex-lawyer turned stand-up comedian and minister.

My one regret? I wish I had realized earlier that my call was not a wrong number. Every person has a call, an invitation to bring all of who we are to the spiritual search. That includes the things that "don't fit the mold"—the tears, the anger, the joy, and the laughter. It's all holy.

We seem to have a much easier time sharing tears and remorse. We come slump-shouldered before God, proudly bearing our shame, our fears, our self-denial, and

---

Rev. Susan Sparks, the only female comedian in the country with a pulpit, is author of *Laugh Your Way to Grace: Reclaiming the Spiritual Power of Humor* (SkyLight Paths). She is senior pastor, and first female pastor, of the historic Madison Avenue Baptist Church in New York City, and won an award from Intersections International for her work to promote justice, reconciliation, and peace among diverse communities.

our suffering. But the part of our humanity that laughs is usually hidden away in shame.

Ironically, people speak of sacred tears. American author Washington Irving wrote: "There is sacredness in tears. They are not the mark of weakness, but of power. They speak more eloquently than ten thousand tongues. They are messengers of overwhelming grief … and unspeakable love." I believe that tears and laughter are almost indistinguishable. Both can offer transformative experiences that cleanse, heal, and restore our spirits. Yet, rarely do we give laughter that chance.

These things that "don't fit the mold" are the very things that give us life and spirit and our very humanity. Swiss psychologist Carl Jung called these the "shadow selves": the parts of us that are alive and well, but that we would prefer to keep on the "q.t." Here is the problem: We can't be made whole if we don't offer up all the pieces. It doesn't matter how wonderful God thinks we are, if we consider parts of ourselves unworthy then we will forever find ourselves slump-shouldered, staring at the floor in holy realms.

Reflection: Laughter and Forgiveness

Laughter, in a way, is about forgiveness. Think of a time when you were able to laugh at your shortcomings rather than judge yourself. How did that change how you felt about yourself? Did giving yourself a break offer a heightened sense of forgiveness for others?

Facing Brokenness

Terry Taylor

For many of us who feel broken, one of the most troubling aspects of our condition is that we feel different from other people, unworthy, not acceptable. There is likely to be a sense of shame involved. Because we tend to internalize our feeling of brokenness and make it part of our identity, our sense of shame isn't limited to whatever we are feeling broken about. Instead, we generalize our feeling of embarrassment to our entire being. In other words, we don't necessarily feel embarrassed about our brokenness, we feel embarrassed at being *ourselves*! When we "let down our guard," with nothing to fill up the space, we may come face-to-face with the emotional pain that often lurks just beneath the surface of our consciousness. This pain is often rooted in the very core of our brokenness and is often clever and tenacious in its hold over us. Because of that, it is important that we acquire some tools to deal with the "emotional sludge" that can ooze up in times of silence or meditation.

I first encountered the interconnected Tibetan Buddhist meditation technique of *maitri* (MY-tree) in the teachings of Pema Chödrön, and I immediately knew I had found a spiritual tool that could be immensely helpful in easing my anguish. *Maitri* is a Sanskrit word meaning compassion, or more literally, "unconditional friendship with oneself."

Making Friends with Yourself

The term *maitri* is used in two different ways. First and foremost, it describes an attitude or spirit of friendliness that you can bring to yourself—your emotional

---

Terry Taylor is a workshop leader and frequent commentator for public radio and other media on topics related to spirituality, peace, and justice. He is executive director of Interfaith Paths to Peace, an organization dedicated to fostering interreligious dialogue, and author of *A Spirituality for Brokenness: Discovering Your Deepest Self in Difficult Times* (SkyLight Paths).

life, your memories, even your very body. Pema calls it a fundamental attitude of nonaggression. Or, to put it another way, it is the mind-set of being sympathetic to yourself, without harshness. *Maitri* is also a specific meditation process in the Tibetan Buddhist tradition through which you can develop this feeling of unconditional friendliness toward yourself—and, I would add, toward your brokenness. I'll explore this in more depth in a minute, but first it's important to grasp how this idea of "befriending yourself" might be a significant spiritual tool for mending your brokenness.

When was the last time you felt relaxed with yourself? Satisfied with who you are? At home with yourself? A friend to yourself? All these are encompassed in the term *maitri*. The idea of learning to feel friendly toward yourself might sound odd at first, but—be honest now—it is probably not something you practice when you are feeling broken. Instead, you probably are far more likely to criticize yourself, or be angry with yourself, or dwell in the depression and shame of "being yourself." Though learning to be friendly toward your pain might sound like a paltry response at first, it is, in fact, a powerful step toward mending your brokenness.

Think about it: if your best friend were feeling anguished or embarrassed, you would offer what any good friend would offer—words of affirmation and love, accompanied by a dose of reality. You certainly wouldn't condemn your friend or tell him or her to "get over it." It is essentially the same process in befriending yourself through *maitri*. You look at your pain the way a close friend would. Or better yet, you look at your misery in the same way you would look at the pain your best friend was feeling. You see your pain through the eyes of compassion rather than criticism or judgment. You are willing to stay with your pain, to befriend it. This is when change can begin. Healthy change. The kind of change that can put you on the road to mending.

Allowing yourself to feel your pain, to really acknowledge its presence, and adopting an attitude of compassion toward yourself can have remarkably positive effects in your life. We want to believe that some healing aid will "cure" us, make us "good as new," yet we're frustrated when the same old hurts or depressions or angers seem to keep plaguing us. The practice of *maitri* invites us to look at our pain—whether physical injuries or emotional memories—not as something to be avoided but as something to be embraced, to be tended, to feel kindly toward. *Maitri* teaches us that our woundedness presents us with an opportunity to begin to care for ourselves in the fullest sense, with compassion for the depth of our anguish, what it is about, and where it is coming from....

You can also learn to get control of the negative behaviors that stem from not acknowledging your pain. You can stop blaming others for your problems. You can stop flying off the handle at loved ones. When you stop burying your anguish, you can let go of the ways you might try to self-medicate your pain through overeating or starving, abusing alcohol or drugs, smoking, overexercising, overworking—whatever your self-destructive coping mechanism is. When you stop trying to escape your pain, you are taking an important step toward an attitude of loving-kindness for your brokenness.

Preparing to Practice

At the beginning of the workshops that I lead about brokenness, I usually ask the participants what coping mechanisms they are using to hide from their brokenness. I find that participants reveal a remarkable variety of (sometimes very creative) coping mechanisms. The one thing they all have in common, however, is that most of the coping mechanisms I hear about involve ways of hiding from brokenness and its pain. The practice of *maitri* does just the opposite: Instead of immediately trying to get rid of pain, *maitri* invites us to lean into the pain and see what happens.

This beginning phase of *maitri* is perhaps the hardest. Allowing your bad memories even a *little* breathing room can feel threatening, even terrifying. If you feel broken, you can easily become overwhelmed by your pain. So before you begin a *maitri* practice, it will be important to know to whom you can go if you do feel overwhelmed. Here are a few more things you can do to help prepare for a rewarding *maitri* experience:

- Be open to just sitting quietly with yourself.
- Don't expect immediate results. Having compassion for yourself involves having patience and letting go of certain expectations.
- Make a commitment to practicing *maitri* on a regular schedule over an extended period of time (days, weeks, perhaps even months). Befriending your pain will probably take time, and it is important not to give up on yourself too early.
- Be as honest as you can with yourself about what you are feeling, especially the intensity of your pain. If it's a ten on a scale of one to ten, recognize that. But if it's a one or a two, be honest in noting that your pain isn't as severe as you expected it might be.

- Try to have a sense of humor about yourself and what yo through. It might be helpful to remember that many com are built around characters going through disastrous eve events can be viewed as tragic or comic, depending on the attitude viewers adopt toward them.
- Embrace the idea of being compassionate toward yourself. Compassion doesn't mean pity; it means "to suffer with." Try to look at your situation the way that you would view the troubles of your closest friend if he or she were suffering.
- Avoid condemning yourself. You've probably already spent enough time beating yourself up.

Practice: *Maitri*—Embracing Your Pain

Are you ready to give *maitri* a try? Here's a suggested step-by-step approach you can use, but keep in mind that these are only suggestions, not rules.

Start by setting a specific length of time for your *maitri*. I use twenty minutes, but find a length of time that works for you … then stick to it!

If possible, find a place to meditate that is quiet and free from distractions.

Either sit on the floor or on a mat in a comfortable position. Or, if you are like me (I have some problems with arthritis) and can't sit comfortably on the floor for extended periods of time, sit in a comfortable straight-back chair for support.

Sit up straight. Don't slouch. If you're sitting on a chair, place the soles of your feet flat on the floor, with your feet a comfortable shoulder-width apart.

Either fold your hands in your lap or place them palms down on your thighs.

Sit facing a blank wall if possible.

Either close your eyes or try to keep them half open and unfocused. You might also try focusing on a single point or object.

Consciously relax all parts of your body step by step, beginning with your feet, moving on to your calves, and continuing upward until you have relaxed your face and head.

Once you have relaxed, begin getting in touch with your feelings, especially your pain (physical or emotional).

Note where you feel your pain and how strong it is.

Try not to let your attention move away from your discomfort. If you find yourself thinking about something else, return your attention to your pain in the same way that you would return to repeating your mantra if you were practicing a form of mindfulness meditation.

Start to think of your pain as a separate entity, a companion within yourself. Consider giving it a name so you can address it.

Talk to your pain. Ask it questions: "Why are you with me? What do you need? Is there something that will make you go away? Do you want to go away? If not, is there something that will soothe you? Do you have something to tell me?"

Listen for your pain's answers. These answers may not come as words, but in dreams, coincidences, or other psychological or emotional phenomena.

Once you have begun thinking of your pain as a companion, try to think of it in a loving way, in the same way you would care about a troubled but lovable relative or partner. It may not be easy to think of your pain in a loving way at first, but do give it time.

Maitri can help you learn to look at your day-to-day life with honesty, humor, and compassion, not condoning or condemning, and it is well worth your time and effort to give it a try.... This process isn't easy at first, but after a while it does soften the pain. *Maitri* won't cure you overnight of your painful memories, your embarrassment, your self-loathing, or whatever painful form your brokenness takes. But *maitri* can ease your journey every step of the way. *Maitri* isn't an end in itself, but rather a step in the process of connecting with your own pain so you can live with it gently and help your wounds mend.

Love Your Enemies

> Preparing to respond to hostility begins from our center, the place inside ourself where we have personal power.... Here and now is the place in which we are powerful. Here and now is the place where hospitality and love begin to change everything, not because we are changing everything, but because love changes everything.
>
> —Rev. Nanette Sawyer

> Once we open ourselves to the perspectives of others, anything can happen.
>
> —John Backman

The idea of loving enemies is at the root of the powerful nonviolent quests for justice in the twentieth century. Loving enemies in your everyday life, though not nearly so dramatic, can also be powerfully healing and freeing (for you—and maybe for your enemy).

Who are your enemies, or people in your life whose primary relationship with you is adversarial? Loving these people is, of course, not particularly natural. You'll fin[illegible] in this section a number of creative, detailed exercises to help prepare you to m[illegible] enemies and adversaries with compassion. Most of these exercises focus on [illegible] ing your perspective: seeing your adversary's human side or "walking a mile [illegible] shoes" can soften your reactions, even as you still disagree—perhaps vehe[illegible]

This section will encourage and equip you not to fear encounters [illegible] or adversaries, but to be centered in your own identity, and to b[illegible] everyone around you with compassion.

eet
shift-
in their
mently.
with enemies
willing to

Hospitality to Enemies

Rev. Nanette Sawyer

How can we love in the face of hatred? How can we prepare ourselves for and then implement hospitality in the presence of hostility? How is it possible to hold receptivity, reverence, and generosity toward those who hold enmity toward us?

Hostility isn't always obvious. Enmity happens at all levels of intensity, from the cold shoulder to the angry stare to brutal violence. Preparing to respond to such hostility begins from our center, the place inside ourself where we have personal power.... The inward preparations that we make will help us in all our outward encounters. The secret is in learning to focus on what is happening and how we are responding *here* and *now*, which in turn enables us to tap into our center of personal power. *Here and now* is the place in which we are powerful. Here and now is the place where hospitality and love begin to change everything, not because *we* are changing everything, but because love changes everything.

Some types of hostility seem too big and too systemic for us to imagine overcoming them with hospitality or love. We have to wonder how we could possibly love someone who hates us. It surely isn't easy; sometimes it feels impossible. But breaking out of the stranglehold of hostility and hatred is the only way that we will ever be spiritually free....

Dr. King said, "I just happened to be here." And Gandhi said, "I am only common clay." They are both telling us—I'm just a person, just like you, doing the best I can, doing my spiritual practices. Our place of power is inside us, rooted and grounded in the here and now of a living power that is love, firmness, and nonviolence....

Rev. Nanette Sawyer, teacher and spiritual counselor, is author of *Hospitality—The Sacred Art: Discovering the Hidden Spiritual Power of Invitation and Welcome* (Skylight Paths) and a founding pastor of Grace Commons, an innovative Christian community in Chicago that holds hospitality as a core value.

Years after Gandhi's teaching empowered a nation and led India to independence from British rule, Martin Luther King Jr. had begun to talk about similar beliefs and methods in Montgomery, Alabama. "Christ furnished the spirit and motivation," Dr. King said, "while Gandhi furnished the method."[1] A year after the Montgomery bus boycott ended, nearly two years after his home was bombed, and twenty-two years after his childhood friend rejected him because of his race, Dr. King preached a sermon at Dexter Avenue Baptist Church in Montgomery called "Loving Your Enemies."[2]

Although King does not use the language of "hospitality" in this sermon, his insight into the challenges of loving our enemies shines a direct light on what it takes to practice hospitality in the face of hostility. Dr. King's sermon takes as its starting point a well-known verse in the Christian Scriptures in which Jesus teaches, "You have heard that it was said, 'You shall love your neighbor and hate your enemy.' But I say to you, Love your enemies and pray for those who persecute you, so that you may be children of your Father in heaven; for he makes his sun rise on the evil and on the good, and sends rain on the righteous and on the unrighteous" (Matthew 5:43–45).

But how can we possibly love those who hate us? In the sermon, Dr. King gives three suggestions about how to love our enemies. First, he says, we must examine ourselves for our possible contributions to the enmity; second, we must try to see the good in our enemies and remember the evil that is in us; and third, we must resist the temptation to defeat our enemies.[3]...

In his sermon about loving our enemies, Dr. King essentially taught how we can prepare ourselves to make a real difference in the world, both personally and socially. Dr. King called it the "redemptive power" of love, and said that this power of love is the only force that can ultimately transform individuals and our world.[4] So let's look at the three foundational steps that Dr. King suggested for loving—or practicing hospitality toward—our enemies.

Why Do They Hate Us?

When considering love, Dr. King encouraged his listeners, and us, to examine ourselves first, because there might be something that we are doing, either on a subtle level or in an explicit way, to stimulate what King called "the tragic hate response."[5] If so, then the only way we'll be able to address and adjust that is by becoming aware of it. It requires us to be relentlessly honest in our self-examination. This is the basic first step of hospitality.

Sometimes when people seem to hate us, it makes no sense. We can't see the reason why. We can't think of anything we have done that would elicit such a reaction. Once I had a job working in an office that was shared by three people, and our work areas were divided into cubicles by freestanding dividers. This meant that we had no privacy, that our phone calls, though we spoke softly, might be overheard by others.

During my first week of work, I heard one of my coworkers refer to me on the phone as "the new chick" and call me "that b—," a very derogatory term, her voice dripping with hostility. I was shocked. I hadn't done anything or said anything mean or hateful. I felt horribly and unfairly judged and somewhat paralyzed by the venomous attitude she began to project onto me.

Why would she hate me like this? At the time it felt so completely unfair. It seemed I had been only kind and open to her. But looking back on it now, I wonder, did I start to dislike her only after she called me awful names to her friends on the phone, or did I dislike her before she started doing that? She was a bit unkempt and somewhat edgy, seeming to spend a lot of her work time surfing the Internet and being sarcastic and irritable. Did I have a subtle judgmental attitude toward her that she sensed and responded to by shutting me out of her inner circle? Was she trying to protect herself against being criticized by criticizing me first? Was she trying to drown out my subtle judgmental "vibe" by criticizing me more loudly or more directly than I was judging her? Maybe there was something in me that had aroused the tragic hate response in her.

Sometimes, though, people hate or dislike us not because of anything that we have done, but because of human tendencies toward jealously, greed, fear, and shame. Could my office mate have hated me because she was insecure and hated herself? Because I reminded her of someone who had treated her badly in the past? Because she felt jealous, fearful, or ashamed? I would never know. In the meantime, what would be an effective response? At the time, I tended to internalize her negativity toward me, feeling bad about myself because she didn't seem to like me. I had enough self-awareness to *try* not to do that, but it is a difficult spiritual practice. I knew that to become angry toward her, adding my own hateful or disdainful attitude to her hostility, would only exacerbate the problem. I was able to act without hostility, but I don't think I achieved generosity. I worked on receptivity and reverence, in the sense of looking for the good in her and looking for the good in me, too, so as not to act hostile toward myself. It was only later that I tried looking for the part of me that might have somehow triggered some of her hostility toward me.

This kind of self-aware examination is something that Dr. King recommended not only at the individual level, but also at the community level and at the level of international relations. The burning issues in his day were different from ours in the particulars, but perhaps similar to ours in the human dimensions. Then, society was facing an ideological struggle between Communism and democracy, embodied in the Cold War between the United States and the Soviet Union.

Now we face other ideological struggles. To be honest in our engagement with these issues and problems, to try to answer the question of "why do they hate us," we need to consider the possibility that we have done something "deep down in our past," as Dr. King said, that has on some level provoked a response of hatred and hostility. If we can't acknowledge what we have done, we deprive ourselves of the opportunity to grow as people and as a culture. We deny ourselves the opportunity to change, to do better, and to improve the hostile situations that we find ourselves confronted with, whether at the personal, communal, institutional, or national level.

Acknowledging our role in interactions is essential to discovering and staying in touch with the source of our power. Our point of power as individuals is based on our self-awareness and our ability to accept the truth about ourselves and others. In exploring this idea, King cited another scripture: "Why do you see the speck in your neighbor's eye, but do not notice the log in your own eye?"(Matthew 7:3). King described this as a tragedy of human nature. It is our tendency to be super aware of the failures and limitations of our adversaries while being woefully unaware or actively in denial about our own failures and limitations. To overturn this tendency is a difficult practice, but if we can develop our capacity to perceive ourselves and our adversaries more accurately, and even to accept them compassionately, then we begin to move into the realm of generous hospitality, extending love in the face of hostility at any level—personal, communal, institutional, or national.

Practice: Self-Examination

Self-examination is a form of awareness practice that can help you develop your capacity for hospitality to enemies. It begins with receptivity through honest perception, but it naturally leads into the realm of reverence and compassionate acceptance if you can keep practicing it. In this exercise, you will be looking for motivating feelings and underlying attitudes that may further enmity rather than hospitality.

Decide how much time you want to spend on this exercise. Five to ten minutes might be all you can manage in the beginning.

Begin by bringing to mind a person with whom you have had hostile interactions. If there is a particular situation you can focus on, all the better. Remember the setting of that event. Whether it was at your workplace, your place of worship, book club, or bowling team, visualize the last place your saw this person.These details will help you get in touch with the memories and emotions.

In your imagination, remember how the person looks, dresses, and does or doesn't approach you.

Now, turn your attention to yourself. Notice how you feel physically while remembering this person or situation. Notice sensations: Clenching teeth? Queasy stomach? Watch whatever sensations you find for a few moments.

Begin to name emotional states that come up, such as anger, frustration, fear, confusion, sadness, shock, rage, grief, and so on.

You may find that you get distracted or lose your focus. Simply return to visualizing the physical place in which you know this individual. Once you're reconnected, you can return to contemplating your physical and emotional reactions.

If one emotion rises to the forefront or seems particularly potent, focus on it more directly for a while. Follow the trail of thoughts that are connected to it and ask yourself questions about it: Where is this anger coming from? What am I afraid of? Why do I feel so sad? Allow yourself to fully witness these feelings and compassionately accept that they exist in you.

As you practice receptivity and reverence toward yourself, your awareness may expand and your adversarial feelings may begin to loosen their grip within you. If and when this happens, you can take the next step and turn your receptive awareness toward your adversary. Can you perceive the Buddha nature or image of God deep within him or her?

As your time begins to draw to a close, notice any changes in how you feel here and now in relation to the person or situation you've been exploring.

Although we may react to people and events outside our control, we do have the power to understand our responses and to make choices about how we direct our thoughts and how we act. With greater self-awareness, we have more freedom to respond proactively from our point of power, rather than reactively from unacknowledged human impulses. Awareness of and receptivity to ourselves and others lays the foundation for transformational hospitality.

Looking for the Evil within Us

Dr. King's second step toward loving enemies invites us to look within for a very specific purpose. He suggested that we look for the good in our enemies and look for the evil that is in us. Dr. King described us as being split up and divided against ourselves as though a civil war were raging inside us. It is the "isness" of our present nature being out of harmony with the eternal "oughtness" that forever confronts us, Dr. King said.[6] In other words, we're not as completely good as we would like to be. If we can recognize that this is true within ourselves as well as within our adversaries, then we can no longer see ourselves as entirely innocent or our adversaries as entirely guilty or evil.

There is no wholly good person, just as there is no wholly bad person. There are only human beings. When we can realize and remember our shared humanity with our adversaries, our attitude can shift, and a little compassion may even rise up within us.

If you would like to explore this particular practice, you can simply add a new step or focus to the earlier exercise of self-examination. Work your way through the same steps of imagining your adversary, and this time look for signs within yourself of hostility, hatred, disrespect, disdain, or anything that undermines the humanity of your adversary by seeing him or her as all bad. Also notice that seeing yourself as all good undermines your own humanity too, because that belief is not based in the complex reality of what it means to be human.

Looking for the Good in Our Adversaries

The words and labels we use for people are important in that they contain many connotations and reinforce beliefs we hold about who other people are at a fundamental level. There's something about calling a person your *enemy* that seems to concretize the hostile relationship, as well as reinforce a belief in the fundamental nature of the other's identity *as enemy*. Then it's not just how he's acting toward you that is problematic; it's his very personhood, the nature of who he is in relation to you. Such an understanding subtly but powerfully precludes a solution to the conflict, or even seeing new possibilities within the relationship.

Calling someone your *adversary* has a different effect, however. Sometimes the people we love the best are our adversaries, when we're disagreeing with them, when we're struggling, even vehemently, over some difference of opinion. An adversary is someone that we are engaging with in a certain way, in an adversarial way, but it doesn't concretize that engagement into a belief about that individual's identity. Our adversarial relationship has the potential to change into a more cooperative relationship, a more connected and less fractured relationship, even a relationship of hospitality. About this process, Dr. King said this:

> The person who hates you most has some good in him; even the nation … [and] even the race that hates you most has some good in it. And when you come to the point that you look in the face of every man and see deep down within him what religion calls "the image of God," you begin to love him.... [Try to] find the center of goodness and place your attention there and you will take a new attitude.[7]

This is a great spiritual practice involving how we use our thoughts to affect our beliefs. Dr. King is suggesting that we place our attention not on hatred, not on evil, not on the worst in another person, but rather on the center of goodness that is surely within each and every created human being. It might be buried deep. It might be something that the person can't even perceive about herself. But looking for it with energy and commitment is a spiritual practice that can literally transform our lives because it can change how we feel, how we act, and how we understand our adversaries, ourselves, and our power and place in the world.

Dr. King would take this even one step further to suggest that placing our attention on the good in our adversaries would ultimately also change them, that our love would draw that goodness out of them. That is the redemptive power of love.

Practice: A Circle of Love (Draw It Large Enough to Include Your Adversary)

So how can we place our attention on the center of goodness in our adversaries? How can we begin to practice loving someone *in spite of*, as Dr. King suggests? How can we extend hospitality rather than hostility, even when hostility is directed at us? It is surely a lifelong spiritual journey to grow adept in these ways, but here is a meditative exercise that can help you practice.

The underlying goal of this exercise is to discover and remember the inherent humanity of the people with whom you are experiencing hostility and to choose to extend hospitality and love. If others are exhibiting hatred toward you, they are, in a sense, rejecting the humanity that they share with you. They are cutting you out of their circle of love and respect, but you can draw your circle big enough to keep them in it.

> Begin by focusing on your heart as the center of your feelings of love.
>
> See with your inner eye the beating of your heart. Imagine that it is pulsing with love. You might imagine the love as a certain color, or as light itself. If you need help feeling the love, you can imagine someone that you love, notice the sensation of love you feel toward him or her, and hold that sensation while releasing the image of the particular person.
>
> Now imagine the light or color of love expanding to fill your whole chest, then your whole body. See it begin to extend out past the limits of your physical form and fill the whole room, then your whole town or city.
>
> See the people everywhere in this area become enveloped in this light of love. Sit with this image for a few moments, allowing it to become stronger.
>
> Now bring to mind an adversary and see him enveloped by this love as well. Know that the source of love is inexhaustible, enough to keep your heart pulsing with it forever. See the light permeating every part of your being, refreshing you. Imagine the same effect on the person you are holding in this light.
>
> As a final step, begin to notice and focus on another light—the heart of the person you are embracing. Let her heart be the symbol of her inner center of goodness. Whatever it looks like, imagine that it, too, is beginning to glow.
>
> As you watch, the light begins to expand and fill her chest, and then her body, and then extends beyond her body and surrounds you. Now the center of goodness—the light of the heart—of your adversary is surrounding you, and the light of your heart is surrounding her.

After holding this inner experience for a while, gently bring your awareness back to where you are sitting. Contemplate your experience. How does this meditation affect your feeling toward this person? The next time you are physically in his presence, remember this exercise. Bring it powerfully to mind and see whether it changes the dynamic between you.

Identify with Your Adversary

Receptivity means developing your awareness of others in addition to your awareness of your inner self. Beginning to identify with your adversaries is taking the next step beyond awareness and into compassionate acceptance. This is the realm of reverence, in which we hold together with tenderness the vulnerable fallible humanity that we all share.

When someone is acting in a hostile manner toward you, try to ask yourself what emotion she seems to be feeling. "Hatred" might be the first and easiest answer that comes up. But push yourself harder. What might she be feeling under and behind the hatred? What other emotions might the hatred be composed of? Consider whether fear, shame, powerlessness, or vulnerability might somehow be all mixed up with her hatred. Besides the emotional content, ask yourself what the mechanism might have been that caused her to act out her hostility toward you. Is there a system or experience of injustice, racism, or classism? Developing awareness of the social systems and expectations that push individuals and groups apart can help us choose to act in different ways. Getting perspective on injustice can also help us remember that some of our experiences of hostility are stemming from external situations that need to be addressed.

Whatever feelings you think might be at play in your adversary, remember times that you have felt those same emotions. Are you feeling them at the moment of the exchange with your adversary? Look for the part of you that is capable of feeling the same feelings as your adversary. This can help you identify with him, remembering your shared humanity.

Sometimes you can even gain insight into what your adversary might be feeling underneath his hostility by noting what you feel on the receiving end of his enmity. For example, if an interaction with someone leaves you feeling powerless and small, consider that he may be trying to create an illusion of power and hostility so *he* won't feel powerless and small—if you feel it, he doesn't have to. It might seem a little crazy, but this is actually a phenomenon that psychologists describe. You can test it by looking for moments in your own life when you have made yourself feel less vulnerable by acting angry at others and making *them* feel vulnerable. Identifying with the humanity of adversaries is taking another step of hospitality, moving toward a posture of welcome and seeking to realize the inherent value or image of God within them.

The Gospel of Matthew on Forgiveness

Translated by Ron Miller

When people ask you for something, give it to them; when they want to borrow something, lend it to them. You've heard it said: "Love your neighbor and hate your enemy." But what I am telling you is to love your enemies and pray for your persecutors. This is how you will become children of your heavenly Parent, who lets his sun come up for bad and good people alike, just as he sends rain both to those who are God-centered and those who are not. What's to your credit in loving just your friends? Don't even the tax-collectors do that? And if you say hello only to your own people, have you done anything extraordinary? Don't even the Gentiles do as much? You should grow to your fullness, becoming whole and holy, like your heavenly Parent.

—Matthew 5:43–48

Ron Miller was chair of the religion department at Lake Forest College in Lake Forest, Illinois, where he has taught for thirty years, and cofounder of Common Ground, an adult education group for interfaith religious study and dialogue since 1975. He is author of many books and articles, including *The Hidden Gospel of Matthew: Annotated & Explained* (SkyLight Paths).

Encountering the Heart of the Enemy

Rami Shapiro

Opening your heart to encounter others means being present in a way that makes you vulnerable to hurt, grief, and suffering. Indeed, it is in your capacity to hurt, grieve, and suffer that you discover your capacity to love. If you can't be hurt, you can't love because you are too defended to let another in. If you can't grieve, you can't love because you have restricted your feelings for another to such a low level that allows for no deep sense of loss if the other leaves or dies. If you can't suffer, you can't have compassion with others who do suffer. Compassion comes from the Latin *com* (shared) *passion* (suffering). Compassion is the capacity to suffer together, and this requires an open heart rather than a constricted one.

Yet here is where most of us fall down. We have compassion for our friends and family, for our neighbors, for those caught up in calamity—hurricanes, tornadoes, earthquakes, famine, disease—but sometimes, too often, our compassion serves our convenience. And sometimes we cannot muster compassion at all. This is why I am more moved by Jesus's admonishment to "love your enemy" (Matthew 5:44) than I am by his (and Leviticus's) command to "love your neighbor" (Leviticus 19:18; Mark 12:31).

Loving my neighbor is relatively easy. I mean, yes, her dogs scamper about the yard at odd hours, and when her nephew and niece are around the scampering becomes bounding and barking, screaming and crashing, and that is ... well, annoying. But in the end, it's minor, and it doesn't really get in the way of our having a perfectly pleasant, neighborly relationship.

Rami Shapiro, a renowned teacher of spirituality across faith traditions and a noted theologian, is a popular speaker on the topics of religion, theology, and spirituality. He is author of the award-winning *The Sacred Art of Lovingkindness: Preparing to Practice* and *Recovery—The Sacred Art: The Twelve Steps as Spiritual Practice* (both SkyLight Paths), among other books.

Loving my enemies, on the other hand, is a hell of a thing. I *fear* my enemies. And with good reason: they're out to get me. That's why we're enemies. To imagine loving them makes me nervous to say the least. What does it mean, anyway? Am I supposed to make peace with them? What if they don't want peace? Or what if the terms of peace are unacceptable? How am I supposed to forgive all the awful things they did to me, and how are they supposed to forgive all the awful things I did to them? The answer is: I'm not. They're not. Jesus doesn't say forgive your enemies. He doesn't say make peace with them. He doesn't even say not to *have* enemies. He tells us, instead, to love them.

So the real question isn't "what does it mean to love my enemy?" but "what does it mean to love at all?" What does it mean to love somebody? When the truth is found to be lies, and everything within you dies, is love the answer? Is love the antidote to despair? Yes and no. No, love isn't the antidote to despair, but, yes, love may be what emerges when you discover that all you thought was true was a lie.

I was once driving too fast through a school zone. I hadn't seen the sign, and was paying no attention to the fact that elementary school kids were being picked up. I sped along the street according to the non-school-zone speed limit. A guy driving behind me in a white Ford F-150 pickup truck honked and waved at me to slow down. I noticed him, realized what I was doing, and quickly cut my speed for the few yards of school zone left to me. I rolled down my window and waved at the man in gratitude and shouted, "Thank you!" I really had been oblivious.

I swear I waved with all five fingers, but he saw only one.

And my "thank you" must have been drowned out in the noise of the school kids, and all he heard was the "k" and the "you." As soon as he was clear of the school zone he revved his engine and the big Ford was after me. I panicked, and picked up speed.

He did the same.

At the time I owned a Porsche 944S. It is important to make note of the *S* (sport) because it made this Porsche more than an entry-level Porsche. If you are going to drive a Porsche, and a red one at that, you don't want people to think you could only afford an entry-level model. Truth is, I didn't buy the car new; in fact, I didn't buy it at all. I ghostwrote a book for a friend who was selling the car, and took it in exchange. The point of all this is to say that a Porsche 944S can outrun a Ford F-150 on any open road. The problem was that we weren't on an open road, and this guy was on my tail no matter what I did.

Finally, I decided to confront him. I slipped into the lefthand lane of a two-lane street, rolled down the passenger-side window as I pulled up to a red light, and waited for the Ford pickup to pull alongside. I kept my hands on the steering wheel where he could see them so he knew I was unarmed, and hoped to God he wasn't packing heat and itching for a gunfight.

The driver of the Ford leaned out of his window menacingly.

The blood was rushing through his face and he was boiling mad.

I smiled, lifted my hand in a wave again and said, "I said, 'Thank you.'" This time he heard me. His face was still red, not with anger this time but with embarrassment. His body softened and he quickly told me that his daughter had been hit by a car racing through that very school speed zone a few months ago. She was okay, but he was a passionate defender of school zone safety.

I think I saw tears in his eyes as he told me about his little girl, and I felt a shock of horror at the thought that I could have hit someone as well. When the light changed, he sat back, waved, and drove off. I let him get ahead of me. I was driving a Porsche 944S—don't forget the *S*—and had nothing to prove.

What does this have to do with loving your enemies? I don't want to make too much of it, but, as he was telling me about his daughter, I was listening with every fiber of my being, and we made a connection. There was love there. Not romantic love; not the love that keeps Viagra in business, but another kind of love: the love that happens when people—even frightened, angry people—let go of their fears and share their truths.

The fellow in the Ford had his truth: I was a narcissistic maniac who put kids in danger and gave the finger and a hearty *f you* to anyone who tried to stop me. When he found this truth to be a lie (sure I'm narcissistic, but the rest of it isn't true) the result was a genuine meeting. He found somebody to love. Me. For a moment.

When Jesus says, to "love your enemies," I think he is challenging us to meet them, to get to know them for who they are rather than who we imagine them to be. Genuine meeting leads to love. This is why Psalm 23 tells us that God prepares a banquet for you in the presence of your enemies (Psalm 23:5).

God isn't doing this to taunt your enemies. You aren't expected to sit down to eat in front of them in a hubristic act of "nah, nah, nah-nah nah." The table is set in front of your enemies so that you can invite them to sit with you and eat, and when they do, and when you start to share your truths, perhaps you will no longer be enemies.

Practice: Dining with the Devil

Make a list of your enemies. If you can't come up with any real enemies, make a list of people whom you strongly dislike. Now invite them to dinner. Not literally, but literarily.

Write about having dinner with these people. Prepare and serve a meal that pleases both you and them. Write about how you would welcome them; how you would explain the invitation and the purpose of the meal. Make it clear that you invited them to hear their truths and share your own.

And write about their truths. Yes, this is an act of fictional writing. You may not know their truths, but do your best to extrapolate their truths from the behaviors you actually see them exhibit in real life. Notice what happens to your body and your heart as you write about their truths. Can you sense your body softening and your heart opening? Do this exercise over and over until you do.

Practice: Dear Hated One

The hardest person to love is someone you define as an enemy. To love the enemy, of course, you have to meet him. This is not always a good idea. Enemies tend to meet over pistols at dawn, and it's very tricky to remain radically open when your safety demands you run for cover or strap on a bulletproof vest. So, rather than trying to track down your enemy for a face-to-face, I suggest meeting him or her in another way: in a love letter.

Two things before you get started on this exercise.

First, let's be very clear: do not mail these letters.... This is an exercise for opening the heart, not baring it to someone else. So, again, do not mail these letters. In fact, if you are writing them on your computer, delete them when you are done. If you are using actual paper, burn them. Or shred them. And if you shred them, then burn them. Just DO NOT MAIL THEM.

I say this because I know people who have mailed them. These people were shredded. And burned. So, please, no mailing.

Second, the goal of this exercise is to awaken your heart to a very specific idea: people, even the people you hate, are doing the best they can with what they've got. This may be a difficult idea for you to swallow. Most of us like to think that people have absolute free will, that they can act however they choose, and that when they act like jerks it is because they choose to act like jerks. I would like to suggest an alternative view.

Free will is a very limited factor in your life. While i
ety of options at any given moment regarding action
your past has conditioned you so powerfully that mos
unchoosable. You do what you do because you have
as simply as I can: most of the time you act on autopi

What is true of you is true of everyone. While there
can be major, most people who hurt you never set out to hurt you. They are just doing what they imagine they have to do in order to get what they imagine they have to get, and you are merely collateral damage.

Think of the last time a close friend did something that hurt you. Perhaps she kept a secret from you, or perhaps you said something and she exploded with such venom that for a moment you had no idea with whom you were talking; your friend was gone, replaced by an alien who had invaded her body. Did she set out to harm you by keeping that secret? Or was she simply protecting herself? Was she looking for an opening to unleash her wrath, or was she as surprised as you at the level of her anger? Only you can say, but only she can know. The aim of this exercise is to imagine what she knows. This is how it works:

> Sit down at your computer, or with paper and pen, and write your friend a letter. Explain the situation as you felt it. Explain how hurt you were, and maybe still are. This event doesn't have to be a recent one. We aren't trying to rekindle old emotions, but to recognize a timeless truth: most often people do what they do because at the moment they do it, doing it is all they can do.
>
> After you have set out your side of the story, shift your imagination to her side. As best you can, write about the situation from her perspective. Don't pretend to be her and write an excuse for her behavior. Write an analysis suggesting why her behavior was, given the situation at that moment, inevitable. This may be difficult—it is meant to be; we are too ready to ascribe premeditation to situations where there is none in order to blame the other for our hurt feelings, and this exercise is going to reveal a different perspective.
>
> Once you have completed your analysis of the other's behavior, take a second look at your own. Why did you feel hurt or angry or betrayed? Could you have felt any other way at that moment, or were you as conditioned as your friend? I think you will find that the latter is true....

[illegible] exercise do for you? It helps you realize that we are all trapped [illegible] conditioned by our past, and victims of habit. This realization need [illegible]se an action, nor is it necessarily the basis for forgiveness. We are doing [illegible]o soften the heart. We are doing this to realize that our hardened hearts are [illegible]ardened automatically by forces beyond our conscious control. We are doing this because as we do it we discover compassion arising: compassion for the other and compassion for ourselves. We realize that we are all doing the best we can with what we've got to work with at the moment, and often what we've got isn't all that wonderful or helpful. But it is what we've got, and who we are, and who the other person is, and we are all trapped and suffering in those traps, and really we need to cry together over our stuckness rather than rage at each other under the banner of an imagined freedom.

A Prayer of Forgiveness for Enemies

Nancy Corcoran, CSJ

All of my life, I have struggled with letting go of resentment. But I was given a mother who does not know the meaning of the word *resentment.*

I remember as a kid going to bed *furious* with her, swearing that I would never speak with her again. The next morning, however, I would go down to breakfast, and there she would be—greeting me cheerfully, as if we had never had a fight. I would forget my pledge of the night before, figuring that I could always go through with it the next time. (And there always was a next time!) But I never could keep that pledge because it just wasn't in my mother's nature to hold a grudge. So when I came across this prayer that was found scribbled on a piece of wrapping paper near the body of a dead child at the Ravensbruck concentration camp in Germany, I marveled at the depth of insight and compassion that has always escaped me. Praying these words opens my heart and stretches my mind to the power of forgiveness.

[O God], remember not only
the men and women of goodwill,
but also those of ill will.
But do not remember all the suffering
they have inflicted on us;
remember the fruits we have bought,
thanks to this suffering—
our comradeship, our loyalty,

Nancy Corcoran, CSJ, leads multifaith workshops and seminars on prayer, meditation, and ritual and is the Catholic chaplain and director of Newman Ministry at Wellesley College and founder of *grass/roots:* Women's Spirituality Center. She is also the author of *Secrets of Prayer: A Multifaith Guide to Creating Personal Prayer in Your Life* (SkyLight Paths).

our humility, our courage,
our generosity, the greatness of heart
which has grown out of all this,
and when they come to judgment
let all the fruits which we have borne
be their forgiveness. Amen.

—*The Oxford Book of Prayer*

A Moveable Feast

Katharine Jefferts Schori

> People will come from east and west and north and south, and will take their places at the feast in the kingdom of God.
>
> —Luke 13:29 (NIV)

I come from a notorious place—the city of Las Vegas. Gambling and prostitution are legal in Nevada, and ministry there means that many congregations host twelve-step programs not just for alcoholics and drug addicts but also for those addicted to gambling. There are a few groups for sex addicts, too. A story quietly circulated when I was bishop there about a priest who encouraged the local madams and their employees to visit the churches he served. One congregation made a warm enough welcome that the women of the night returned frequently. Other congregations acted more like Jesus's fellow dinner guests did when a woman of ill repute showed up, as told in Luke 7:36–50: "Who let *her* in here?" The women didn't return to those dinner tables.

In some circles The Episcopal Church has the reputation for being a place where you have to dress correctly and know how to act—you really *should* know all the responses in the worship services by heart, and be able to find your way around the several books we use in worship—or you shouldn't even bother walking in the front door. I'll admit that there are a few places like that, where the local pew-sitters are more afraid than their potential guests, but there are lots more communities where all comers are not just invited, but welcomed with open arms.

Katharine Jefferts Schori is the presiding bishop of The Episcopal Church, and the Anglican Communion's first female primate. She is author of *The Heartbeat of God: Finding the Sacred in the Middle of Everything* and *Gathering at God's Table: The Meaning of Mission in the Feast of Faith* (both SkyLight Paths), among other books.

It's hard work to get to the point where you're able and willing to see the Lord of love in the odorous street person next to you in the pew. It can be just as hard to find him in the unwelcoming host.

What makes us so afraid of the *other?* There's something in our ancient genetic memory that ratchets up our state of arousal when we meet a stranger—it's a survival mechanism that has kept our species alive for millennia by being wary of the unknown. But there's also a piece of our makeup that we talk about in more theological terms—the part that leaps to judgment about *that* person's sins. It's connected to knowing our own sinfulness and our tendency toward competition: *Well, she must be a worse sinner than I am—thank God!*

That woman who wanders into Simon's house when Jesus is dining there comes with her hair scandalously uncovered (Luke 7:36–50). The dinner guests assume that she's a woman of the street, and in their view, she confirms it by acting in profoundly embarrassing ways, crying all over Jesus's feet and drying them with her hair and covering him with perfume. Jesus's host—and the rest of the dinner guests—were horrified that this was taking place in a "proper" house—they were more than a little worried about the gossip it would cause and appalled at the sort of person Jesus must be to let this woman do such things to him.

The scorn that some are willing to heap on those who are judged to have loved excessively or inappropriately is still pretty common. Yet it is this woman's loving response to Jesus that brings her pardon, and leads to Jesus's celebration of her right relationship with God. She doesn't even have to ask. Jesus seems to say that evidence of her pardon has already been given—full measure, pressed down, and overflowing—just like her tears and hair and cask of perfume.

It's the same message Jesus offers over and over: "Perfect love casts out fear" (1 John 4:18). It's actually our fear of the wretchedness within our own souls that pushes us away from our sisters and brothers.

Fear is the only thing that keeps us from knowing God's love—and we most often discover it in the people around us. Jesus wasn't afraid to eat with sinners—Simon and the other dinner guests were sinners, too—and he wasn't afraid of what the woman of the city would do to his reputation.

The forgiven woman of the city is sister to the prodigal son who begs his father's forgiveness. They are both our siblings, and their experience is ours, too. Like them, we can rejoin the family if we're willing to let go of the fearful veneer of righteousness that covers our yearning to be fully known, because we don't quite think we're lovable.

That veneer is the only thing between us and a wholehearted "welcome home." It's risky to let that veneer be peeled away, but all we risk is love. The veneered self simply can't be vulnerable enough to receive the love that's being offered. Can we see the human heart yearning for love in *that* person over there? Can we recall our own yearning, and find the connection? That's what compassion is—opening ourselves to love.

Practicing compassion rather than judgment is one way the layers start to fly off. Think about all those dinner guests. The party's going to be far more interesting if we can find something to love about the curmudgeonly host and his buddies. Rejecting them is going to shut down any real possibility of compassion. It's risky, yes, but the only thing we risk is our own hearts, and the possibility they'll overflow as readily as that woman's tears. It's a big risk to let the layers go, but the only thing we risk is discovering a brother or sister under the skin.

Jesus invites us all to his moveable feast. He leaves that dinner party with Simon and goes off to visit other places in need of prodigal love and prodigious forgiveness. Those who know the deep acceptance and love that come with healing and forgiveness can lose the defensive veneer that wants to shut out other sinners. They discover that covering their hair or hiding their tears or hoarding their rich perfume isn't the way that the beloved act, even if it makes others nervous. Eventually, it may even cure the anxious of their own fear by drawing them toward a seat at that heavenly banquet. There's room for us all at this table; there are tears of welcome and a kiss for the wanderer, and the sweet smell of home.

Want to join the feast? We are all welcome. Love has saved us, so enter in peace.

Praying with the Angels

Imam Jamal Rahman

Praise be to Allah … Who made the angels messengers with wings.

—Qur'an 35:1

Ours is a universe of astonishing mystery. According to the Qur'an, our planet is visited and populated by all kinds of invisible energies—angels, *jinn,* and the "slinking whisperer"—who have been with us since the beginning of Creation. If we think of ourselves as too sophisticated to believe in such superstitions, Rumi advises us, "Sell your cleverness and buy bewilderment!" God creates "as He pleases," says the Qur'an in a verse celebrating both visible and invisible creation: "Praise be to Allah, Who created out of nothing the Heavens and the Earth, Who made the angels messengers with wings" (35:1). It is righteousness and an article of Islamic faith to believe in these genderless, luminous, and invisible beings who act as intermediaries between God and humanity.

The Qur'an mentions hosts of unnamed angels who "celebrate His praises night and day" (21:20), who "sustain the Throne of God" (40:7), and who "celebrate the Praises of their Lord, and pray for forgiveness for [all] beings on Earth" (42:5). Two important angels are Ridwan (meaning "good pleasure"), the guardian of Paradise, and Malik ("master"), the overseer of Hell....

There is a mystifying account of two angels named Harut and Marut who were somehow caught up in esoteric knowledge in Babylon, the ancient center of astronomy and other sciences (2:102). Theologians disagree on what actually

---

Imam Jamal Rahman, beloved teacher and retreat leader, is author of *Spiritual Gems of Islam: Insights & Practices from the Qur'an, Hadith, Rumi & Muslim Teaching Stories to Enlighten the Heart & Mind* and *Sacred Laughter of the Sufis: Awakening the Soul with the Mulla's Comic Teaching Stories & Other Islamic Wisdom* (both SkyLight Paths), among other books.

happened, but one legend has it that angels in Heaven complained to God about the inequities that humans committed on earth and God replied that if angels possessed free will as humans did, they also would succumb to earthly temptations. The angels chose two of their best members, Harut and Marut, and God sent them down to earth endowed with free will. Eventually, Harut and Marut became corrupted and committed grave sins.

Chastened by the experience of Harut and Marut, angels have been asking God to forgive humanity ever since because they realize that free will is an awesome and burdensome responsibility.

(An alternative interpretation offered by the respected commentator Yusuf Ali is that Harut and Marut were not angels at all, but angelically good humans who lived in Babylon and unknowingly imparted esoteric knowledge to ill-intentioned men who used it fraudulently for evil purposes. The lesson in this interpretation is that we have a moral responsibility to pursue and use knowledge wisely and responsibly.)

The Qur'an contains numerous revelations about the countless angels who bless us, watch over us, and nudge us toward wise and responsible choices. Each of us has a "protector" (86:4) and angels "before and behind" to guard and to guide in the lifelong work to "change what is within [our]selves" (13:11) and to record our deeds, good or bad (50:17–18, 82:10–12). The Prophet added, "They mind your works: when a work is good, they praise God, and when one is evil, they ask God to forgive you."[1]...

When we praise and thank God with all our hearts we join a resounding chorus of invisible beings aligned in a powerful vibration and connection with our incomparable Creator. Similarly, we can join with the angels who pray for our forgiveness by praying sincerely for God to forgive those who have wounded or disappointed us.

The Qur'anic verse at the beginning of this chapter, "Praise be to Allah ... Who made the angels messengers with wings," goes on to say that those wings number two, three, or even four pairs (35:1). In Islamic spirituality wings are a symbol of soul tenderness. If we humans join our prayers to forgive those who have wronged us with the angelic prayers for humankind, we too shall develop metaphorical wings that will lift us above our burdens of anger and pain.

Forgiveness, Justice, and Peace

Each of us has the power to promote peace in the world today. How? We can do this by tapping into our Divine Source as spiritual beings with the spark of divine life and the seed of peace within us.

—Molly Srode

Sometimes putting a face with a prayer opens us to a new level of compassion. You may realize that your enemy belongs to a loving and worried parent. You may find that the oppressor carries an unhealed wound. You may realize that the one you have trouble praying for is still God's child, still loved by God.

—Rev. Larry J. Peacock

Forgiveness can bring healing and freedom to those who have been wounded, but, particularly in the case of deep wounds, horrible wrongs, and oppression, there is still also very much a need for justice. Forgiveness is not about letting evil continue to exist in the world. If you need justice in your own situation, find a community that will support you as you seek it. But lest the oppressed become the oppressor, first seek compassion in your heart for the one who wronged you. Justice must also be tempered by mercy. There must be a way to healing for all involved.

Sometimes it's not clear who or what to forgive, but it is clear that there is a need for forgiveness, as in the case of racial reconciliation or interfaith healing. And clearly humanity has wounded the earth in profound ways. But how to ask (or grant) forgiveness for these things? We must focus on facing the truth and making amends, on living out the forgiveness we seek. This is repentance; this is the goal of asking forgiveness. We have to make choices that allow us to live daily reconciled to the earth, and to those we may have somehow participated in wronging.

This section presents strategies for seeking forgiveness and justice on both large and small scales. Rev. Dr. Joan Brown Campbell asks what is needed for reconciliation in communities that have been ripped apart by violence, while Rev. Donna Schaper examines the need for forgiveness and mercy in how we create and enforce our laws. John Philip Newell reflects on our need to be at peace with the earth. Molly and Bernie Srode ponder how to be peacemakers in the everyday.

Seek justice and cultivate peace in your own heart and relationships. But don't let it stop there: widen the circle and see what the next level of living out forgiveness and reconciliation is. This is the way to peace, freedom, and justice for all.

Seeking Justice on the Path to Forgiveness

Marie M. Fortune

The single most common pastoral concern that I hear expressed by victims and survivors of sexual or domestic violence is their anxiety about forgiveness, which often focuses on a sense of obligation regardless of circumstances. Reframing our understanding of forgiveness is a fundamental task of feminist and womanist theology, biblical studies, ethics, and pastoral care.

In contemporary Christian teaching and practice, the burden to forgive seems always to be placed solely on the shoulders of those who have suffered physically and emotionally. This is the most common response that victims or survivors hear from family, friends, and the church. The first thing anyone who is trying to be helpful wants to discuss is forgiveness, meaning that the one victimized should simply forgive and then be rewarded magically with healing.

In Judaism, the burden rests with the one who causes harm. Medieval Jewish philosopher Maimonides explained that the Day of Atonement, Yom Kippur, provides corporate atonement for sins against God. But sins against one's neighbor (c intimate partner) are not pardoned unless the offender compensates the victim a apologizes. This means confession, taking responsibility, repentance, and restitu to the one harmed.[1] Repentance is real when there is an opportunity to repe offense and the offender refrains from it because of his or her repentance because of fear.[2] In fact, the teachings of Jesus in the Gospels are congruent

---

Marie M. Fortune is a pastor, an educator, an author, and a practicing theologi She contributed to *New Feminist Christianity: Many Voices, Many Views* (S and is a founder and senior analyst at the FaithTrust Institute, where she ad domestic violence in faith communities.

teachings of Judaism on this issue. In Luke 17:3–4, Jesus says, "If another disciple sins, you must rebuke the offender, and *if* there is repentance, you must forgive." And then the seven times come in: if that one "sins seven times *and* repents seven times, you must forgive." Fundamentally, both Judaism and Christianity link the expectation of forgiveness on the part of the one harmed to genuine confession and repentance on the part of the offender. This is the context of justice that we shall examine as necessary for real forgiveness and healing to occur.

The problem for Christians is that somehow the notion and practice of forgiveness have been romanticized and placed in a vacuum due in large part to the canonization of "forgive and forget" theology. Although "forgive and forget" is not biblical, it has struck a resonant chord in the public psyche.[3] I believe that is precisely because it is simplistic and allows us to ignore the power dynamics of the situation in which harm has been done by one to another.

If the expectation of agency in response to harm done by one to another is passed to the one harmed and away from the one causing harm, then three things happen:

- No one (including bystanders) ever has to make the offender accountable. This is particularly advantageous for the nonrepentant offender.
- Victims, whose priority is their own healing, can decide that they have the power to bring about this healing by their agency in the "act" of forgiving. This is a cruel hoax for victims.
- The bystanders (often ministers and many members of our churches) can stand by and do nothing, self-righteously reassured that we have no lines in this play.

As a result, the victim is shamed or cajoled into saying the magic words, "I forgive him," convinced by us that now she will feel better. Now God will love her, and now she can remain in good standing within her church. And the bystanders don't have to do anything.

Forgiveness is God's gift for victims and survivors. Any benefit that it brings to offenders is a bonus. Likewise, any benefit it brings to the bystander is a bonus. For-iveness brings the *possibility* of healing to those harmed....

Justice is a necessary precursor to forgiveness. As a pastor, I began to learn at justice looked like when I slowed down long enough to listen to survivors. I rned to ask them the question, "What do you need in order to find some heal- and resolution from the abuse that you suffered?" If, as a helper and an advo- we bother to ask this question, they will usually have a fairly straightforward er.

They say that they need:

- "My abuser to acknowledge what he did to me."
- "A chance to tell the bishop what the priest did to me."
- "An apology from my uncle."
- "To be sure that he won't do this to anyone else."
- "Compensation for my expenses as a result of all this."

If we think categorically about these concrete requests, we begin to see what justice looks like:

- Truth telling: the chance for the victim/survivor to tell her story.
- Acknowledgment: a response from someone who matters to the victim/survivor, who stands beside her as an advocate (for example, "What he did to you was wrong").
- Compassion: to suffer with the victim/survivor—not to pass by.
- Protection of the vulnerable: to do everything we can to ensure that no one else is harmed by this perpetrator.
- Accountability for the offender: to call the offender to account either in the church and/or legally.
- Restitution to the survivor: material compensation to the survivor for the cost of the harm done.
- Vindication for the survivor ("to be set free"; the outcome of justice making is to be set free and restored to one's community).

So, if we understand that some experience of justice (imperfect though it may be) is a prerequisite for forgiveness, then we see that forgiveness does *not* condone or pardon harmful behavior or assume any degree of future relationship with the person who caused the harm. Forgiveness is:

- Letting go so that the immediacy of the painful memories can be put into perspective.
- Possible in a context of justice making and the healing presence of the Holy Spirit.
- God's gift to those who have been harmed, for the purpose of healing.

Women who have been victimized do not need platitudes, sentimentality, and offers of cheap grace. They do not need to be urged "to forgive"; in fact, in many cases they need to be urged not to forgive so quickly. They need guidance and support to help them face head-on the painful realities and memories of violence and abuse in their lives. They need to hear about a God who stands with the exploited and abused; who calls the powerful to account; who offers justice and forgiveness as the tools of healing; who expects bystanders to support victims and call abusers to account.

Wise Justice, Merciful Hearts

Rev. Donna Schaper

What is wisdom? Surely a large part of wisdom is the capacity to have mercy. What wise nation would spend $80,000 per year to incarcerate a juvenile offender instead of $30,000 to give him a college education? What wise nation would keep a person convicted of a drug arrest ineligible for financial aid for a college education? Has anyone noticed the federal financial aid form for colleges lately? It says, "Have you ever been convicted of possession or selling illegal drugs? If you have, answer 'Yes.' Complete and submit this application and we will send you a worksheet in the mail for you to determine if your conviction affects your eligibility for aid. Do not leave question 23 blank."

In 2001, forty-seven thousand of the ten million applicants for federal student aid lost eligibility for some or all of their assistance because of past drug convictions or because they failed to answer a question about drug use on the application. Of those forty-seven thousand, more than 60 percent lost financial aid for the entire year; 20 percent left the question blank and did not get any aid; and a little under 20 percent lost financial aid for part of the year. Why do these figures matter? Because they are merciless. Because they aren't wise. Because they put kids already in trouble into more trouble. Because they are based in punishment rather than in mercy. Questions like number 23 are the opposite of sacred speech: They close doors and create fear. They are not wise.

No, I am not condoning (listen for the punitive language) or recommending light penalties for drug use. But I know a young man named John who would like

---

Rev. Donna Schaper is widely recognized as one of the most outstanding communicators in her generation of Protestant clergy. Senior minister at Judson Memorial Church in New York City, she is author of several books, including *Sacred Speech: A Practical Guide for Keeping Spirit in Your Speech*, and coauthor of *Labyrinths from the Outside In: Walking to Spiritual Insight—A Beginner's Guide* (both SkyLight Paths).

to be a student at a local community college. He did do drugs in high school; he spent one night in jail and was fined a hundred dollars for possession of marijuana when he was sixteen. He doesn't do drugs anymore. He is twenty-three. He worked for two years and now wants to get a degree. He received a letter from the education department saying that he would not be eligible for student aid because of a previous drug conviction. Now he will have to drop out of school and get a job. What do you really think will happen to John because of this punishment for his crime? Will John contribute to society all that he could? Or will John be just another wasted talent, someone who took a stupid risk and has to pay too long for it? If we are lucky, John will find a wise person to help him through his anger, his resentment, his guilt, his trouble. That person will know mercy. If we are not lucky, John will go back to drugs. He may even rob you to get them.

Forgiveness may be the highest pragmatism as well as something very, very holy.

In my experience, people also have difficulties with punishments that do not "fit the crime." Sabotage of a career, for instance, is not appropriate punishment for a stupid practical joke played by a drunken conventioneer who should have known better but didn't.

But how do we know? And when is it as unwise not to punish as it is to punish? Even in our otherwise perfect family (ha!), things have happened to test us. An incident last fall involved my teenage son borrowing the car and driving it when his name was not on the insurance policy. He knew that was the case, and, of course, he had a fender bender that evening while driving six of his friends to hear Ralph Nader speak. He thought his destination would pacify me. It did not.

He not only had a fender bender, but he also ran into a man whose middle name, apparently, was Litigious. For several months we awaited the astronomical repair bill that was surely coming. It never arrived. Should we wisely assume that was sufficient punishment for our darling? I thought not. A larger consequence than just "getting lucky and getting off" should prevail. Thus, this child of mine got the car keys back on June 1 and not sooner.

Don't confuse mercy with wisdom. Sometimes mercy means punishment. Sometimes appropriate punishment can prevent future drug use, car-key stealing, and midnight pranks. Appropriate punishment can be wise. Inappropriate punishment, on the other hand, is rarely wise.

How do we apply these principles to the risks we have to manage? How do we keep ourselves from shooting ourselves in the foot, so to speak, while aiming at a terrorist or an addict? How do we use punishment in a sacred way, a way that eventually winds down the road to forgiveness and reconciliation? How do we keep ourselves from protecting democracy through undemocratic means, making peace by waging war, sending kids to jail to learn how to be better criminals? How do we let wisdom temper punishment so that mercy will prevail? Surely we start with Representative Mark Souder of Indiana, the author of the drug law, who says its application has been much more severe nationwide than he intended. He has since made attempts to correct the law. That is mercy in action, and we can commend him.

We also learn to do what he is doing. We can learn the fine art of saying, "Whoops, I made a mistake." We become merciful toward ourselves. That is the basis for mercy for others. Indeed, forgiveness is not something that we direct only toward others. The art of sacred speech in the matter of forgiveness has to do with being ready to admit mistakes, to say we are wrong, to say "whoops" and mean it. Saying "whoops" is sacred speech.

Control is rarely wisdom. Companionship and participation are often wisdom. Hanging in with somebody is almost always wisdom. It is also merciful....

Psalm 90 is probably my favorite psalm. Basically the psalm says, "Life is short, so get wise soon." Getting wise late doesn't help you—and thus that marvelous transition phrase between the strophes of the psalm: "O satisfy us early with thy mercy so that we may be glad all our days." And, "So teach us to number our days that we may apply our hearts early to wisdom." Early wisdom, early mercy: sacred speech gets to the words of forgiveness as quickly as it can after something bad happens.

Thus, a proper reading of Psalm 90 would tell us to hang in with kids who take stupid risks, such as using drugs. When our very short lives are over, we can hope to stand on the merciful, not punitive, side of the ledger. "Teach us, O God, an early wisdom." Life is short—get wise early....

In public, as well as in intimate life, forgiveness is an important art. Those who have been oppressed by racism or sexism or homophobia are also in great need of the art of forgiveness. Otherwise, they internalize the oppressor's power.

By the way, it may also at times be holy and sacred to litigate. But when oppression is the norm, we need other arrows in our quiver than mere justice. God defends us with anger and with relief from anger.

Sacred speech opens doors, even when the gates of oppression are locked. It does so by letting us take the next step, to "go on" and not get stuck in anger or fear or depression. Sacred speech clears away the confusion and creates futures for people who think they have none. Sacred speech maximizes love, minimizes fear, and creates the links that let people move toward each other and toward God.

The Book of Common Prayer on Forgiveness

Our Father in heaven,
hallowed be your Name,
your kingdom come,
your will be done,
on earth as in heaven.
Give us today our daily bread.
Forgive us our sins
as we forgive those
who sin against us.
Save us from the time of trial,
and deliver us from evil.
For the kingdom, the power,
and the glory are yours,
now and for ever. Amen.

—The Lord's Prayer, contemporary version,
from *The Book of Common Prayer—*
Annotated & Explained

Reconciliation, Retribution, and Justice in Islam

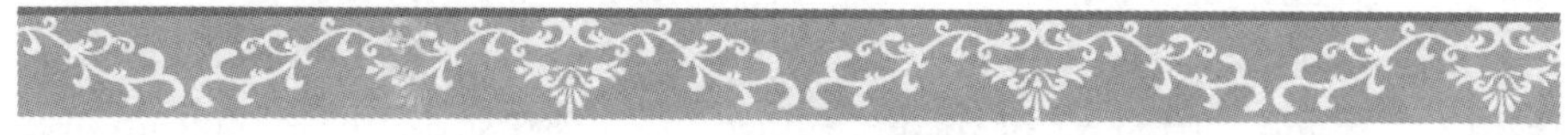

Annotated by Sohaib N. Sultan

> The recompense for an injury is an injury equal thereto [in degree]; but if a person forgives and makes reconciliation, his reward is due from God, for God loves not those who do wrong. But indeed if any do help and defend themselves after a wrong has been committed against them, there is no blame against such a person. The blame is only against those who oppress men and commit wrongdoing and insolently transgress beyond bounds through the land, defying right and justice, for such there will be a penalty grievous. But indeed if any show patience and forgive, that would truly be an exercise of courageous will and resolution in the conduct of affairs.
>
> —Qur'an 42:40–43

The Qur'an recognizes the value of justice and in making right the wrongs of the past in order to reach a position of reconciliation. Therefore, it is permissible for victims of injustice to seek just retribution. However, the higher moral position is with the person who chooses forgiveness and reconciliation over his or her right to justice, because such a course facilitates the path to peace, which is the ultimate goal of all reconciliation projects.

What is unacceptable is for a victim of injustice to seek out more in retribution than what he or she was made to suffer, and to use the victim mentality and position to unleash oppression on others. Here the Qur'an, in its teachings on reconciliation,

---

Sohaib N. Sultan is a freelance journalist, public speaker, and author of *The Qur'an and Sayings of Prophet Muhammad: Selections Annotated & Explained* (SkyLight Paths). In 2005, he was appointed as the first-ever Muslim chaplain at Yale University.

is attempting to break the common historical pattern of the oppressed becoming oppressors, and victims of evil turning into perpetrators of evil.

At the heart of the Qur'anic prescription for reconciliation is the principle of forgiveness even when we are angry, because forgiveness has a powerful healing quality. Forgiveness liberates the soul from the burden of anger, and it is an absolute requirement in mending relationships.

Therefore, the next step in reconciliation, after opening the door to its possibility, is actually going out and seeking forgiveness from each other, and overcoming the feelings of anger. The most beautiful way for reconciliation to occur is by warding off and getting rid of the ill feelings and mistrust that have built up over time. This can be done by doing something good and kind for the person, group, or nation with whom you are attempting reconciliation.

The exchanging of gifts, charitable acts, and kindness helps replace bad memories and ill feelings with good thoughts and warm feelings. In this way, the path to reconciliation is paved, and the possibility for converting hatred into intimate friendship becomes real.

> For good and evil are not equal: Promote what is better, and then one between you and whom there was enmity will become like intimate friends. But no one will be granted such goodness except those who exercise patience and self-restraint, none but persons of the greatest good fortune. So if an incitement to discord is made to you by the Evil One, seek refuge in God, for God hears and knows all things.
>
> —Qur'an 41:34–36

Prodigals and the Path to Peace

Rev. Dr. Joan Brown Campbell

> The son said to him, "Father, I have sinned against heaven and before you; I am no longer worthy to be called your son."
>
> —Luke 15:21

Once upon a time there was a prodigal son. Everybody knows the parable about forgiveness and reconciliation that Jesus told. It's in the Bible, and it's played out every day in somebody's family, in somebody's community, all around the world. It's a family drama, a very human story that pulls at our hearts and at our experience just as much now as it did twenty centuries ago.

It goes like this: There was a family with two sons. The elder was a model child who stayed home to work the family farm; the younger one asked for his inheritance and headed out for a more glamorous life. But when his money and friends ran out, the prodigal came back home, humbled and remorseful, and asked his father for a job in his fields. Instead of punishing him, his father greeted him with joy, killed the fatted calf, and threw a welcome-home party.

It has always been easy to put myself into this parable. I was a dutiful first child with a sister who tested my parents at every turn. I did what I was told. I was a good girl; I did my homework and got good grades and helped with the household chores. I didn't give my parents anxiety attacks—and deep down, I guess, I expected some appreciation for all my efforts. My sister, on the other hand (whose missionary work, I've often said, was penance for her early days of misbehavior),

---

Rev. Dr. Joan Brown Campbell is a highly sought-after lecturer and author of *Living into Hope: A Call to Spiritual Action for Such a Time as This* (SkyLight Paths). She currently serves as chair of the Global Peace Initiative of Women and is one of the founding members of the Council of Sages for Karen Armstrong's Charter for Compassion initiative.

kept my parents constantly on edge. If the curfew was midnight (and it was in those days), I would be home five minutes early, while Betty would roll in about half past twelve. Betty got her share of lectures, but my mother was always so relieved to see her, she would greet her with a hug and a prayer of gratitude for her safety. I was glad she got home in one piece, but I confess that, like the elder child in the parable, I was a bit resentful. I identified totally with the pious older brother in the story. I had been a good child, and there did not seem to be much reward in being good when all the attention went to my sister. It just didn't seem quite right....

In this parable, we usually focus on the father's forgiveness, which is instantly and wholeheartedly offered to his younger son. But the parable is also about confession and the process of reconciliation. Even as we long for a confession from the wayward one, we need to confess our own unworthiness too. It's the saintly—maybe even self-righteous—older brother who has difficulty being reconciled.

The wayward younger brother confesses his sins with sincere remorse, and the father forgives him before the words are even uttered. The older brother, though, feels he has nothing to confess.

With the party plans in full swing, the older boy, in a fit of pique, confronts the father, demanding, "What is all this music and dancing and carrying on? This boy, this son of yours, who gave us so much difficulty—you've *embraced* him?" The older brother's reaction is totally human. I know now, even as I knew as a child, that it was right for my parents to embrace my wayward sister. And looking back, I realize she really wasn't all that wayward—and she was, after all, a member of the family. She was loved and treasured even when she exasperated my parents. In the parable, the father replies to the jealous older brother, "Son, you are always with me, and all that is mine is yours. But we had to celebrate and rejoice, because this brother of yours was dead and has come to life" (Luke 15:31–32).

The father acted out of his understanding of forgiveness and of family. He prepared a feast, brought out the party clothes, and put a ring on this younger son's finger. When the boy protested, "I am no longer worthy to be called your son," the father warmly welcomed him home anyway. The text does not say for sure, but it hints that the wayward son was reconciled to God, to his father, and finally to his older brother.

Yet in many ways the older brother was the one most in need of reconciliation to his God. The younger brother's salvation was in his confession—his mistakes were so clear to him that it was a simple matter to admit his unworthiness. He claimed for himself no sense of privilege; his only claim was his need for forgiveness. He became, as Paul writes in his second letter to the Corinthians, "a new creation" (2 Corinthians 5:17). But the older brother had to come to grips with the reality that he, too, needed forgiveness. His goodness, which had become his pride, his birthright, his sense of privilege, had to give way for him to be able to lay claim to the generous gift of love. This, really, is what the story is all about.

Pope John Paul II, in "Reconciliation and Penance," spoke about this parable in a very helpful way:

> If the parable is read from the point of view of the other son, it portrays the situation of the human family, divided by forms of selfishness. It throws light on the difficulty involved in satisfying the desire and longing for one reconciled and united family. It therefore reminds us of the need for a profound transformation of hearts through the rediscovery of the Father's mercy and through victory over misunderstanding and over hostility among brothers and sisters.[1]

It may not be easy for those of us who are the "good" and dutiful members of the family to believe we are all loved equally by God, but that is our only hope for reconciliation and for peace. This was the consistent message that Desmond Tutu, the Anglican archbishop of Cape Town, South Africa, spoke as he worked against apartheid.

Archbishop Tutu is a tiny man, except when he preaches—then he is very tall indeed. I remember his speaking to the General Board of the National Council of Churches while I was the general secretary. Desmond was looking out at an audience of three or four thousand people who were at the gathering, saying, "God loves you." And the people there must have thought, "We've paid to have him come all the way here from South Africa to say that? We know that!" And then he stopped, looked at his listeners, and declared, "God loves everyone." That's the tough part. How ironic—the wayward younger brother who wasted his father's money is also God's child.

John Hope Franklin, a wise man who chaired President Clinton's panel on racism, once attended a dinner party at Jesse Jackson's home. I also attended this party. One of the guests asked Dr. Franklin the provocative question whether he thought the nation should apologize for slavery.

Dr. Franklin was a courteous, well-bred man. I recall that he was very quiet for a while and then he answered, "I do not intend to put my time into that. I won't do that because it is not slavery that perpetuates racism in this nation. It is white people's sense of privilege, of entitlement, of an exaggerated sense of self-worth that is the problem. For the nation's wounds to be healed, for equality to be realized, white people must recognize their sense of privilege that grants them special status and denies equality to others." In the same way, the self-righteous older brother in the parable teaches all who arrogantly claim their birthright that they too need forgiveness.

The Truth and Reconciliation Commission established in South Africa following the fall of apartheid, the system of racial segregation that was in place in that country between 1948 and 1994, is a good example of this need for forgiveness. South Africa's black community had every right to be angry, perhaps even to hate, for their lives had been made a living hell. Their children had been denied their God-given potential. They had been damaged by the cruel system of apartheid, created by the government and sanctioned by the church.

But Nelson Mandela and Desmond Tutu saw a more excellent way.... Both Tutu and Mandela believed that punishing the criminal would not alone create a climate of reconciliation; rather, it was important that crimes be admitted and the truth be told.

Reconciliation will not happen unless we speak the truth of our fears, our hopes, and our transgressions to one another. This is the root of the South African Truth and Reconciliation Commission: Truth must be spoken before forgiveness can be made real. Forgiveness must be offered before reconciliation is possible.

The power of confession cannot be overstated. Our equality before God may not be easy. It may not be easy for those of us who are older brothers or older sisters, but it is in fact our only hope for peace. Reconciliation may be a gift from God, but our calling is to respond to the generosity of this gift by loving one another, especially those who are difficult to love. The unattractive qualities we see in both the older brother and the younger brother are everywhere, but so is the capacity to forgive and to rise above our foolish ways.

The search for reconciliation takes us out of ourselves and focuses us on the gifts and graces of the other. That, of course, is what the father asked of the older brother when he said, "He [your brother] was lost and has been found" (Luke 15:32). The father was really saying, "Step out of yourself. Take a look at your brother. See what it is that he has to offer his family." The idea that God loves us all hardly seems fair. But if we fail to believe this deep down, if we continue to hold grudges against one another, or consider ourselves superior, the possibility for a peaceful society diminishes.... In forgiveness lies the only way to peace.

Reconnecting with the Earth

John Philip Newell

The first modern Christian prophet of the sacredness of the universe was Pierre Teilhard de Chardin (1881–1955), a French Jesuit priest and scientist. I use the term *modern* prophet because there have been earlier prophets in the Christian tradition who have clearly articulated the sacredness of all being—Hildegard of Bingen in the twelfth century, for instance, or John Scotus Eriugena in the ninth century, to name but a few. But Teilhard was the first in the modern period to remember what these earlier teachers had known, that "at the heart of matter is the heart of God."[1] The deeper we move into the mystery of any created thing, the closer we come to the Divine Presence. He also believed that what the Christian doctrine of the Incarnation teaches us to see is that "We can be saved only by becoming one with the universe."[2] The story of the incarnate Christ points to the oneness of heaven and earth, the Divine and the human, spirit and matter. It points not to an exclusive truth, but to the most inclusive of truths. It does not limit the sacredness to one man at one moment in time. It reveals the essential sacredness of every person and everything that has been created....

I still meet Roman Catholic priests today who were training in the late 1950s. They have memories of reading Teilhard's forbidden material at night under the covers by flashlight in their seminary dorms, and of strapping his books under their mattresses by day. This is exactly what theology should be—so exciting, so relevant to the human journey and the unfolding story of the universe, that we will

---

John Philip Newell, internationally acclaimed teacher, retreat leader, and speaker, is author of *The Rebirthing of God: Christianity's Struggle for New Beginnings* (SkyLight Paths), among other books. Formerly warden of Iona Abbey in the Western Isles of Scotland, he is now companion theologian for the American Spirituality Center of Casa del Sol at Ghost Ranch in New Mexico and the cofounder of Heartbeat: A Journey Towards Earth's Wellbeing.

read it no matter who tells us not to! One of the themes to emerge in the posthumous writings of Teilhard was his belief that Christianity was "reaching the end of one of the natural cycles of its existence."[3] It needed to be "born again."[4] The most prominent feature of a reborn Christianity, he said, was that Christ would be viewed not as a "deserter" of the earth but as a lover of the earth.[5] The "primacy of humility" would be seen as the foremost mark of our Christhood and Christianity's primary blessing to the world—living in relationship to the sacred *humus* of the earth.[6] Oneness with the Divine, Christianity's greatest goal, would be experienced not as a looking away from the earth but as "communion with God through earth."[7] "We must "let the very heart of the earth ... beat within us," he wrote.[8]

Perhaps it is John the Beloved who best articulates Christianity's gift for the world when he writes that "you cannot hate your brother or sister and love God" (1 John 4:20; adapted). You cannot do it because they are one. Teilhard's version of this would have been to say that we cannot hate the earth, we cannot neglect or abuse the earth, and claim to love God. We cannot do it because they are one. Not only do we need a new way of seeing, but we also need to forge a new way of living. We must usher in a radical rebirth of our relationship with the earth and its creatures if we are to thrive.

If Teilhard can be described as the first modern Christian prophet of earth's sacredness, then Thomas Berry (1914–2009), a student of Teilhard's writings, can be described as the first Christian prophet of the protection of the earth. Teilhard *saw* the sacredness. Berry called on us to *protect* it. A theologian and cultural historian by training, Berry preferred to call himself a "geologian."[9] Earth was God's great work, he said, and to serve in that great work is humanity's highest calling.[10] As a prophet, Berry did not shy away from drawing attention to the "extinction spasm" that we are in the midst of.[11] Over three hundred species a week are becoming extinct, in part because of how we are choosing to live—or, more precisely, because of how we are choosing *not* to live—in relationship with the earth. In the last century we have undone much of what it took the earth four billion years to evolve.

Berry loved the Christian household well enough to criticize it and call on it to change. Responsibility for the degradation of the earth was not to be laid solely at the door of Western Christianity, but he saw clearly that we have been complicit in the crime. The nations at the forefront of our planetary degradation over the last hundred years have been predominantly Christian nations. Given the excessive orientation in our religious inheritance toward transcendence, we have tragically failed to protect the sacredness of the earth. What we now need, he said, is a theology of radical immanence. "We need to move from a spirituality of alienation from the natural world to a spirituality of intimacy with the natural world."[12] And rather than viewing ourselves as separate from the earth, we need always to remember that we are "Earthlings," he said.[13] We do not have the capacity in and by ourselves to save the earth. We do, however, have the capacity to serve the earth and to nurture its deep energies for healing, to allow it the space and the time to renew itself.

The Qur'an includes a beautiful description of the creation of humanity. It describes God as drawing us forth from the dark, moist soil. When the first man and woman have emerged from the fecundity of earth's womb, God instructs the angels to bow down before them. The angels prostrate themselves, with one exception. The greatest angel, Satan, refuses. He says to God, "I will not bow to a human being whom You created from the mud" (Al-Hijr Valley 15:33).

Is this not the root of our falseness, refusing to bow to the sacredness of what comes forth from the earth? Is this not the pattern in most of our division as nations and as a human species—the refusal to honor what is deepest in others? Satan chooses the way of hubris, of pride, of lifting himself up over the other. Think of the hubris of our nations, our religious traditions, of humanity's arrogance over the earth. It is the beginning of Satan's falseness and it is the heart of our betrayal of one another.

We need to be aware of our failures. This is essential to the way forward. Equally important, we must be aware of our successes. When the Christian household gets it right—that is, when we embody our vision for justice, live our commitment to the poor, move in harmony with the earth—we can get it right like no other entity in the Western world.

A few years ago I was invited to the Cathedral of St. John the Divine in New York City for St. Francis's Sunday. I was staying in the cathedral cloisters, and when I got up early on Sunday morning to go out for coffee, there on the street in front of me, hours before the service was to begin, were hundreds of people lined up with their dogs, cats, and pets of every description. They were waiting to get into the cathedral for the great celebration of the blessing of the creatures, a liturgy that happens every year on the Sunday closest to St. Francis's feast day on October 2.

The cathedral was full that day, packed to the gunwales. It is fuller on St. Francis's Sunday than on Christmas or Easter. New Yorkers come there by the thousands—many of them for their one and only day of church attendance all year to celebrate the sacredness of the earth and its creatures.

The service overflowed with creativity. Paul Winter, the composer of the *Missa Gaia,* was there. He had woven wolf and whale sounds into the sung liturgy. At one point in the celebration, dancers from a New York contemporary dance troupe leapt in front of the altar and all around it as creatures of earth, sea, and sky. Throughout the service parakeets perched on people's shoulders and magnificent macaws squawked raucously in response to the choir. It all felt like true worship—alive, vibrant with the yearnings of this moment in time, and inclusive of the whole of creation.

Toward the end of the liturgy we moved into what is called the Silent Procession of the Creatures, silent to honor them but also so as not to startle them as they enter. The huge west-facing doors opened and in came the wonderful train of creatures, both large and small, exotic and domestic, wild and tame. Leading the procession was a camel, its long neck reaching forward to look from side to side. One wondered who was on display here! A boa constrictor followed the camel, then a pig, a goat, and the whole spectrum of God's creatures. At times it felt like being on a *Lord of the Rings* film set. I almost expected great trees to come walking down the central aisle. Of course, the cathedral can host a procession on this scale, its Gothic proportions being those of nature.

I was not prepared to be as moved as I was that day by the presence of the creatures in the cathedral. I know that the tears that welled up in my eyes when I saw them entering the west-facing doors were shared by thousands of others at that moment. But what impressed me most that morning was that the Church was not telling the people what to believe. They already knew what they believed. That was why they were there. The Church's role was to serve that deep knowing and to help translate it into how we live together with the earth.

Too often in the past our approach to truth has been to assume that we have it and others do not. Consequently, we have thought that our role is to tell people what to believe. We are being invited instead into a new humility, to serve the holy wisdom that is already stirring in the hearts of people everywhere, the growing awareness of earth's interrelatedness and sacredness. We must remember that the well of truth is not ours. It is deep within the earth and deep within the heart of humanity. Our role is to be a servant at that well.

Thomas Berry said that we are living in a moment of grace.[14] By that he meant that we are living in the midst of an awareness of earth's oneness, the likes of which humanity has never known before. We are experiencing a way of seeing that is vital to the healing of the earth. The question is whether we will translate this seeing into action, whether we will apply this awareness to the holy work of transformation. But as Berry went on to say, moments of grace are transient.[15] They are passing. In other words, will we meet this moment or will we miss it?

Interfaith Forgiveness

Pastor Don Mackenzie, PhD, Imam Jamal Rahman, and Rabbi Ted Falcon, PhD

The famous professor of comparative religion Huston Smith wrote that when we view something only from one angle, we miss the deeper vision we can get only by viewing it from many perspectives. When people begin to share their faiths more deeply with others, it can be eye opening to see that similar truths are expressed through different cultures, with different names, different stories, different characters, and different rituals. Often, people are amazed to find the same basic stories emerging from more than one tradition. Though our histories, our paths, our traditions may be different, when we recognize that we pursue the One Life we share, we find ourselves on common ground.

When the three of us hosted our yearlong Interfaith Talk Radio show in Seattle, we had the remarkable opportunity of sharing, for an hour a week, teachings from many traditions. The guests we invited to join us on the show brought information from traditions other than our own. We talked about comfortable things and about things that were not so comfortable. We probably talked too much, but we also learned much. And we took special care to listen carefully to the experience of others and not be judgmental of other spiritual paths.

Our guests helped to reinforce one of our strongest convictions: there are many spiritual paths and *they are all authentic.*

Pastor Don Mackenzie, PhD, Imam Jamal Rahman, and **Rabbi Ted Falcon, PhD**—now known as the Interfaith Amigos—started working together after 9/11. They have written two books together: *Getting to the Heart of Interfaith: The Eye-Opening, Hope-Filled Friendship of a Pastor, a Rabbi and a Sheikh* and *Religion Gone Astray: What We Found at the Heart of Interfaith* (both SkyLight Paths). Their work is dedicated to supporting more effective interfaith dialogue that can bring greater collaboration on the major social and economic issues of our time.

Many of them are extremely different from ours, different from what we are used to. On our show, we always looked for the universals that brought us together and the particular teachings in our traditions that supported those universals....

Inclusive Spirituality

For us, inclusive spirituality relates to the realization of Oneness, the Oneness toward which each of our faith traditions leads us. The One we seek is a shared One—there is only One. We believe the One, usually called "God" or "Allah" in our three faith traditions, is the One Universal Life that contains all that exists, yet is infinitely more than all that exists. To the extent that we realize ourselves as integral parts of that One, we are moving toward the spiritual side of the scale, as Rabbi Ted would describe it.

This inclusive spirituality is crucial because it leads to a very particular way of being in the world. When we are connected to each other and interconnected with all beings, we naturally begin to care better for others and for our planet. This spiritual consciousness allows us to see ourselves in all others and to understand that when we bring pain to another, we are actually bringing pain to ourselves. When we support another, we are also supporting ourselves. A strong ethic naturally flows from an inclusive spirituality, and this is the ethic we seek to celebrate together. In our interfaith work, we have realized again and again that the more deeply we share, the better we are able to appreciate the Universal we all seek to serve....

Honoring the Spirit

During the course of our interfaith journey, we have shared our stories and our deepest beliefs. We have wrestled with the problems and the promises of our faith traditions. We've gone beyond what is "safe" and moved to a different level of understanding in matters of the Middle East, where tensions and tempers are so very volatile.

We have shared in each other's rituals and practices. In each of the stages of the journey, we have been taking steps toward participating in an authentic spiritual experience through a tradition other than our own. This dimension of honoring the Shared Universal is the most challenging. Sometimes we are not able to appreciate the true depth of an experience until we actually *live* it. This was surely the case for us in what turned out to be a moment that integrated the major elements of our work together.

It started casually enough. Pastor Don had invited Ted and Jamal to help him lead a preworship forum on interfaith and social action at his church. About a month before that, Don realized that since the three of us were going to be at the church anyway, we could preach together on the golden rule as the sermon during worship. It seemed a safe enough topic.

But about two weeks before that service, Don realized that it was to be a communion Sunday. What to do about that? Then he remembered an experience from our Israel-Palestine trip where we had visited and taught at the Mount of the Beatitudes in Galilee in northern Israel. It had been a Friday afternoon, so Ted had concluded the teachings with the *Kabbalat Shabbat*, the traditional Welcoming of the Sabbath with wine and bread. Immediately, it had become clear to both Ted and Don how similar the ritual was to the traditional words and symbols of the sacrament of communion for Christians.

It had been a remarkable experience of the convergence of three traditions in that special moment and place. Jamal had also offered some reflections from his tradition, explaining the significance of Friday in Islam as the day God created Adam and his spouse, placed them in Paradise, and sent them to earth. Friday is also the Day of Judgment. On Fridays, when Muslims gather in community to praise and remember God, their prayers, especially at midday, have enhanced spiritual merit.

As Don sat reflecting on these events, he began to conceive of the possibility of including Rabbi Ted and Imam Jamal in the communion service. When he consulted with his colleagues on the pastoral staff at his church, they agreed that Ted and Jamal should be invited to serve the bread at the communion service. Step by step, little by little, that ritual moment was coming together.

But on the morning of that Sunday, as he was driving to church, Don began considering how he was going to introduce the communion moment. He certainly didn't wish to compromise the integrity of communion. The congregation would already have had a few surprises—leaders from the three Abrahamic faiths standing together, sharing the sermon, showing how the core teaching of the golden rule appeared in each tradition.

Don decided to start by introducing the "Open Table" to which his church welcomes all who wish to share. He reminded the congregation that communion is a sacrament, a moment when we are more deeply aware of the presence and the love of God through the person and teachings of Jesus. He talked about the way communion invites us all to experience forgiveness and, with love, to build loving community within a life of faith. The meal remembered and represented by the sacrament brings people together around a table, a ritual that exists in different ways in all religious traditions.

Then he said that Rabbi Ted and Imam Jamal would help serve the bread, and he asked people to reflect on how the presence of a rabbi and an imam could remind them of the greater embrace of a loving God and a welcoming community.

Pastor Don administered the sacrament at the communion table with the words from the United Church of Christ *Book of Worship*, "Through the broken bread we participate in the body of Christ," which is considered to be loving community, and "through the cup of blessing we participate in the new life Christ gives," indicating the openhearted love and compassion, which is identified as this new life.

Four pairs of people then took their places at the front of the sanctuary, one holding the cup and the other holding a basket of bread. Jamal and Ted stood with the center two pairs, each holding a basket of bread. Don had worried that too few people would accept the bread from Ted and Jamal, but actually very few came to his own basket of bread. The lines in front of Jamal and Ted were far longer than the others! Afterward, many expressed deep emotion about the reconciling presence of these two religious leaders in the midst of the sacrament.

For Don, it was a dramatic step away from a long history of repudiation of other faiths and a step toward honoring other spiritual paths without any need to feel coerced or defined by them. He knew that what happened that Sunday morning bridged the tension between the sacrament of communion as a symbol dedicated only to Christian community, and the need—suggested at the heart of Jesus's teachings—to be welcoming to all people. In the great mystery of the sacrament, this communion represented what Jesus taught: love, forgiveness, and loving community.

Jamal expressed his heartfelt gratitude to the congregation. He was aware of the deep spiritual significance of the sacrament to Christians, and as a Muslim, he felt blessed to participate because he felt a closeness to Jesus as a revered prophet, a connection with the ceremony, and a humble aspiration to experience community.

A verse in the Qur'an tells us that if we remember God, God remembers us (2:152). The Prophet added that when people remember the Divine in community, God remembers them better. The sacred community created by this communion was truly a circle of love and beauty. Jamal was deeply moved by the large number of Christians enthusiastic about receiving communion from a Muslim, and it reaffirmed for him the power and majesty of hospitality and openheartedness.

Perhaps the moment was most complicated for Rabbi Ted. Communion ceremonies clearly excluded him; taking communion meant that you were Christian. But over the years, Ted's relationship to Christians and to Christianity had changed. As he stood in Pastor Don's church that morning, he thought about the literal symbol: Jesus, a Jew, was sharing bread with other Jews. And he let that symbol expand so that a Jew was sharing bread with more than Jews, with those who would later be identified as his followers and be called Christians. While it was true that over centuries, the symbols of communion had developed deeper theological meanings and served to distinguish Christians, in the context of Pastor Don's teachings that morning, the bread and the wine could also be bread and wine. Like the bread and wine shared to welcome Shabbat, this bread and wine could celebrate sacred community and universal spiritual truth. This communion could represent a community, a place of nourishment, a place of forgiveness, of compassion, and of love. Standing at the front of that United Church of Christ, wearing *kippah* and *tallit*, Rabbi Ted was not Christian and was not pretending to be. He was a Jew honoring the church community with whom he was sharing. He was a Jew honoring the God of Love.

We are not recommending that interfaith participation in communion be standard practice. But the freedom to step into that place of Spirit on that communion Sunday was a blessing for the rabbi, for the imam, and, of course, for the pastor.

The Future of Interfaith Dialogue and Celebration

Interfaith dialogue and relationships have many stages, from separation and suspicion to embracing each other's spiritual practices. We have walked this path—from resistance to healing—and we have come, many times, to the sacred place of being humbly able to honor each other's spiritual paths. We have shared the stages of our particular journeys, but now it's in your hands. It's in your heart. You have precious opportunities of finding your own way on this interfaith journey. We hope what we have offered will support you on your unique path toward the deeper realization of the Life we all share. We want to leave you with a few thoughts as you take those amazing steps on your own path.

> *Listen:* Practice listening to others and encourage them to share their stories. Begin dialogue on issues that are of greatest concern to you and to others. See how well you can identify with another's

journey—particularly with those who seem most different from yourself. Allow yourself to move beyond suspicion and separation.

Learn: See if you can identify the shared universals that transcend every particular path but nourish us all. Look for the nature of oneness, love, compassion, and forgiveness in another's tradition. Learn how the particulars of a faith can, in fact, support universals we are all able to celebrate. As you inquire more deeply, you may learn more about your own tradition as well.

Discover: As you share, you will discover further opportunities for cooperation and collaboration. Learn to focus on these, and invite others to see them. Discover the ways in which you and those with whom you share can contribute to expanding levels of understanding and appreciation within your communities. This deeper level of discovery includes sharing both the comfortable and the uncomfortable aspects of our traditions.

Appreciate: The more you can be open to appreciating the particulars of another tradition, the better able you will be to perceive and to share the universals. The ground of mutual understanding can make it clear that no one needs to convert anyone else and that there are many authentic spiritual paths. Here you may find yourself moving beyond safe territory, but the groundwork you have created will support this deeper dimension of your journey.

Celebrate: Seek to celebrate the Universal together. If God is One, then we are all part of that One. Interfaith spirituality can allow you to support others as you climb to the top of the mountain. Taste the fruits that spring forth from your particular oasis. Celebrate an inclusive spirituality that can dispel distrust and suspicion and create pockets of peace wherever you go. Sometimes spiritual practices from another tradition can profoundly deepen your appreciation of your own faith.

It's time. We need each other more than ever, for we understand now how much we share. We have responsibilities to others and to our planet. Inclusive spirituality invites us to live less wastefully, to internalize simple truths of planetary ecology. It invites us to compassionate action in the world. It opens our hearts and promotes true compassion for others. It gives rise to visions of fulfilling basic human needs without resorting to violence. Inclusive spirituality naturally supports full access to all human and civil rights for everyone.

We are beings of deep faith. Our traditions provide us with communities and with continuity. But our traditions need to reach out beyond themselves. We are in this together.

It is our hope that our relationship and our teachings can be a gift to help you on this journey. As we strive to appreciate both the blessings and the griefs of each of our faiths, we dedicate ourselves to envisioning together a world of greater understanding, acceptance, compassion, and love. We dream of a world awakening to the essential Oneness that contains us all.

It's a matter of our survival.

Peacemaking in Our Own Hearts

Molly and Bernie Srode

Each of us has the power to promote peace in the world today. How? We can do this by tapping into our Divine Source as spiritual beings with the spark of divine life and the seed of peace within us.

For some, like Jimmy Carter, Martin Luther King Jr., or Mother Teresa, that seed was nurtured and grew into a mighty tree. For many, the seed has blossomed into a fruitful plant. In others, who display violent behavior, the seed lies dormant but not destroyed.

Millions of people throughout the world are nurturing the seed of peace within themselves. They are people who go about their everyday duties—at their place of work, in their home, and in their community. We do not see them profiled in the media; nonetheless, they are making the world a better place. If we want to understand the bigger picture, we have to see their place in it.

These are the teachers who daily go about their work of molding the future generations. These are the hundreds of service providers who show up at our door to fix the furnace, install carpet, or take care of a plumbing emergency. They are the retirees who volunteer their time at the local school, hospital, or wherever they're needed. They are the elderly who live in retirement centers and spread goodwill each day with their smiles, words of appreciation, and kindness to others. We are these people, members of a mighty army of peace that marches on in spite of the violence in the world.

I am convinced that there is more peace than violence in the world. As we hear about wars and read about violence in the news, we should make an effort to balance

---

Molly Srode, a retired hospital chaplain, and her husband, **Bernie Srode**, a former priest, are publishers of the *Senior Spirituality Newsletter* and coauthors of *Keeping Spiritual Balance as We Grow Older: More than 65 Creative Ways to Use Purpose, Prayer, and the Power of Spirit to Build a Meaningful Retirement.*

ents with a vision of the millions of people who con-
r world by daily nurturing the seeds of peace within.
n lives to further the cause of peace? We do not start
t by changing ourselves. We begin by giving our own
t vestiges of anger, resentment, and hatred lie hidden in
s? Are we angry with someone in our own family? Are
will not speak to us? Have we failed to forgive someone
who has hurt us?

How do we sweep out and let go of these feelings that seem perfectly justified? Sometimes the words or actions of another person provoke an immediate angry reaction in us. If we respond in an angry way, the interaction escalates. Isn't this what is happening in the world today? We have the ability to take a step back and refuse to respond with the same emotional intensity that was aimed at us. This takes awareness and a willingness to keep our feelings in check, but it can be done. It takes a strong act of our own will to say, "I will not go there anymore. I will no longer rehearse the wrongs that others have done to me. I will no longer proclaim my 'just' anger to others. I will no longer hold grudges toward those with whom I have had a misunderstanding.

"I will embrace the compassion of God who is the Parent of all. I will acknowledge that there is much I do not know about those who perpetrate violence, and I will let go of my propensity to judge them. I will examine my own attitude and root out any anger or hatred that I may be harboring."

As we discuss changes in our personal life, you might wonder what this has to do with the world scene. I am reminded of the award-winning movie *A River Runs Through It.* As I watched the characters of the movie joined and defined by that river, it reminded me that all of humankind was connected. A great, mighty river runs through all humankind, and while it contains life and hope for humanity, it has been polluted by violence. That river runs through all of us, and as it passes through, we can add our own gift of love, compassion, and forgiveness. In our own way, through our own lives, we can make a difference.

Let us do what we can to root out any negativity in our own hearts so that the gift we offer may be as loving as possible. Then we can join together and pray in our own faith tradition and in our own way for the coming of peace on earth.

Practice: Affirmations for Personal Peacemaking

I let go of any negativity in myself that does not lead to peace.

I recognize and emulate the peacemakers I see every day.

I am a peacemaker in my family, my community, and my world.

Dancing Peace and Forgiveness

Cynthia Winton-Henry

At one time in my life, dancing was the only place I sensed the possibility of peace. It healed my wounds and helped release the obstacles my body had inherited from generational wounds. At each step in my development, my dedication to freedom and peace in the world intensified. Dancing became my form of activism. Because of my addictive tendencies to overdo everything, I put twelve-step practices alongside dancing and InterPlay, and I was constantly reminded to let go and let God.

That is when the dream of peace became most real for me. That of which I had dared not dream became a reality. My hope for you is that a dance practice can cultivate peace for you in the following ways.

Use dance to cultivate personal peace.

"Let peace begin on earth, let it begin with me," say the lyrics of a popular song. Movement can help recenter you in your body and unlock your innate wisdom. This peace is the peace to be who you are without worry. It is not a staged or pious peace. It isn't forced or controlled. It is a personal peace that loosens yo and brings you back to the heartbeat of humanity. To develop peace in your makes you the best peace mediator you can be. As Kenneth Cloke, directo the Center for Dispute Resolution, says, "It is easier to assist conflicted parti being authentic and centered with one another if we are authentic and cent [ourselves]." ...

Cynthia Winton-Henry teaches people to unlock the wisdom of the body th movement and creativity. She is author of *Dance—the Sacred Art: The Joy of Moven as a Spiritual Practice* (SkyLight Paths) and is cofounder of InterPlay, an internation not-for-profit organization with locations in over fifty cities on five continents.

Use dance to release negative emotional buildup.

As the Dalai Lama suggests, "To make peace in the Middle East, we must decrease negative emotions." This is good advice not only on a national but also a personal level. I think of my husband. When he is distressed about work, he gets depressed. But when he does an uninhibited dance, letting his frustration come out in crazy sounds and faces, letting his whole body dance, his experience shifts. Immediately afterward, he sighs and says, "That feels better." The negative emotions have moved on.

When African bushmen experience a conflict, their elders convene a *xotla,* a public meeting that all adults attend. The parties are allowed to express grievances before the assembled community. Sometimes their group tensions are best resolved through dance. As people sing and clap, while the dancers dance, the *xotla* can go on for days, until all parties literally exhaust their negative feelings.

One women's spirituality group uses another strategy for tension. Mad? "Sing it! You won't be able to stay mad." I would add, "Move it!" If you can let your body speak, once it's had its say, most often you'll want to move on....

Use dance to redirect disdainful actions.

In *Dancing in Conflict,* Patrick Koop, founder of the Peace Agents Foundation, reflects on aikido, a Japanese martial art created as an art of peace by Moriher Yesheiba during World War II in one of the darkest periods of human history. Koop says aikido teaches people "not to look at the opponent as an enemy," but to focus on "neutralizing destructive energies." He describes the movement as a "step in or step out" to "outbalance the opponent." Fifth-degree black belt holder George Leonard puts it this way: "The genius of aikido is to transform the most violent attack, by embracing it, into a dance." Similarly, when you dance, you can pay attention to energy, step in or away when a conflict exceeds your capacity, and learn to move *with* rather than *against* the people around you.

Use dance to create distance from conflict zones.

step away from geographies of pain is a basic principle of reducing conflict. ething as simple as stepping back or walking away from aggression is a reli-a strategy. Taking this one step further, when you make a neutral place, a dance zo, you can soften up tensions. This is one purpose of a ritual environment. It ca allow you and the one you're in conflict with to reflect, choose how to act according to a higher good, rehearse and even transform your way of acting. Rituals both set apart and bind together our experiences.

Trying to create peace in a place where hatred runs rampant is like putting medicine in a bleeding wound. Not until the wound is bound up and has had time to close can you treat it. A dance can be an act of binding or a means of taking pressure off a wound. It is necessary to let peace and love dance the other areas of the body, lest the whole body become a war zone.

Use dance to help you forgive and move forward.

One of the most difficult steps in peacemaking is to show up after you've been hurt. I was furious when the head of a dance organization banned my friend over a piece of choreography. As soon as I heard about it, I spoke my mind. Disgusted with the organization's judgmental response, I indignantly withdrew my membership.

Years later, the dance group coaxed me to return. The invitation was compelling, and I wanted to forgive and forget. I agreed to give it a try. On the first night, the dancing began and I wept. I remembered that these dancers were like my extended spiritual family. I had left over a shortcoming. In dancing, my animosity finally melted, I confessed my sorrow aloud, and the rift was healed. Dancing led the way.

Rose Berger and Julie Polter visited Corrymeela, Cornerstone Community, and Currach in Northern Ireland where Catholics and Protestants touch "fingertips in an arch over the desolate cyclone fencing, razor wire, and bricks of the 'peace line.'" They saw dances of peace being enacted where "memory-carrying people can remember yet forgive, where human frailty and weighted histories might turn in a fresh step, where the bones of Northern Ireland, dry for so long in broken tenements and divided suburbs, may yet raise themselves up … as they strive to translate small reconciling gestures into oratorios of movement." This was more than poetry for them. These people literally danced forgiveness.

Practice: Inner Peace Dance—80 Percent Stillness

Take a deep breath. Let it out with a sigh.

With one arm or your whole body, make a shape.

Breathe into the shape, becoming present to it.

Shifting from one shape or posture to another, it is important to indulge the stillness.

Incorporating music, dance with 80 percent stillness (or whatever is the best percentage for you right now). Your shapes can transition with quick energetic shifts or slow ones.

It is essential to breathe. Sometimes sighing or "toning" while moving keeps the breath alive and the quiet energy flowing.

Dancing with gestures and stillness, invite forgiveness for yourself or others. Lift those you cannot forgive to your higher power.

If you like, imagine creating ripples of peace out into the world.

Intercession and Justice

Rev. Larry J. Peacock

> This poor soul cried, and was heard by the Lord, and was saved from every trouble. —Psalm 34:6

The poor have long cried to God; later in Psalm 34 we find the testimony that God draws near to the brokenhearted and crushed (Psalm 34:18).

In the 1970s, Christians, led by the Roman Catholic Church, made a serious attempt to address the plight of the poor in Central and South America. A new theology of liberation developed in which oppressors were confronted and the poor organized. Those who benefited from keeping the poor enslaved—often an unholy alliance of the rich, the government, and the military—fought back and targeted religious leaders.

Rutilio Grande (1928–1977), an El Salvadoran priest, encouraged the church to minister to the poor. His death prompted newly appointed Archbishop Óscar Romero to speak out against government-sanctioned violence and to advocate that the church must care for the oppressed. The death of Father Grande became the first of many in El Salvador, and it would be some time before the last part of Psalm 34:6, "saved from every trouble," was carried out.

> Many are the afflictions of the righteous, but the Lord rescues them from them all. —Psalm 34:19

Saint Patrick (c. 389–c. 461), kidnapped by Irish pirates and taken from Britain to Ireland, escaped from slavery and became a priest. When he returned to Ireland to convert the nation, he baptized thousands of people and ordained hundreds

---

Rev. Larry J. Peacock is a retreat leader, writer, and advisory board member at the Academy for Spiritual Formation. He is author of several books, including *Openings: A Daybook of Saints, Sages, Psalms and Prayer Practices* (SkyLight Paths) and is executive director of Rolling Ridge Retreat and Conference Center in North Andover, Massachusetts.

of priests. Legend says that Patrick drove all snakes out of Ireland and gave the shamrock religious significance.

Sometimes God seems to take a long time to perform the rescue. Kidnapped from England and sold into slavery in Ireland, Patrick had to wait six years before he could escape. He went home a changed person, now a man of faith who went on to study for the priesthood, much to the surprise of his family. In his dreams he heard the call to go back to Ireland, not to seek revenge but to preach the gospel. For thirty years he preached, established churches, baptized thousands, and changed the course of the nation. The legends about him may stretch the truth, but there is no doubt that Patrick lived as a remarkable servant of Christ.

Intercessory prayers often go hand in hand with action to address problems. In times of injustice and social oppression, when the gap between the rich and the poor widens, prayers of intercession for change become linked with letter-writing campaigns, marches and sit-ins, and the creation of alternative models.

If Patrick at first prayed for revenge on his captors, his intercession eventually changed from anger and bitterness to reconciliation and conversion. When we pray for our enemies, God may help us see them in a new way, perhaps as part of God's own family.

Today lift up to God a situation of pain or hurt in the world. Pray for leaders who could make a difference. Pray for people who are hurt, oppressed, and ignored. Pray for those whose actions contribute to the pain. Pray for the church to involve itself as an agent of change, a voice of reconciliation, and a partner in healing.

Practice: Intercession Collage

Create a photo collage of people and situations that you include in your prayers. Sometimes putting a face with a prayer opens us to a new level of compassion. You may realize that your enemy belongs to a loving and worried parent. You may find that the oppressor carries an unhealed wound. You may realize that the one you have trouble praying for is still God's child, still loved by God. Create your photo collage and use it in your prayer time.

Cultivating a Forgiving Heart

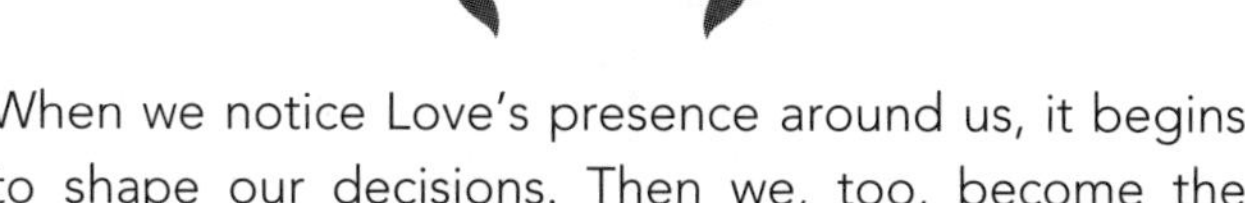

> When we notice Love's presence around us, it begins to shape our decisions. Then we, too, become the embodiment of God's love.
>
> —Nancy L. Bieber

Forgiveness for others grows out of compassion, being at peace with yourself, and feeling loved and accepted enough to let go of judgment. When you have a heart at peace, you'll find it easier to forgive in the moment, and every day will be full of the freedom that comes from forgiveness.

In this section, you'll find practices for wiping the slate clean each night, for cultivating compassion for yourself and everyone you encounter, for letting things go—not denying hurt or pretending not to mind, but genuinely learning not to take things personally and so not needing to react with bitterness or defensiveness. Diane M. Millis, PhD, encourages you to see everyone as a stranger with whom you have no baggage, no negative history; and Yoland Trevino and Rev. Nanette Sawyer share the power of seeing all strangers as part of our family. Every shift in perspective that the contributors suggest ultimately is in pursuit of one goal: to live and react and love out of openness and forgiveness.

May you find a little more compassion and forgiveness in the world—and in your own heart—each day.

Lovingkindness Meditation to Open the Heart and Mind

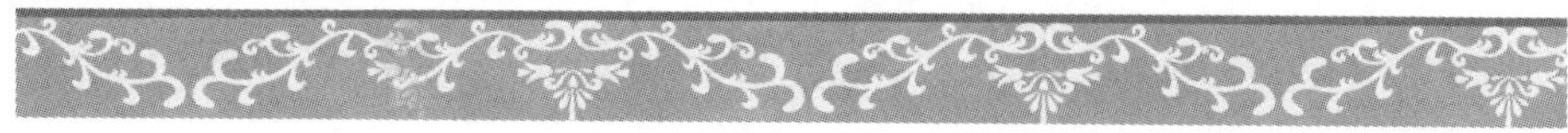

Louise Silk

Lovingkindness is a meditation practice taught by the Buddha to develop the mental habit of selfless and altruistic love. It brings about positive attitudinal changes as it systematically develops the quality of loving acceptance. It frees the troubled mind from its pain and confusion. Hatred cannot coexist with lovingkindness and dissipates if supplanted with loving thoughts. Lovingkindness has the immediate benefit of changing and sweetening old habituated negative patterns of the mind. Through this practice we befriend ourselves.

The innocent mistake that keeps us in our own particular style of unkindness is that we do not see clearly what is. Our basic misunderstanding is the belief that by improving ourselves, by trying to be better than we are, we will avoid pain and be happy.

The original name of this practice is *mettabhavana,* which comes from the Pali language. *Metta* means love in a nonromantic sense—friendliness, kindness, or lovingkindness. We feel it in our hearts. *Bhavana* means development or cultivation. Lovingkindness meditation produces four qualities of love: *metta* or friendliness, *karuna* or compassion, *mudita* or appreciative joy, and *upekka* or equanimity. The quality of friendliness is expressed as warmth that reaches out and embraces others. As our lovingkindness practice matures, it naturally overflows into compassion as we empathize with other people's difficulties. This positive expression of empathy is an appreciation of other people's good qualities or good fortune or

---

Louise Silk is a spiritual teacher, integrated kabbalistic healer, and professional quilter. She is author of *The Quilting Path: A Guide to Spiritual Discovery through Fabric, Thread and Kabbalah* (SkyLight Paths).

appreciative joy. It is not feelings of jealousy or pity. This series of meditations comes to maturity as equanimity. Ultimately, we remain kindly disposed and caring toward everybody with an equal spread of loving feelings and acceptance in all situations and relationships.

Practice: *Mettabhavana* Meditation

Lovingkindness meditation supports keeping an open mind. When I am troubled and people are getting on my nerves, I go to this practice. The first step to lovingkindness is loving myself. I am not being vain or selfish but attempting to generate my own sense of well-being and love of self.

When in doing this I experience resistance, I recognize the presence of my very familiar feelings of unworthiness. The design of the practice helps me overcome my feelings of self-doubt or negativity. The practice goes on to develop lovingkindness toward others. There are three types of people to develop lovingkindness toward. The first is a respected or beloved family member, friend, or teacher. The next is a neutral person, somebody I know and have no special feelings toward, such as my neighbor or someone who performs a service for me. The third is a hostile person, someone I am currently having difficulty with.

> Begin the practice by spending five minutes meditating at each stage. In the first stage, feel *metta* for yourself. Become aware of yourself, focusing on feelings of peace, calm, and tranquility. Let these feelings grow into feelings of strength and confidence, and then develop these into love within your heart. You can use an image such as golden light flooding your body. Or repeat a mantra or phrase over and over again, either out loud or silently, such as "May I be well and happy." Another method is making an affirmation, a positive statement about yourself in your own words. These are all ways of stimulating the feeling of *metta* for yourself.
>
> For the next stage, think of a good friend. Bring them to mind as vividly as you can. Describe their good qualities. Feel your connection with your friend—how much you love him or her—and encourage these feelings of love to grow by repeating "May this friend be well and happy." You can also use the image of a light shining from your heart into your friend's heart, or form a mental picture of you and that person with a joyous feeling of love surrounding both of you.

> Reflect on the positive qualities of this person and the acts of kindness he or she has done. These visualizations and reflections are dependable devices for arousing positive feelings of lovingkindness. When the positive feelings arise, switch from the devices to the feelings. The feelings are the primary focus.
>
> Keep the mind fixed on the feeling. If it strays, bring it back to the device, or if the feelings weaken or are lost, then return to the device to bring back or strengthen the feeling. Use these techniques of a phrase, an image, or a feeling in the next two stages as well.
>
> For the third stage, think of someone you do not particularly like or dislike, someone for whom your feelings are neutral. This may be someone you do not know well but have contact with. Reflect on their humanity and include them in your feelings of *metta*.
>
> Next think of someone you actually dislike. Instead of getting caught up in feelings of hatred, think of this person positively and send your *metta* to him or her as well.
>
> Finally, think of all four people together—yourself, the friend, the neutral person, and the adversary. Now extend your feelings further to everyone around you in your neighborhood, your town, your country, and so on throughout the world. Feel waves of lovingkindness spreading from your heart to everyone, to all beings everywhere. Then gradually relax out of meditation and bring the practice to an end.
>
> Systematically sending lovingkindness into the universe breaks down barriers. It will affect the divisions within your mind, which are the source of most conflicts.

How did it feel? Were you able to be with yourself without harshness or embarrassment? Did you discover a piece of your innate wisdom that exists along with your neurosis? Our brilliance, spiciness, and completeness is right beside our confusion, dissatisfaction, and harsh judgment. If we try to rid ourselves of our negative aspects, we also lose our wonderful idiosyncrasies and uniqueness. As your practice grows, your mantra will become: "I am grateful for who I am just as I am in this very moment." Cultivating gentleness and the ability to let go of small-mindedness opens our thoughts, emotions, minds, and hearts.

Escaping the Blame Cycle

Gordon Peerman

Whether we are angry at ourselves or someone else, we usually have a story of blame consolidated around a believed thought that somebody is wrong, someone is bad. But underneath that story of blame, there is some point of vulnerability in us, some unmet need, something that wants kind attention. The "trance of blame," as my teacher Tara Brach describes it, is our attempt to anesthetize the pain of what lies underneath, to create a false refuge from this underlying pain. When we can be mindful of the energies of blame—in our mind and our body—we can let go of the story of blame, open to the vulnerability underneath, and come out of the trance in which we find ourselves.

Let's say, for example, that you've just learned someone has been gossiping about you, saying some very unkind things that, in your view, badly misrepresent your motives. And now this person is going about publicly besmirching your name. You find yourself feeling outraged. You're thinking how unfair he is, how wrong he is about you, what a *!#@* he is, how you'd like to retaliate by saying a few things about him. Self-righteously, you imagine setting him straight or beating him up, but only after having made him pay by having others think poorly of him. Your believed thought is that, once justice is served, you'll have made him pay and you'll feel better. But, as Tara points out, *justice never heals the wound of loss.*

Instead, thoughts of retribution will generate deeper suffering in you, squeezing out the pleasures of your life. When you are in the grip of blame, you have no relief. Even though you might recognize that you can never feel comfortably at home in your life as long as you are blame-storming, it is still easy to keep fanning

---

Gordon Peerman is an Episcopal priest, psychotherapist, and teacher. He is author of *Blessed Relief: What Christians Can Learn from Buddhists about Suffering* (SkyLight Paths) and is an adjunct faculty member at Vanderbilt Divinity School.

the flames of blame. Blame both feeds you and consumes you. You may not even want to stop blaming.

Tara uses the Buddhist image of the two arrows of suffering to explain how blame works. In this example, the first arrow is the shot of physical and emotional pain you feel when you initially learn that someone is gossiping about you. The pain of this wound cannot be avoided; it has already happened.

But if you attempt to anesthetize the pain of the first arrow with, of all things, a second arrow—blame—you are taking a false refuge from the rawness of the original wound. You might think you'll feel better by blaming: "My suffering is his fault. If he hadn't gossiped, I wouldn't be feeling this way. He's bad." You may hope to anesthetize the pain, but you actually multiply your suffering. Your blame harms you far more than the person who wounded you. You can make a different choice that will lessen your suffering. You can choose to wake up from the trance of blame. This, Tara says, is a true homecoming, an exile's return from the land of demanding that life be other than it is.

An acronym for this practice that my Buddhist teachers have offered has been hugely helpful to me when I'm caught in the middle of a blame cycle. It is the acronym *RAIN,* which stands for *Recognition, Acceptance, Investigation,* and *Nonidentification.*

The intention to "bring RAIN to blame," as Tara puts it, is a powerful antidote to the suffering of blaming.

The first step of RAIN is *recognition,* which means simply noting that this is a moment of anger, that anger is like this, in the mind and in the body. It is an observation that you have a mind filled with rage, or at least what Tara calls "uncharitable mental commentary."

The second step, *acceptance,* is a matter of acknowledging that this moment of anger cannot be otherwise. You may not like it, you may want it otherwise, but "it is what it is," and you stop demanding that it be something else. How you recognize and accept the emotion (and your resistance to the emotion) makes all the difference. If you can accept anger with the mental tone of kindness or hospitality, you are practicing compassion.

Acceptance often comes down to this question: Can I simply be with this emotion and let go of the hope that it will soon depart? If I am able to do this, spaciousness in which the emotion is simply allowed to be can arise.

The third step, *investigation,* is a shift to curiosity about your physical and mental experience of this moment of anger. You check out where you are feeling vulnerable, where the blame resides in your heart, mind, and body. How do I feel it in my body? What thoughts am I having right now? What story am I believing? Can I drop the story line and simply be with the physical sensations of the emotion? Once you start exploring what this feeling is like, you've removed your focus from that "bad" person out there and introduced a new tone to the experience, that of simple curiosity. Noticing where bodily tension arises, staying with it for a few minutes to watch how it changes, and attending to the breath at the same time can be especially helpful.

The fourth part of RAIN, *nonidentification,* means just that: don't identify with the emotion. There is always more to you than the moment's fear, anger, or sadness. This feeling does not exhaust the fullness of who you are. Whatever emotion you are having, it is a cloud that, for the moment, covers the luminous spaciousness of what the Tibetans call "the sky-like mind," or big mind. Small mind is covering big mind. You realize that this "mind moment" is not *me* or *mine,* but rather an impermanent energy passing through. You see anger not as *my* anger and personal, but as *the* anger and impersonal, something afflicting many other persons on the planet. When you can disidentify with the feeling, the spaciousness of the big mind can shine through. Remembering what lies behind the cloud of anger can be like getting a peek at the blue sky after days of overcast weather.

Nonidentification is the essential step in self-transcending. Suffering exists and you are present to it, but there is more to you than your suffering. You can be present to your hurt and vulnerability, but the hurt and vulnerability are not you. And the blame is not you. You are the awareness of the contents of your mind, but you are not exclusively identified with any particular content or wound. You are the consciousness of the emotion and not the emotion itself. And in this awareness, your identification with the emotion dissolves and you transcend the way you conventionally understand yourself.

Go back for a moment to the gossiping example. If you were to put RAIN into practice, the scenario might go something like this. When you first learn of someone gossiping about you, you simply *recognize,* without judgment, your initial flash of anger. You *accept* that multiple causes and conditions have come together to make this moment the way it is; the next moment may be different, but this one cannot be. Then you begin your *investigation:* When you first learned about the gossip, what believed thoughts came with your anger? What needs of yours were not being met—the need to be understood? the need to be treated fairly? the need to be respected? Rather than focusing on what the other person said, you choose to be present to the physical sensations of vulnerability in yourself, to your body's response to not having your needs met. You check it out by asking, What is happening in my body when

I tell this story? Who would I be and how would my body feel without this st How long have I felt this way? Does this feel familiar? You allow yourself to feel the "ouch" of the pain without resorting to blaming the one who hurt you. Finally, you invite *nonidentification.* You realize that this anger, even with all its intensity is not *you* or *yours.* You see it as *the* anger, an impermanent energy moving through your mind and body, but not something that defines who you are. You are more than this passing energy. You are the awareness of this energy.

By bringing RAIN to blame, you undermine your story of blame along with its strategy of keeping you from feeling vulnerable. You begin to *feel* your vulnerability, in the body and in the mind. As you hold that vulnerability in mindful, loving presence, it will begin to heal. When you can let go of the story of blame, your healing can begin. You will understand viscerally just how much suffering is hidden under the layers of blame. When you can bring loving presence to that suffering, you can wake up from the trance of blame and come home to yourself. The fruit of this homecoming is known as forgiveness, and it is the very heart of Jesus's teaching.

Jesus's willingness to drink the cup he was given and to bear his own cross with forgiveness marks the self-transcending step in handling anger. Jesus's self-transcending love moved *through* his anguish, his vulnerability, and the anger of others, not *around* them. In the language of theologian Reinhold Niebuhr's Serenity Prayer, "accepting what we cannot change" is a movement of self-transcending. In this surrender, we let go of our own preferences and simply bear reality. We carry what we must without resistance and without blame, not demanding that things be other than what they are. We commit ourselves into the hands of a greater spirit.

A problem for some is making the move to surrender or self-transcending *before* engaging in self-soothing and self-defining. This is a false surrender, a spiritual bypass that often results in passive accommodation to abuse or injustice, or in playing the victim role with the attempt to induce guilt. Not only does this spiritual bypass masquerade as genuine surrender, it also fails to address unfairness and injustice both interpersonally and within the community. This false surrender is *not* an instrument of peace. Only when self-soothing and self-defining have taken place is it truly possible to let go, as Jesus did in his passion, to engage in self-transcending.

We can become instruments of Jesus's peace when we are present to our own anger and that of others, learning with mindfulness to transform the energy of anger into compassion and peace. Self-soothing contains the angry urge to strike back. Self-defining converts the energy of anger into powerful presence.

nscending commits us to a loving awareness beyond our personal endas, surrendering our anger to God's peace and reconciliation. ; threefold path, we find a way through discord to unity, through hatred to love, through injury to pardon. We become instruments of peace.

Practice: Working with RAIN

The RAIN acronym is an especially valuable tool in bringing mindfulness to strong emotions. The next time you find yourself in the middle of an emotional hijacking by anger (or another strong emotion, such as sadness or fear), try this RAIN technique to help you see into and through the storm of the emotion to a larger and more spacious awareness.

> *Recognition*: When you find yourself on emotional overload, this simple "stop, look, and listen" step is a fundamental place to start. All you need to do is recognize the emotion that you are feeling, to simply acknowledge the anger (or whatever the feeling is). Here is anger—it's just a fact. Try saying to yourself, "Anger is like this ... it's here." The key is to be nonjudgmental and open about what, in fact, is taking place.
>
> *Acceptance*: This is the time to turn your inner critic off. You may not like how you feel, but you can acknowledge that it is what it is and you can stop demanding that it be other than it is. Try saying to yourself, "I accept the presence of this anger; I will let it be and I will let my resistance to anger be." This is the necessary first step in letting go of your emotion's hold on you.
>
> *Investigation*: Here is where it gets interesting. Think of this step as a wide-open invitation for your curiosity. With kind exploration, ask some questions. What is this anger like in my mind? At what exact moment did this anger arise? What triggered it? What thoughts accompany my anger? What is this anger like in my body? Specifically, where does the energy of anger show up in my body? How does the bodily energy of anger change moment to moment? How big is this anger in my body? Is this energy stationary or moving, hot or cold? If it had a color, what color would this energy be? What believed thoughts come with the story of anger? All of these questions are ways to investigate, to witness, to hold your anger without letting it take over you.

Nonidentification: This is the time to sort out "who's who." Nonidentification is a matter of remembering that your feelings are not you. A clever way of practicing nonidentification is to imagine for a moment that this feeling you are having belongs to someone else. This strategy is a way to temporarily distance yourself from the delusion that you are nothing but this feeling. Most important, let yourself rest in the awareness of the anger. Let the anger be just one mental content flowing down your mind stream. Notice what other contents are also in your mind stream, and recognize that you are more than any passing content. Your anger has come, and gone, and will come again. But your awareness remains.

Meditations of Marcus Aurelius on Forgiveness

If a person is mistaken, instruct her kindly and show her the error. But if you are not able, blame yourself, or blame not even yourself.

—Meditations of Marcus Aurelius, X:4, from
The Meditations of Marcus Aurelius:
Selections Annotated & Explained

Bedtime Forgiveness Prayer

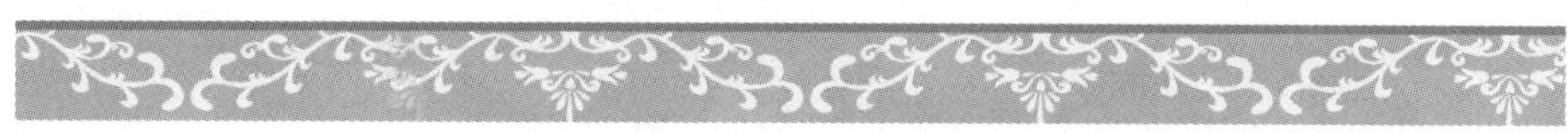

Tamar Frankiel, PhD, and Judy Greenfeld

Master of the universe,
I hereby forgive each person who angered or antagonized me, or sinned against me—
whether against my body or my property, my honor or anything of mine,
whether accidentally or willfully, carelessly or purposely,
whether by speech or deed, thought or fantasy,
whether in this incarnation or in another incarnation—
may no one be punished because of me.
May it be Your will,
Adonai my God and God of my ancestors,
that I may sin no more.
Whatever my error before You,
may it be blotted out in Your abundant mercies,
but not through suffering or severe illness.
May the expressions of my mouth
and the thoughts of my heart
be pleasing to You, Adonai, my Rock and my Redeemer.

—Traditional Jewish Prayer of Forgiveness

Tamar Frankiel, PhD, is president of the Academy for Jewish Religion, where she also lectures on Jewish mysticism. **Judy Greenfeld** is cantor at the Academy for Jewish Religion and founded the Nachshon Minyan, a community that reaches out to the unaffiliated. They coauthored *Entering the Temple of Dreams: Jewish Prayers, Movements, and Meditations for the End of the Day* (Jewish Lights).

The meditation that follows on the traditional Jewish Forgiveness Prayer can be used as part of a bedtime prayer ritual to help you learn, little by little, how to release pain, to be grateful for whatever lessons you have received, and to give the ultimate outcome—whatever that may be—over to God.

We highly recommend doing a forgiveness meditation frequently, concluding with a reading of the traditional forgiveness prayer, or whatever portions of it you find comfortable. Recognize that as you prepare to say the prayer, you may not be willing to grant complete forgiveness to even one person. You may instead prefer to say to God, "I am reading this prayer even though I cannot yet do what it says. Help me be willing to forgive more and more."

We suggest that you start with one person who has affronted you in a minor way so you can become accustomed to the dynamic of forgiving. Often it's too difficult to start by trying to forgive an abusive parent or a person you face in your life every day.... When you find that you cannot forgive a certain person, again ask God to help you be willing to forgive in the future. Put that incident or relationship aside and continue with others, returning to the more difficult ones at a later time.... Of course, you can adapt the meditation and visualization to your own needs, using different images or words, after you become familiar with the process. The most important thing is to do the exercise—and do it regularly.

Practice: Bedtime Forgiveness Meditation

Close your eyes and breathe deeply, in and out. Let your body settle into your chair or bed. Become aware of your physical body and how you are sitting or lying. What is the temperature of your body? What is the taste in your mouth? Is there fear or tension in your body? Gently tell your body that it is okay to relax now because you have finished your day. Give thanks to God for helping you complete a day to the best of your ability.

Now close your eyes. You are ready to open your inner eyes and experience a place where you have the gift of inner vision. Inwardly imagine yourself in a *sukkah* (outdoor shelter) of peace. As you rest, notice that on one side of it the curtains part, and you see before you a magnificently moonlit beach. See yourself stepping out of the *sukkah* onto a path made of natural stones, which is also lit by the moon. As you place your feet on the smooth stones, the light glistens and illuminates your feet as well. You become aware of a warm blanket being placed around your shoulders to protect and comfort you. You can hear the sound of the ocean as you approach. The air is fresh and cool against your nostrils.

Breathe in and breathe out. Open your arms wide like a bird. The breeze blows right through you, cleansing away any tension or residue from the day. It takes away any impurities, blocks, or resistance from your inner being. They seem to dissolve into the air.

A sense of freedom and expansiveness fills you. Notice whether there are any places where the wind, the Spirit, cannot blow freely. Gently focus on that area and send the breeze lovingly to that place. Notice what the breeze feels like as it blows through your mind and senses ... your throat, your heart ... your solar plexus, your belly, hips, pelvis, groin. It blows through your spine and the muscles of your back, arms, and legs. You become a hollow reed as it moves freely through you.

If you are ready, it is now time to do some forgiveness work. Ask yourself: Am I ready to let go and untie myself from what does not serve my soul's mission in this world? From relationships and experiences that drain my energy? If the answer is yes, you are ready to "for-give" this to God so you can learn, release, and move forward in wisdom.

Begin to notice the beauty of the vast dark ocean before you. The moonlight begins to shine on the waves in a way that brings up pictures of the day's events—people you encountered, business you were involved in, everyday tasks. The scenes may shift to the past week or to events from the past year. Trust whatever presents itself. Perhaps nothing will appear, and that is fine, too. Just keep making the space for whatever or whoever needs to appear. Ask God to help you be willing to face and heal the feelings inside you.

Whoever appears before you will be the one from whose painful acts, betrayal, or abandonment you need to be healed. It doesn't matter if this is a highly significant person in your life, or someone you met only once in the grocery store. The important thing is that the encounter left you with a certain emotional resonance.

When the person's image becomes clear enough for you to recognize, thank the person for coming. Try not to judge what you are feeling about the person. Simply allow the painful feeling to arise.

Imagine that a strand of light extends from your heart or solar plexus to the same area on the other person's body. This strand may be as thick as a rope or as thin as a thread. It represents the energy that attaches you to this person. Feel the energy of the event that caused you pain. Do not judge it. Just feel it. This is energy that is being taken from your body and psyche to sustain your attachment to this event with this person. What does it feel like? Is it leaking out in dribbles, or pouring out like a flood of tears? Is it blocked? Try to name the feeling of your pain. Describe your perception of it. Tell the person before you about your feelings, remembering to stay with your feelings. Avoid getting involved in talking about their feelings, remembered or imagined. For example, "I feel angry that you walked out of my life and started a new one." "I feel betrayed that you spend time on your work instead of with me." "I feel resentful that you did not protect me." Keep the feelings in the present tense. Be clear about the event or experience.

How did it harm you? Did it harm your body, your property, your honor, or your self-esteem? Did the injury come through your friends or family? Was it done accidentally or willfully? Through speech or through an action? Did it occur in this incarnation or perhaps in another? Once you have stated the feelings, try to see whether there was a lesson to learn, a life experience you needed to face and master through your encounter with this person. Now that you have named it and seen it clearly, you are ready to let go. You have the choice to stop carrying this burden.

Now we are ready for giving this experience to God, Ruler of all souls, to judge and heal.

Keep breathing. Look at this person and thank them for the experience they brought into your life. Tell them that you have learned your life lesson and that you are ready to move on now. Thank God for the lesson and for Divine help to move on. Take a long deep breath and slowly exhale it.

Look again at the strand of light that connects you to this person. Notice that midway along it there is a bow that ties the strands together. Reach out with your right hand and pull on the strand that releases the bow, untying the knot. The strand of light will now spiral back counterclockwise into the center of your own body. It warms, soothes, and relaxes the muscles of your stomach.

As you breathe, the relaxation moves into your chest, relaxing the muscles around your heart and lungs. The warmth and light and relaxation now spread into your arms and legs, hands and feet, then into your face, relaxing the muscles around your mouth and eyes. With it comes confidence and strength.

You are free. You have let go. You may notice that the image of the person before you has changed, softened, or even faded. The other person is now free to do his or her own work with God.

Now say the Prayer of Forgiveness.

The Fruit of Love

Nancy L. Bieber

God is love, and when we are willing, attentive, and responsive to God, we grow in love. We notice it around us, and we grow in giving and receiving it. Even when God is not named, the presence of love testifies to the presence of God.

When we are attentive to Love, we see more of God's presence around us. We see it in the tenderness of relationship between lovers, the listening and laughter between friends, the amazing patience in parents of small children, the welcome extended to one who lingers on the edge of the circle. When we're aware of Love, we notice God's presence in the smallest of details. On frosty nights while I sleep, my husband covers me with an additional blanket even though he's not cold. But he knows I chill easily, and he is saying "I love you" with this small act of lovingkindness.

When we notice Love's presence around us, it begins to shape our decisions. Then we, too, become the embodiment of God's love. Ed's story is an example of this. He needed to decide what to do about his difficult next-door neighbor. They shared a small backyard, and the neighbor's dog kept digging holes all over it, with a special interest in Ed's carefully tended flowerbeds. Ed and his neighbor had had previous exchanges about a blaring television, so Ed knew how quickly his neighbor could get angry.

When Ed opened the situation to God, willing to be attentive to whatever he might see, the first thing that he noticed was how important this dog was to his neighbor. His neighbor never seemed to go out with friends, and Ed wondered if the dog really *was* his neighbor's best friend. Ed decided that the first step would be

---

Nancy L. Bieber is a Quaker spiritual director, retreat leader, psychologist, teacher, and author of *Decision Making and Spiritual Discernment: The Sacred Art of Finding Your Way* (SkyLight Paths). She also teaches at Lancaster Theological Seminary and is a core leader with Oasis Ministries for Spiritual Development.

to make friends with the man's dog. Then he would have a basis for talking more comfortably with his neighbor and he could speak of his concern for their yard.

Love was the fruit of Ed's discernment. As he gave love and attention to the dog (and received it, too!), he found a compassionate love growing in him for his neighbor. He saw more clearly who his neighbor was, not just the owner of this animal that was destroying his flowers, but a person who was somewhat shy and hid behind a gruff and angry exterior.

In paying attention to his neighbor, Ed's love showed itself through compassion and through forgiveness. Compassion is the love that feels another's distress and brokenness. Compassion does not eliminate our sense of judgment, but it enlarges our awareness so that we can understand others better and care for them as they are. We understand better how other people—our brothers and sisters—have experienced the world and how they are struggling.

Forgiveness—whether giving or receiving it—is a decision of love. We humans hurt each other in all kinds of ways. When we forgive, we are letting go because we love. It may be an act of love to one who hurt us, but it is also an act of love directed within to decide to release the hurt rather than clutch it to ourselves. Though we still see clearly the reality of the injury, we can choose to lay down the burden of resentment. Forgiveness is often a long, slow process of turning away from anger or bitterness, but the ability to forgive is a powerful gift of the God of love.

Living in Love

The Rev. Peter Wallace

Love is clearly the centerpiece, the heart, of life for Jesus, and he invites those who wish to live fully and authentically to follow him in the passionate way of love. So what sort of love does Jesus call us to experience and share throughout the gospels?

> *Jesus's love is uninhibited and freely shared.* You know he loves you simply from his gaze, his touch, his words, his warmth, his very presence.
>
> *Jesus's love is actively expressed*—with acts of service, with healing, with sacrifice. It means something. It isn't merely an emotion felt; it is an action fulfilled.
>
> *Jesus's love is authentic, real, and trustworthy.* There is no doubt, no uncertainty. He doesn't offer his love with ulterior motives. His love is clean, clear, and true.
>
> *Jesus's love is forever,* from the beginning of time to the end of infinity. Unwavering. Unshakable. Undiminished. Eternal.

This love involves compassionately serving anyone who is in need. It involves actively doing good to everyone, even our enemies. It involves avoiding the self-approving judgment of others who are different. It involves forgiveness and reconciliation. It involves sharing all our resources with those with whom we live in community.

But this love is more than that. As we can see in the gospels, Jesus possesses a heart of love full to bursting. He wholly knows the character of God, and he knows

---

The Rev. Peter Wallace is author of *The Passionate Jesus: What We Can Learn from Jesus about Love, Fear, Grief, Joy and Living Authentically* (SkyLight Paths), among other books, and is executive producer of *Day1,* an acclaimed ecumenical radio ministry.

that all men and women are made in God's image. Out of that knowledge flows a love that must be expressed, given away, multiplied.

The basis for Jesus's entire ministry was a sacrificial, healing love for others deeply rooted in the Jewish understanding of God's compassion for all who are created in God's image. This sort of love is not a general, ethereal, otherworldly love for all humanity; it is a genuine love for each person Jesus encountered, because Jesus saw his or her infinite value in God's heart.

It is not enough to know whom and how Jesus loved, or what he taught about love. It is not even enough to accept the reality that Jesus loves us even now. This love is not a one-way street. It must have an outlet. We must follow Jesus's example in expressing our holy love passionately, in sharing it, receiving it, and living in and through it.

Think about how you share love with those in your circles of life. Your lover. Your family. Your friends. Your colleagues. Your fellow congregants. Your neighbors. Strangers on the street. On and on in outwardly rippling circles. How free and uninhibited and healing is your love? How actively and sacrificially is it given? How authentic and real and trustworthy is it? How long will it last? In short, what kind of love is Jesus passionately calling all of us to experience and share?

Love Your Enemies

Jesus also taught that we are not to pay back our enemies according to what they do to us. Rather, we are to love them no matter what (Luke 6:27–36). "But I say to you that listen, Love your enemies, do good to those who hate you, bless those who curse you, pray for those who abuse you. If anyone strikes you on the cheek, offer the other also; and from anyone who takes away your coat do not withhold even your shirt. Give to everyone who begs from you; and if anyone takes away your goods, do not ask for them again. Do to others as you would have them do to you." Such a teaching must have shocked the listening crowd; perhaps some even laughed at it. Who could do such things? Jesus's way of love is utterly counter to the ways of the world. He sets the bar for a fulfilling life of love far higher than we might set it.

Jesus explains why he encourages this radical lifestyle: "If you love those who love you, what credit is that to you? For even sinners love those who love them. If you do good to those who do good to you, what credit is that to you? For even sinners do the same." In other words, our loving those who love us is only natural.

But Jesus calls us to a higher, a supernatural love: "Love your enemies, do good, and lend, expecting nothing in return. Your reward will be great, and you will be children of the Most High; for he is kind to the ungrateful and the wicked. Be merciful, just as your Father is merciful." We are to live as merciful people, as loved and loving people, following the example of Jesus.

This kind of love is sacrificial and giving; it is meant to build up the other person, not to use him or her for some ulterior selfish purposes. It involves caring and serving. It is passionate and holy work. It is not mere romance or friendship, or any of our culture's weak and empty fabrications of love. We must know in our hearts that this love is the most genuine reality in the universe.

This kind of love demands honesty and authenticity. It is expressed fully and openly without holding back. As a result, it can overturn cherished notions and practices. It offers a revolutionary way of life, of putting aside self for others, for the common good, for Jesus's sake.

This kind of love puts us together into families of faith. Jesus brought people together to love and support and teach and learn from one another, to serve one another no matter what. Jesus puts people together in loving relationships that go beyond the routine and the expected. Our Jesus-like love is multiplied exponentially when it is channeled through families of faith, our congregations, our efforts to serve, our important relationships.

This kind of love costs us everything. Jesus demands all—every part of us—not that we become imprisoned by standards of behavior we don't want to or can't fulfill. Rather, Jesus frees us to become all we were created to be. He enables us to engage life passionately at every level, even when we know that such engagement often involves tremendous risk. Ultimately we are in God's hands, but the traditional, worldly understanding of safety and security—often involving wealth and possessions—evaporates in the loving will of God.

This kind of love is radiated through our every word and deed. In Jesus's case, his love colors every emotion he felt and expressed, even his anger and fear. Love is the foundation of all the other passions. Love seeps into every breath he took, every gesture he made, every word he spoke, and it can do so with us as well.

We can follow Jesus's example of selfless, sacrificial, authentic love. We can gratefully, with understanding and appreciation, accept that kind of healing love when it is shared with us. We can find ourselves in the big picture of eternity and universality, part of the web of loving care God has spread throughout all existence. We can live in love forever.

Reflection: Loving and Being Loved

Have you ever felt unloved? What was the cause? Do you recall how lonesome, perhaps desperate, you felt?

Can you identify individuals in your community, your workplace, your religious community who are unloved? What would it mean for you to love those individuals as Jesus loves us?

Can you recall a time when you failed in love? Has a lover ever failed you? How did you learn to love again?

Have you ever fallen out of love with God? What was the cause? Have you found your way back to God's full embrace? How did that happen, or how do you think it might happen?

When was the last time you embraced lovingly an enemy or an unlovely and unloving person? What would enable you to embrace that person?

Meeting Everyone as a Stranger

Diane M. Millis, PhD

Do not call to mind the former things,
or ponder things of the past
Behold, I will do something new,
Now it will spring forth;
Will you not be aware of it?

—Isaiah 43:18–19A (NASB)

"At every meeting we are meeting a stranger."[1] T. S. Eliot's words seemed to jump off the page. I set my book down and paused to take some deep breaths. I then picked the book up and began reading the chapter titled: "I take up the way of speaking of others with openness and possibility."

As I read, I thought to myself, this precept would have been great to include in my book, *Conversation—The Sacred Art*. However, I had just sent the final manuscript to my editor. I finished the chapter, passed the book to Mark and said, "Read this." (Mark and I thrive on discussing books. It all started on our first date with *Zen and the Art of Motorcycle Maintenance*.) So, being the great husband that he is, he set down his iPad, took the book from my hands, and read the chapter. As he handed the book back to me, I asked, "Isn't that amazing? Imagine if we could consistently put that into practice: to meet others as strangers." He nodded.

Meeting the stranger invites us to continually press the refresh button on our perceptions of others and ourselves. Diane Eshin Rizzetto underscores the paradoxical nature of meeting the stranger. "In order to truly know someone, we have

---

Diane M. Millis, PhD, is an inspirational speaker, workshop and retreat leader, organizational consultant, and spiritual director. She is author of *Conversation—The Sacred Art: Practicing Presence in an Age of Distraction* (SkyLight Paths) and is founder and director of the Journey Conversations Project.

to be open to the possibility of change, and admit that we can only truly know that person in the present moment."[2] Although it's never easy, I often find it less difficult to meet a literal stranger *openly and with possibility* than to meet the stranger in those with whom I live and work. Moreover, it's only in the past couple of years that I've grown to appreciate the strangeness I encounter in myself, those parts of me that are new and unfamiliar. I know I'm not alone.

We tend to freeze our perceptions of others and ourselves rather than encounter the unknown and unfamiliar. "You know how men *are*, they're clueless about feelings." "Oh, that's just how Aunt Sherice *is*; the only person she's concerned about is herself." "I *am* too emotional. I'm afraid I'll never get a job in sales because I can't take rejection." We can blame it on our brains. Neuroscientists are discovering that the natural tendency of our brains is to take an idea or action that is unfamiliar to us and reconceive it as something we are already familiar with. For example, if I have never met a man who has disclosed his feelings, I may reject the notion that men want to and therefore never consider inviting any man to do so. If I perceive Aunt Sherice to be self-absorbed because she has never inquired about my life or offered to do anything for me, I may overlook or fail to notice behaviors that counter my view. If I believe that I am so emotional that anyone's rejection will cause me to crumble, it isn't likely that I'll recall times when I haven't.

It's important to cultivate our awareness of what is being revealed in our heart, in another's heart, and in between us as we engage in conversation. I increasingly realize that the sacred art of conversation is a spirituality of beholding and meeting the stranger. As the opening epigraph from the Hebrew Scriptures reminds us, the Spirit is beckoning us to behold, to be aware of, the *something new* in ourselves, in others, in our relationships, and in our world. We are practicing the

When we meet others as strangers, our hearts are open to possibility, change, and reconciliation. We haven't decided what one another is, and only know that person as she presents herself in this very moment. Yesterday, you may have exchanged a few harsh words and thought her disagreeable but today, in this moment, where is disagreeable? I like to think of our faultfinding as tinted glasses obscuring a clear view of who or what we meet at any given time. If you meet that person with the words of yesterday echoing in your mind, then your glasses are tinted disagreeable. You cannot meet the other as the stranger. How do we assume or not assume that a person has changed since yesterday? As long as we insist on seeing him through our memories, those glasses will not allow us to meet him openly and with possibility.

—Diane Eshin Rizzetto, *Waking Up to What You Do*

sacred art of conversation whenever we encourage one another to behold, to be on the lookout for the myriad ways in which the sacred is springing forth in our lives—both those that seem familiar and especially those that appear to be strange.

This theme of meeting the stranger keeps recurring in the conversation in my heart and in conversations with my husband. Over the past month at various points throughout our daily conversations, Mark grins and then interjects:

"It's about the stranger, right?"

I respond with delight, "Yep, it's about the stranger."

Seeing a World Where There Is No "Other"

Yoland Trevino

In Lak'ech Ala K'in. In my Mayan tradition this sacred greeting serves to honor another and means "I am another yourself" or "I am you, and you are me." Another meaning is "I bow to the Divine within you." When this greeting is given, there is always an action of placing the hands over the heart. In the Hindu tradition the greeting *Namaste,* which I learned through my work and connection with spiritual teachers in India, corresponds and is similar to the Mayan greeting. It is a philosophical statement affirming that the doer of everything is not me but the gods. With these greetings I embrace the blessings of diversity....

My grandmother taught me about the inherent value of life—a concept I would later come to know as *ahimsa,* a Sanskrit word meaning "nonviolence"—as she refused to kill even an ant. Instead, she fed them so they would leave the house on their own. As a child, observing my grandmother's reverence for all life taught me the spiritual views and values by which I live today.

I have also been deeply influenced by the spiritual teachings experienced throughout my travels in India, where I came to fully appreciate the Living Universal Consciousness. This expansive worldview recognizes the Divine within each one of us. As we feel the blessings of what each of us brings—our divine expression of who we are—we can mirror that in one another. In Mayan tradition we believe that we are all related to one another, not just in an abstract sense but as real family. As I look at nature and its wondrous expressions, I am in awe and

Yoland Trevino is a familiar participant in international interfaith and intercultural efforts. She is a contributor to *Women, Spirituality and Transformative Leadership: Where Grace Meets Power* (SkyLight Paths) and cocreator, coordinator, and faculty member of the international program Cities in the 21st Century: People, Planning, and Politics, based in India.

delighted about the colorful array. The same is true of our human family—how boring it would be if we were all uniform and without our own unique definitions. My knowledge and experiences have been deeply influenced by the spiritual awareness I learned as a young girl. Later I discovered that even contemporary men of science have expressed an understanding of the subtle spiritual nature of reality: "Everyone who is seriously involved in the pursuit of science becomes convinced that a spirit is manifest in the laws of the universe—a spirit vastly superior to that of men."[1] I believe that the challenges of living with diversity grow from a cultural socialization that promotes separateness as opposed to oneness.

I believe that this perception of separateness is the biggest challenge, as it creates the false view that my manifestation, my religion, my country is better than yours. In this way it serves to divide people. In Guatemala there was a sense that people, ideas, religions, and other things that were of European origin were inherently better. This can create for many the belief that Native ways, people, and beliefs are to be avoided or forgotten, which is very sad. Of course, this was fueled by many religions promoting the old European concept that Native indigenous people were savages to be dominated, Christianized, or killed. To this day, this perception continues to fuel a division between the indigenous people and those of mixed Native and European ancestry.

For me, the blessing of diversity is to experience ourselves as interconnected, integrated in all that lives. We are called to experience the gift that when we stand for each other, greatness can bloom before our eyes. When we accept that every member of the human family has an ultimate reason and a purpose for being on the planet at this time, only then can we joyously experience existence. When I can be my unique self by embracing who I am at my highest, I can offer the same divine right to the rest of the world. I believe that "we are each of us angels with only one wing, and we can only fly by embracing one another."[2] How can we reconcile the challenges and blessings of diversity? Our first challenge is in recognizing when we slip into judging, distancing ourselves from walking a mile in other people's shoes, and slipping into a place of separation from that oneness. Separation eventually leads to despair. The blessing is our opportunity to embrace "what is" without wanting to change it into something else....

In this world, where there is so much emphasis on money, power, prestige, and fame, when the TV news is largely tragic and undermining our happiness, it can be easy for some to forget our true divine nature. When we get caught up in the world of pain and loss, it is sometimes easy to forget the wonder and joy of our cosmic heritage ... that many of the very elements that make up our bodies were fused within stars in the distant past … that we are all one, and one with all there is. Keeping this knowledge alive in our hearts through ritual and ceremony can help us step outside of our small selves and experience the world and its people as sacred.

My values and spiritual traditions take me to far and distant lands to meet with authentic indigenous leaders, where I may sit at their feet and in ceremony remember who I really am, and bring forth the innate wisdom whispered by my ancestral spiritual guides. My spiritual values were shaped by the traditions and practices with which I was raised—yet my cultural and spiritual identity continues to evolve throughout my life by my learning, sharing, and celebrating the diverse traditions of others. Perhaps the greatest blessing of diversity is that it is a great teacher—for in appreciating our differences, we come to realize in some fundamental way at our very core, within our heart of hearts, that we are all brothers and sisters on the road of life. In this way we consecrate the path we tread as we make our way in the world. Each one of us has a higher purpose as a sacred manifestation of the Divine. When we pursue this purpose, we contribute to manifesting a world in balance, where women and men can fully express their divine origin as being complementary opposites in a world where there is no "other."

Pursuing Kinship Rather than Estrangement

Rev. Nanette Sawyer

We often feel a basic human sensation of separation and "otherness." When we see people as strangers, we have a choice about whether we will see them as fundamentally different from us or as intrinsically similar. It's a question of how we understand the differences between us. Dwelling on the distinctions between us can concretize or harden them. This thought process reinforces our belief in our identity as "different" and others as "strangers." Comparing ourselves to others by emphasizing the contrasts always leads to the same state, says Buddhist teacher Henepola Gunaratana—"estrangement, barriers between people, and ill feeling."[1]

Gunaratana describes inner "hindrances" that prevent us from seeing things the way they truly are and from resting in our Buddha nature. Buddha nature is our ultimate essence, which Gunaratana describes as "pure, holy, and inherently good."[2] When we are able to rest in this nature, we experience ourselves as fully alive, taking nothing for granted, experiencing everything with vitality as a living, changing process. As a Christian, I correlate this idea of Buddha nature with my understanding of the image of God at the core of every human being. It's that "pure, holy, and inherently good" quality that is somehow intrinsically present in us, but which we often do not fully realize or embody in our lives.

The hindrances, such as greed, lust, hatred, and aversion, keep us from resting in that pure, holy, inherently good nature that is somehow our ultimate essence. Fear is another hindrance.

Rev. Nanette Sawyer, teacher and spiritual counselor, is author of *Hospitality—The Sacred Art: Discovering the Hidden Spiritual Power of Invitation and Welcome* (SkyLight Paths) and a founding pastor of Grace Commons, an innovative Christian community in Chicago that holds hospitality as a core value.

Gunaratana also calls these hindrances "defilements," because they cloud the purity of our Buddha nature. All of these hindrances reinforce our belief that we are inherently separate from others. "Greed and lust are attempts to get 'some of that' for me; hatred and aversion are attempts to place greater distance between 'me and that.' All the defilements depend upon the perception of a barrier between self and other, and all of them foster this perception every time they are exercised."[3] Rather than focus on the distinctions between people, Gunaratana suggests that it is better to replace this unskillful state of mind with a more skillful one. Through awareness practices, we can center our attention on things that are universal human experiences; this will bring us closer to others, rather than pushing us apart. This kind of comparison "leads to feelings of kinship rather than feelings of estrangement."[4] The universal human experiences that Gunaratana suggests we look for, and that can lead to feelings of kinship, are the internal processes that have to do with how we think and how we react to things. When we encounter something (a person or a thought or an object—it doesn't matter), a reaction rises up in us. It can be a positive, negative, or neutral response. It can be a feeling—anger, pride, fear, affection, fascination. It can be a memory of the past or a fantasy of the future. Though the contents may differ from person to person or culture to culture, the process itself is the same; when we encounter something, a reaction rises up in us.

Becoming aware of this process, and seeing that it is a fundamentally human process, leads us to an acceptance of ourselves and others. There is a kind of forgiveness inherent in this kind of acceptance. We let go of judging because we see that this is how people are, ourselves included. When feelings of anger come up in us, we can say to ourselves, "Oh, I'm having this very human experience of anger. This is what people do." Becoming *aware* and *accepting* it at this level can then lead to us being more responsible about *how we express* our anger (or any emotion)—*awareness, acceptance, action*—our old triadic friend. Accepting that our experience is human doesn't mean giving permission for acting out. Instead, it creates space for forgiveness and compassion, which in turn creates the opportunity for us to respond to our feelings rather than react. In other words, we become more free and able to choose how we will act.

Becoming aware of these human processes and tendencies will help us grow in hospitality. Gunaratana describes some of these beneficial transformations: "We become very understanding people as a result. We no longer get upset by the 'failings' of others. We progress toward harmony with all life."[5] This kind of understanding will enable us to see past our illusions of estrangement, and to extend welcome and hospitality in reverent, generous ways, human to human, bozo to bozo, bus-mate to bus-mate. On this fundamental level, no one is a stranger. We are all on this bus together.

Credits

Unless otherwise stated, all quotations from the Bible are from the *New Revised Standard Version Bible*, © 1989, Division of Christian Education of the National Council of the Churches of Christ in the United States of America. Used by permission. All rights reserved.

The contents of this book originally appeared in materials published by SkyLight Paths and Jewish Lights and are reprinted with permission.

Nancy L. Bieber, "Naming Your Hurts and Fears" and "The Fruit of Love," are excerpted from *Decision Making and Spiritual Discernment: The Sacred Art of Finding Your Way.* (SkyLight Paths Publishing, 2010).

Carolyne Call, "Forgiveness and Grace after Divorce" and "Questions in Asking for Forgiveness," are excerpted from *Spiritually Healthy Divorce: Navigating Disruption with Insight & Hope* (SkyLight Paths Publishing, 2010).

Joan Brown Campbell, "Prodigals and the Path to Peace," is excerpted from *Living into Hope: A Call to Spiritual Action for Such a Time as This* (SkyLight Paths Publishing, 2012).

Nancy Barrett Chickerneo, "Clearing the Wellspring," is excerpted from *Woman Spirit Awakening in Nature: Growing into the Fullness of Who You Are* (SkyLight Paths Publishing, 2008).

Paul Wesley Chilcote, "Offering All to God," is excerpted from *The Imitation of Christ: Selections Annotated & Explained* (SkyLight Paths Publishing, 2012).

William Cleary, "You Accept Us—At Times of Self-Doubt," is excerpted from *Prayers to an Evolutionary God* (SkyLight Paths Publishing, 2004).

Nancy Corcoran, "A Prayer of Forgiveness for Enemies," is excerpted from *Secrets of Prayer: A Multifaith Guide to Creating Personal Prayer in Your Life* (SkyLight Paths Publishing, 2007).

Linda Douty, "What's Stopping You?" is excerpted from *How Did I Get to Be 70 When I'm 35 Inside? Spiritual Surprises of Later Life* (SkyLight Paths Publishing, 2011).

M. F., "Prayer for Our Mothers," is excerpted from *Honoring Motherhood: Prayers, Ceremonies and Blessings* (SkyLight Paths Publishing, 2012).

Marcia Ford, "It Starts with You," "Setting Boundaries," and "Granting Yourself Absolution," are excerpted from *The Sacred Art of Forgiveness: Forgiving Ourselves and Others through God's Grace* (SkyLight Paths Publishing, 2006).

Marie M. Fortune, "Seeking Justice on the Path to Forgiveness," is excerpted from *New Feminist Christianity: Many Voices, Many Views* (SkyLight Paths Publishing, 2012).

Tamar Frankiel and Judy Greenfeld, "Bedtime Forgiveness Prayer," is excerpted from *Entering the Temple of Dreams: Jewish Prayers, Movements, and Meditations for the End of the Day* (Jewish Lights Publishing, 2000).

Edwin Goldberg, "How to Let Go of Resentment," is excerpted from *Saying No and Letting Go: Jewish Wisdom on Making Room for What Matters Most* (Jewish Lights Publishing, 2013).

Caren Goldman, "Reconciliation in Your Own Heart," is excerpted from *Restoring Life's Missing Pieces: The Spiritual Power of Remembering and Reuniting with People, Places, Things and Self* (SkyLight Paths Publishing, 2011).

Steven Greenebaum, "A Prayer for Forgiveness," is excerpted from *Practical Interfaith: How to Find Our Common Humanity as We Celebrate Diversity* (SkyLight Paths Publishing, 2014).

Kent Ira Groff, "Four Rs for Relinquishing," is excerpted from *Honest to God Prayer: Spirituality as Awareness, Empowerment, Relinquishment and Paradox* (SkyLight Paths Publishing, 2012).

Diana L. Guerrero, "What Animals Can Teach Us about Letting Go," is excerpted from *What Animals Can Teach Us about Spirituality: Inspiring Lessons from Wild and Tame Creatures* (SkyLight Paths Publishing, 2003).

Karyn D. Kedar, "Crossing the Bridge," is excerpted from *The Bridge to Forgiveness: Stories and Prayers for Finding God and Restoring Wholeness* (Jewish Lights Publishing, 2011). "You Are Living a Good Story," is excerpted from *God Whispers: Stories of the Soul, Lessons of the Heart* (SkyLight Paths Publishing, 2000).

Kay Lindahl, "Listening for Reconciliation," is excerpted from *The Sacred Art of Listening: Forty Reflections for Cultivating a Spiritual Practice* (SkyLight Paths Publishing, 2001).

David Lyon, "The Privilege of Asking Forgiveness," is excerpted from *God of Me: Imagining God throughout Your Lifetime* (Jewish Lights Publishing, 2011).

Don Mackenzie, Jamal Rahman, and Ted Falcon, "Interfaith Forgiveness," is excerpted from *Getting to the Heart of Interfaith: The Eye-Opening, Hope-Filled Friendship of a Pastor, a Rabbi & an Imam* (SkyLight Paths Publishing, 2009).

Marcus Aurelius, "Meditations of Marcus Aurelius on Forgiveness," is excerpted from *The Meditations of Marcus Aurelius: Selections Annotated & Explained* (SkyLight Paths Publishing, 2007).

Maximos, "The Philokalia on Forgiveness," is excerpted from *Philokalia—The Eastern Christian Spiritual Texts: Selections Annotated & Explained* (SkyLight Paths Publishing, 2006).

Ron Miller, "The Gospel of Matthew on Forgiveness," is excerpted from *The Hidden Gospel of Matthew: Annotated & Explained* (SkyLight Paths Publishing, 2004).

Diane M. Millis, "Meeting Everyone as a Stranger," is excerpted from *Conversation—The Sacred Art: Practicing Presence in an Age of Distraction* (SkyLight Paths Publishing, 2013).

Timothy J. Mooney, "A Choice and a Gift," is excerpted from *Like a Child: Restoring the Awe, Wonder, Joy and Resiliency of the Human Spirit* (SkyLight Paths Publishing, 2014).

John Philip Newell, "Reconnecting with the Earth," is excerpted from *The Rebirthing of God: Christianity's Struggle for New Beginnings* (SkyLight Paths Publishing, 2014).

Linda Novick, "Repainting Your Story," is excerpted from *The Painting Path: Embodying Spiritual Discovery through Yoga, Brush and Color* (SkyLight Paths Publishing, 2007).

Larry J. Peacock, "Trusting God's Forgiveness" and "Intercession and Justice," are excerpted from *Openings: A Daybook of Saints, Sages, Psalms and Prayer Practices*, 2nd ed. (SkyLight Paths Publishing, 2014).

Gordon Peerman, "Escaping the Blame Cycle," is excerpted from *Blessed Relief: What Christians Can Learn from Buddhists about Suffering* (SkyLight Paths Publishing, 2008).

M. Basil Pennington, "The Psalms on Forgiveness," is excerpted from *Psalms: A Spiritual Commentary* (SkyLight Paths Publishing, 2008).

Jan Phillips, "Letting Go of Old Illusions," is excerpted from *Divining the Body: Reclaim the Holiness of Your Physical Self* (SkyLight Paths Publishing, 2005).

"The Qur'an on Forgiveness," is excerpted from *The Qur'an and Sayings of Prophet Muhammad: Selections Annotated & Explained* (SkyLight Paths Publishing, 2007).

Susan Quinn, "Finding Peace in Letting a Relationship Go," is excerpted from *Women, Spirituality and Transformative Leadership: Where Grace Meets Power* (SkyLight Paths Publishing, 2014).

Jamal Rahman, "Developing Self-Compassion" and "Praying with the Angels," are excerpted from *Spiritual Gems of Islam: Insights & Practices from the Qur'an, Hadith, Rumi & Muslim Teaching Stories to Enlighten the Heart & Mind* (SkyLight Paths Publishing, 2013).

Marty Richards, "Forgiveness in Caregiving," is excerpted from *Caresharing: A Reciprocal Approach to Caregiving and Care Receiving in the Complexities of Aging, Illness or Disability* (SkyLight Paths Publishing, 2010).

C. K. Robertson, "Prayers for Marriage," is excerpted from *The Book of Common Prayer: A Spiritual Treasure Chest—Selections Annotated & Explained* (SkyLight Paths Publishing, 2013).

Nanette Sawyer, "Hospitality to Enemies" and "Pursuing Kinship Rather than Estrangement," are excerpted from *Hospitality—the Sacred Art: Discovering the Hidden Spiritual Power of Invitation and Welcome.* (SkyLight Paths Publishing, 2007).

Donna Schaper, "The Sacred Speech of Forgiveness" and "Wise Justice, Merciful Hearts," are excerpted from *Sacred Speech: A Practical Guide for Keeping Spirit in Your Speech* (SkyLight Paths Publishing, 2004).

Katharine Jefferts Schori, "A Moveable Feast," is excerpted from *The Heartbeat of God: Finding the Sacred in the Middle of Everything* (SkyLight Paths Publishing, 2010).

Rami Shapiro, "Encountering the Heart of the Enemy," is excerpted from *Writing—The Sacred Art: Beyond the Page to Spiritual Practice* (SkyLight Paths Publishing, 2012). "A God Who Desires to Forgive" is excerpted from *Perennial Wisdom for the Spiritually Independent: Sacred Teachings—Annotated & Explained* (SkyLight Paths Publishing, 2013). "More Than Apologizing" is excerpted from *Recovery—The Sacred Art: The Twelve Steps as Spiritual Practice* (SkyLight Paths Publishing, 2009). "Proverbs on Forgiveness" is excerpted from *Proverbs: Annotated & Explained* (SkyLight Paths Publishing, 2011).

Louise Silk, "Lovingkindness Meditation to Open the Heart and Mind," is excerpted from *The Quilting Path: A Guide to Spiritual Discovery through Fabric, Thread and Kabbalah* (SkyLight Paths Publishing, 2006).

Susan Sparks, "Laugh at Yourself," is excerpted from *Laugh Your Way to Grace: Reclaiming the Spiritual Power of Humor* (SkyLight Paths Publishing, 2010).

Aaron Spevack, "Ghazali on Forgiveness," is excerpted from *Ghazali on the Principles of Islamic Spirituality: Selections from* The Forty Foundations of Religion*—Annotated & Explained* (SkyLight Paths Publishing, 2011).

Elie Kaplan Spitz, "Forgiving Suicide," is excerpted from *Healing from Despair: Choosing Wholeness in a Broken World* (Jewish Lights Publishing, 2010).

Molly and Bernie Srode, "Peacemaking in Our Own Hearts," is excerpted from *Keeping Spiritual Balance as We Grow Older: More than 65 Creative Ways to Use Purpose, Prayer, and the Power of Spirit to Build a Meaningful Retirement* (SkyLight Paths Publishing, 2004).

Tom Stella, "Humbly Embracing Imperfections" and "Letting Go of a Vengeful God," are excerpted from *Finding God Beyond Religion: A Guide for Skeptics, Agnostics & Unorthodox Believers Inside & Outside the Church* (SkyLight Paths Publishing, 2013).

Sohaib N. Sultan, "Reconciliation, Retribution, and Justice in Islam," is excerpted from *The Qur'an and Sayings of Prophet Muhammad: Selections Annotated & Explained* (SkyLight Paths Publishing, 2007).

Terry Taylor, "Facing Brokenness," is excerpted from *A Spirituality for Brokenness: Discovering Your Deepest Self in Difficult Times* (SkyLight Paths Publishing, 2009).

Yoland Trevino, "Seeing a World Where There Is No 'Other,'" is excerpted from *Women, Spirituality and Transformative Leadership: Where Grace Meets Power* (SkyLight Paths Publishing, 2014).

Jane E. Vennard, "Leaving the Past Behind," is excerpted from *Fully Awake and Truly Alive: Spiritual Practices to Nurture Your Soul* (SkyLight Paths Publishing, 2013).

Peter Wallace, "Living in Love," is excerpted from *The Passionate Jesus: What We Can Learn from Jesus about Love, Fear, Grief, Joy and Living Authentically* (SkyLight Paths Publishing, 2012).

Cynthia Winton-Henry, "Dancing Peace and Forgiveness," is excerpted from *Dance—The Sacred Art: The Joy of Movement as a Spiritual Practice* (SkyLight Paths Publishing, 2009).

Notes

What's Stopping You?

1. Frederick Buechner, *Wishful Thinking* (New York: HarperSanFrancisco, 1973), 2.

How to Let Go of Resentment

1. Donald McCullough, *Say Please, Say Thank You: The Respect We Owe One Another* (New York: G. P. Putnam, 1998), 258.
2. Michael McCullough, "Getting Revenge and Forgiveness," *On Being*, American Public Media (May 24, 2012).
3. Stephanie Dowrick, *Forgiveness and Other Acts of Love* (New York: W. W. Norton, 1998), 291–292.
4. Ibid., 292.

A Choice and a Gift

1. Lewis B. Smedes, *Forgive & Forget: Healing the Hurts We Don't Deserve* (San Francisco: HarperOne, 1996), excerpted *by Spirituality & Practice*, www.spiritualityandpractice.com/books/excerpts.php?id=14077 (accessed March 23, 2014).

Four *R*s for Relinquishing

1. Joyce Rupp, *Praying Our Goodbyes* (Notre Dame, IN: Ave Maria Press, 1988), 83–93.
2. See Eugene Gendlin, *Focusing* (New York: Bantam Books, 1981) and Ann Weiser Cornell, *The Power of Focusing* (Oakland, CA: New Harbinger Publications, 1996).

Letting Go of Old Illusions

1. Coleman Barks, *The Essential Rumi* (San Francisco: HarperSanFrancisco, 1995), 191.

It Starts with You

1. Marian Anderson, *My Lord, What a Morning: An Autobiography* (New York: Viking Press, 1956), ch. 28. Quoted on www.bartleby.com, citing Robert Andrews, Mary Biggs, and Michael Seidel, et al., *The Columbia World of Quotations* (New York: Columbia University Press, 1996), Quote 3500.

The Sacred Speech of Forgiveness

1. Robert Folger, "Trust and Controversy," *Chronicle of Higher Education* (April 12, 2002), B13.

Forgiving Suicide

1. *Arukh Ha Shulkhan* 345:5. This rabbinic conclusion was taken one step further when, in 2004, leaders of Judaism's Conservative movement ruled that a suicide is "to be treated like any other death, with the right of burial in a cemetery and the same rituals of mourning." The *teshuvah* was

composed by Rabbi Kassel Abelson and approved by the Rabbinical Assembly Committee on Law and Standards in September 2005. A dramatic example of an Orthodox ruling on interment despite suicide is the ruling of the Sephardic chief rabbi of Israel, Shlomo Amar, who permitted the interment of Zionist founder Theodor Herzl's children, Pauline and Hans, alongside their father in Jerusalem on September 20, 2006. Seventy-six years earlier, Pauline, who had suffered from morphine addiction leading to multiple hospitalizations, took her life in Bordeaux, France, with a tranquilizer overdose. The next day, Hans killed himself. Rabbi Amar ruled that mental instability and the psychological stress upon learning of his sister's death allowed each of them to be buried in the national Jewish cemetery.

2. Harold S. Kushner, *When Bad Things Happen to Good People* (New York: Avon, 1981, 1983).

Letting Go of a Vengeful God

1. William Johnston, *The Cloud of Unknowing* (New York: Doubleday, 1973), 23.
2. Thomas Merton, *The Way of Chuang Tzu* (Boston: Shambhala Publications, 1992), 26.
3. Thomas Merton, *The Sign of Jonas* (New York: Image Books, 1956), 54.

The Privilege of Asking Forgiveness

1. Abraham ben Samuel Abulafia, *The Penguin Book of Hebrew Verse*, ed. and trans. T. Carmi (New York: Penguin Books, 1981), 419.

Humbly Embracing Imperfections

1. Kerry Walters, *Rufus Jones: Essential Writings* (Maryknoll, NY: Orbis Books, 2001), 18.
2. C. S. Lewis, *Surprised by Joy* (New York: Harcourt Brace, 1956), 226.
3. Annie Dillard, *Teaching a Stone to Talk* (New York: HarperCollins, 1982), 94–95.

Granting Yourself Absolution

1. Lewis B. Smedes, *The Art of Forgiving: When You Need to Forgive and Don't Know How* (Nashville: Moorings, 1996).
2. Ibid.

Hospitality to Enemies

1. Martin Luther King Jr., *The Autobiography of Martin Luther King Jr.*, ed. Clayborne Carson (New York: Warner Books, 1998), 67.
2. Martin Luther King Jr., "Loving Your Enemies," in *A Knock at Midnight: Inspiration from the Great Sermons of Reverend Martin Luther King Jr.*, ed. Clayborne Carson and Peter Holloran (New York: Warner Books, 1998), 41–60.
3. Ibid., 42, 46, 47.
4. Ibid., 57.
5. Ibid., 43–44.
6. Ibid., 46.
7. Ibid.

Praying with the Angels

1. Quoted in "The Angels," by Sachiko Murata, www.islamawareness.net/Angels/murata.html (accessed January 13, 2013).

Seeking Justice on the Path to Forgiveness

1. Maimonides, *Mishnah Torah, Book One: Knowledge: Repentance*, ed. Philip Birnbaum (New York: Hebrew Publishing, 1944), 2.9.
2. Ibid., 2.1.
3. It appears in Shakespeare's *King Lear*, act 4, scene 7.

Prodigals and the Path to Peace

1. Pope John Paul II, "Reconciliation and Penance," postsynodal apostolic exhortation, Rome, December 2, 1984.

Reconnecting with the Earth

1. Pierre Teilhard de Chardin, *The Heart of Matter*, trans. R. Hague (London: Collins, 1978), 15.
2. Pierre Teilhard de Chardin, *Christianity and Evolution*, trans. R. Hague (London: Collins, 1971), 128.
3. Ibid., 94.
4. Ibid., 95.
5. Pierre Teilhard de Chardin, *The Prayer of the Universe*, trans. R. Hague (London: Collins, 1977), 88.
6. Ibid., 86.
7. Ibid., 41.
8. Pierre Teilhard de Chardin, *Le Milieu Divin*, trans. R. Hague (London: Collins, 1967), 154.
9. Walter Schwartz, "Thomas Berry Obituary," September 27, 2009; www.guardian.co.uk/world/2009/sep/27/thomas-berry-obituary (accessed April 6, 2012).
10. Thomas Berry, *The Great Work* (New York: Bell Tower, 1999), ix.
11. Ibid., 164.
12. Thomas Berry, *The Sacred Universe* (New York: Columbia University Press, 2009), 133.
13. Ibid., 69.
14. Thomas Berry, *The Great Work* (New York: Bell Tower, 1999), 201.
15. Ibid.

Meeting Everyone as a Stranger

1. T. S. Eliot, *The Cocktail Party*, I, iii (London: Faber and Faber, 1950), 72–73.
2. Diane Rizzetto, *Waking Up to What You Do: A Zen Practice for Meeting Every Situation with Intelligence and Compassion* (Boston: Shambhala, 2005), 72.

Seeing a World Where There Is No "Other"

1. Albert Einstein, *The Human Side: New Glimpses from His Archives*, ed. Helen Dukas and Banesh Hoffman (Princeton: Princeton University Press, 1981), 33.
2. Luciano de Crescenzo, "Thus Spake Bellavista," *Magill Book Reviews* (Ipswich, MA: Salem Press, 1989), 15.

Pursuing Kinship Rather than Estrangement

1. Henepola Gunaratana, *Mindfulness in Plain English* (Boston: Wisdom Publications, 1992), 48.
2. Ibid., 186.
3. Ibid., 185.
4. Ibid., 48.
5. Ibid., 49.

Women's Interest

She Lives! Sophia Wisdom Works in the World
By Rev. Jann Aldredge-Clanton, PhD
Fascinating narratives of clergy and laypeople who are changing the institutional church and society by restoring biblical female divine names and images to Christian theology, worship symbolism and liturgical language.
6 x 9, 320 pp, Quality PB, 978-1-59473-573-8 **$18.99**

Birthing God: Women's Experiences of the Divine
By Lana Dalberg; Foreword by Kathe Schaaf
Powerful narratives of suffering, love and hope that inspire both personal and collective transformation. 6 x 9, 304 pp, Quality PB, 978-1-59473-480-9 **$18.99**

Women, Spirituality and Transformative Leadership
Where Grace Meets Power
Edited by Kathe Schaaf, Kay Lindahl, Kathleen S. Hurty, PhD, and Reverend Guo Cheen
A dynamic conversation on the power of women's spiritual leadership and its emerging patterns of transformation.
6 x 9, 288 pp, Quality PB, 978-1-59473-548-6 **$18.99**; HC, 978-1-59473-313-0 **$24.99**

Spiritually Healthy Divorce: Navigating Disruption with Insight & Hope
By Carolyne Call A spiritual map to help you move through the twists and turns of divorce. 6 x 9, 224 pp, Quality PB, 978-1-59473-288-1 **$16.99**

New Feminist Christianity: Many Voices, Many Views
Edited by Mary E. Hunt and Diann L. Neu
Insights from ministers and theologians, activists and leaders, artists and liturgists offer a starting point for building new models of religious life and worship.
6 x 9, 384 pp, Quality PB, 978-1-59473-435-9 **$19.99**; HC, 978-1-59473-285-0 **$24.99**

Bread, Body, Spirit: Finding the Sacred in Food
Edited and with Introductions by Alice Peck 6 x 9, 224 pp, Quality PB, 978-1-59473-242-3 **$19.99**

Dance—The Sacred Art: The Joy of Movement as a Spiritual Practice
By Cynthia Winton-Henry 5½ x 8½, 224 pp, Quality PB, 978-1-59473-268-3 **$16.99**

Daughters of the Desert: Stories of Remarkable Women from Christian, Jewish and Muslim Traditions *By Claire Rudolf Murphy, Meghan Nuttall Sayres, Mary Cronk Farrell, Sarah Conover and Betsy Wharton*
5½ x 8½, 192 pp, Illus., Quality PB, 978-1-59473-106-8 **$14.99** Inc. reader's discussion guide

The Divine Feminine in Biblical Wisdom Literature
Selections Annotated & Explained
Translation & Annotation by Rabbi Rami Shapiro; Foreword by Rev. Cynthia Bourgeault, PhD
5½ x 8½, 240 pp, Quality PB, 978-1-59473-109-9 **$18.99**

Divining the Body: Reclaim the Holiness of Your Physical Self
By Jan Phillips 8 x 8, 256 pp, Quality PB, 978-1-59473-080-1 **$18.99**

Honoring Motherhood: Prayers, Ceremonies & Blessings
Edited and with Introductions by Lynn L. Caruso
5 x 7¼, 272 pp, Quality PB, 978-1-58473-384-0 **$9.99**; HC, 978-1-59473-239-3 **$19.99**

Next to Godliness: Finding the Sacred in Housekeeping
Edited by Alice Peck 6 x 9, 224 pp, Quality PB, 978-1-59473-214-0 **$19.99**

The Triumph of Eve & Other Subversive Bible Tales
By Matt Biers-Ariel 5½ x 8½, 192 pp, Quality PB, 978-1-59473-176-1 **$14.99**

Woman Spirit Awakening in Nature: Growing Into the Fullness of Who You Are
By Nancy Barrett Chickerneo, PhD; Foreword by Eileen Fisher
8 x 8, 224 pp, b/w illus., Quality PB, 978-1-59473-250-8 **$16.99**

Women of Color Pray: Voices of Strength, Faith, Healing, Hope and Courage
Edited and with Introductions by Christal M. Jackson
5 x 7¼, 208 pp, Quality PB, 978-1-59473-077-1 **$15.99**

Personal Growth

The Forgiveness Handbook
Spiritual Wisdom and Practice for the Journey to Freedom, Healing and Peace
By the Editors at SkyLight Paths; Introduction by The Rev. Canon Marianne Wells Borg
Offers inspiration, encouragement and spiritual practice from across faith traditions for all who seek hope, wholeness and the freedom that comes from true forgiveness. 6 x 9, 256 pp, Quality PB, 978-1-59473-577-6 **$18.99**

Decision Making & Spiritual Discernment: The Sacred Art of Finding Your Way *By Nancy L. Bieber*
Presents three essential aspects of Spirit-led decision making: willingness, attentiveness and responsiveness.
5½ x 8½, 208 pp, Quality PB, 978-1-59473-289-8 **$16.99**

Like a Child
Restoring the Awe, Wonder, Joy and Resiliency of the Human Spirit
By Rev. Timothy J. Mooney
Explores Jesus's counsel to become like children in order to enter the kingdom of God. 6 x 9, 160 pp, Quality PB, 978-1-59473-543-1 **$16.99**

Secrets of a Soulful Marriage
Creating & Sustaining a Loving, Sacred Relationship
By Jim Sharon, EdD, and Ruth Sharon, MS
An innovative, hope-filled resource for developing soulful, mature love for committed couples who are looking to create, maintain and glorify the sacred in their relationship. Offers a banquet of practical tools, inspirational real-life stories and spiritual practices for couples of all faiths, or none.
6 x 9, 192 pp, Quality PB, 978-1-59473-554-7 **$16.99**

Hospitality—The Sacred Art
Discovering the Hidden Spiritual Power of Invitation and Welcome
By Rev. Nanette Sawyer; Foreword by Rev. Dirk Ficca
Discover how the qualities of hospitality can deepen your self-understanding and help you build transforming and lasting relationships with others and with God.
5½ x 8½, 208 pp, Quality PB, 978-1-59473-228-7 **$16.99**

The Losses of Our Lives
The Sacred Gifts of Renewal in Everyday Loss
By Dr. Nancy Copeland-Payton
Shows us that by becoming aware of what our lesser losses have to teach us, the larger losses become less terrifying. Includes spiritual practices and questions for reflection.
6 x 9, 192 pp, Quality PB, 978-1-59473-307-9 **$16.99**; HC, 978-1-59473-271-3 **$19.99**

A Spirituality for Brokenness
Discovering Your Deepest Self in Difficult Times
By Terry Taylor
Compassionately guides you through the practicalities of facing and finally accepting brokenness in your life—a process that can ultimately bring mending.
6 x 9, 176 pp, Quality PB, 978-1-59473-229-4 **$16.99**

The Bridge to Forgiveness
Stories and Prayers for Finding God and Restoring Wholeness
By Karyn D. Kedar
Inspiring, deeply personal stories, comforting prayers and intimate meditations gently lead you through the steps that allow the heart to forgive.
6 x 9, 176 pp, Quality PB, 978-1-58023-451-1 **$16.99***

Conversation—The Sacred Art
Practicing Presence in an Age of Distraction
By Diane M. Millis, PhD; Foreword by Rev. Tilden Edwards, PhD
5½ x 8½, 192 pp, Quality PB, 978-1-59473-474-8 **$16.99**

*A book from Jewish Lights, SkyLight Paths' sister imprint

About SKYLIGHT PATHS Publishing

SkyLight Paths Publishing is creating a place where people of different spiritual traditions come together for challenge and inspiration, a place where we can help each other understand the mystery that lies at the heart of our existence.

Through spirituality, our religious beliefs are increasingly becoming a part of our lives—rather than *apart* from our lives. While many of us may be more interested than ever in spiritual growth, we may be less firmly planted in traditional religion. Yet, we do want to deepen our relationship to the sacred, to learn from our own as well as from other faith traditions, and to practice in new ways.

SkyLight Paths sees both believers and seekers as a community that increasingly transcends traditional boundaries of religion and denomination—people wanting to learn from each other, *walking together, finding the way.*

For your information and convenience, at the back of this book we have provided a list of other SkyLight Paths books you might find interesting and useful. They cover the following subjects:

- Buddhism / Zen
- Catholicism
- Chaplaincy
- Children's Books
- Christianity
- Comparative Religion
- Earth-Based Spirituality
- Enneagram
- Global Spiritual Perspectives
- Gnosticism
- Hinduism / Vedanta
- Inspiration
- Islam / Sufism
- Judaism
- Meditation
- Mindfulness
- Monasticism
- Mysticism
- Personal Growth
- Poetry
- Prayer
- Religious Etiquette
- Retirement & Later-Life Spirituality
- Spiritual Biography
- Spiritual Direction
- Spirituality
- Women's Interest
- Worship

Or phone, fax, mail or email to: SKYLIGHT PATHS Publishing
Sunset Farm Offices, Route 4 • P.O. Box 237 • Woodstock, Vermont 05091
Tel: (802) 457-4000 • Fax: (802) 457-4004 • www.skylightpaths.com
Credit card orders: (800) 962-4544 (8:30AM–5:30PM EST Monday–Friday)